With Compliments,
Howard Wolk

To write a review: https://www.amazon.com/Launchpad-Republic-Americas-Entrepreneurial-Matters/dp/1119900050

To order additional books:

Amazon: https://www.amazon.com/Launchpad-Republic-Americas-Entrepreneurial-Matters/dp/1119900050

B&N: https://www.barnesandnoble.com/w/launchpad-republic-howard-wolk/1141020241?ean=9781119900054

Bookshop.org: https://bookshop.org/books/launchpad-republic-america-s-entrepreneurial-edge-and-why-it-matters/9781119900054

For bulk orders, please contact Aaron Schleicher at aaron@porchlightbooks.com or Silvana Bouhlal at sbouhlal@ccgroup.com

Additional Praise for *Launchpad Republic: America's Entrepreneurial Edge and Why It Matters*

"For all their vision and drive, entrepreneurs are but seedlings who require fertile soil to flourish. Melding a smart and sprightly historical survey of American politics with a successful practitioner's keen eye for competitive dynamics, Wolk and Landry offer a compelling argument about how formal and informal rules of the game have long sustained the world's most entrepreneurial society. Anyone interested in better understanding U.S. entrepreneurial success – and how to hold on to it – should read this engaging book."

—**David B. Sicilia**,
Henry Kaufman Chair of Financial History,
University of Maryland

"Amidst the deafening noise of polarized politics, economic uncertainty, and rising social challenges, *Launchpad Republic* offers a signal of optimism and hope. Wolk and Landry remind us that limited government, protection of property rights, and a rebellious spirit are critical drivers of America's dynamism. A must-read for policymakers and citizens alike!"

—**Vikram Mansharamani**,
Lecturer, Harvard University, author of
*Think for Yourself: Restoring Common Sense in
an Age of Experts and Artificial Intelligence*

"The timing of this book is perfect. We need a reminder, or more appropriately, a reeducation of how the ideas, events, culture, and institutions came together to create unprecedented progress and prosperity. The scholarly recount of history that led to this amazing outcome highlights the important role of America's unique brand of entrepreneurship. This book is an important defense of entrepreneurship and ideas and institutions that have well proved their value."

—**Ray Stata**,
Founder, Analog Devices,
technology industry pioneer

"In this important book, Wolk and Landry deftly explain how the United States can address its current social issues and preserve its moral authority and global leadership role. The solution is not 'big government' but, on the contrary, leveraging America's entrepreneurial edge: the talent and the energy that have been the source of a remarkable revolution."

—**Marco Magnani**,
Economist, LUISS University, author of
Making the Global Economy Work for Everyone

"Wolk, a successful entrepreneur himself, and Landry, an experienced business historian, trace the free-enterprise arc ingrained in America's culture that produces innovation and innovators time and again. In a thorough and well documented way, they demonstrate how upstarts change norms and adaptability prevails in the past and present and therefore likely will in the future."

—**David Cowen**,
President & CEO, Museum of American Finance,
co-author of *Alexander Hamilton on Finance, Credit and Debt*

"*Launchpad Republic* is the definitive review of America's journey to become the world's entrepreneurial engine. Wolk and Landry expertly uncover the combination of political, economic, and social tensions that bind our colonial origins, our industrial past, and our digital present. This well-researched and thoughtful retrospective of American economic history should be required reading for anyone interested in maintaining our nation's entrepreneurial edge."

—**Sunil Dhaliwal**,
Founder and General Partner,
Amplify Partners, Silicon Valley

"*Launchpad Republic* provides a rich historical and contextual understanding on entrepreneurship in America. With practical case studies illustrating the birth and journey of startups across eras, the book provides a useful reference for educators and learners globally. The book is also a must-have for policy makers working on initiatives to spark or scale local entrepreneurship."

—**Jonathan Chang**,
Former Executive Director, Lien Centre for Social Innovation
at Singapore Management University,
Former Executive Director, Entrepreneurship Centre and the
Overseas Colleges at National University of Singapore

LAUNCHPAD REPUBLIC

LAUNCHPAD REPUBLIC

AMERICA'S ENTREPRENEURIAL EDGE AND WHY IT MATTERS

Howard Wolk
John Landry

WILEY

Published by John Wiley & Sons, Inc., Hoboken, New Jersey.
Published simultaneously in Canada.

For general information on our other products and services or for technical support, please contact our Customer Care Department within the United States at (800) 762-2974, outside the United States at (317) 572-3993 or fax (317) 572-4002.

Wiley also publishes its books in a variety of electronic formats. Some content that appears in print may not be available in electronic formats. For more information about Wiley products, visit our web site at www.wiley.com.

Library of Congress Cataloging-in-Publication Data is Available:

9781119900054 (Hardcover)
9781119900078 (epdf)
9781119900061 (epub)

Cover Design: Wiley
Cover Image: © George Inness, The Lackawanna Valley, c. 1856,
National Gallery of Art, Gift of Mrs. Huttleston Rogers

SKY10034743 070722

For Candice, Addison and Berkeley, and Deanna and Sidney
— HW

For Carolyn Landry, and in memory of Walter Landry Sr.
—JL

Contents

Preface   xiii

Acknowledgments   xxi

About the Authors   xxiii

1   Bigger, Better, Faster, Cheaper   1
Why Entrepreneurship Is More Vibrant and Sustained in the United States Than Elsewhere

2   Gorillas and Guerillas   23
How Start-ups and Established Companies Make Each Other Better

3   European and Colonial Foundations   43
Where America Got Its Crazy Ideas About Property Rights and the Right to Compete

4   Upstart Nation   63
How the Bickering New States Created a Constitution of Competing Interests

5   Building the Entrepreneurial Republic   81
How America Balanced the Race to Get Ahead with the Desire to Stay There

6   The Evolution from Small Business to Big   103
How Upstarts Challenged Incumbents to Create the First Unicorns

7   The Age and Aging of Incumbents   125
What Happens When Giants Fall Asleep

8   The Entrepreneurial Revolution   147
It's Cool to Get Rich, Man

9   The Inflection Point?   169
    Avoiding Pitfalls in Tackling Social Issues

10 Maintaining the Entrepreneurial Advantage   189
    Pursuing Shared Prosperity Without Killing the Goose

Index   207

Preface

Entrepreneurship is often a form of rebellion.

Many people think of entrepreneurs as builders, which is certainly true. It takes a Herculean effort to launch a company, and most successful entrepreneurs have a relentless drive to create, sustain, and develop their enterprises. They work continually on growth and planning for the future. They invest extraordinary amounts of time and resources, and they take on great risks.

But underneath this effort, entrepreneurship is frequently an act of dissent, an attack on the status quo, and sometimes even a political manifesto. The attack may be subtle, through an unserved niche in the market or a product idea that incumbents are neglecting, rather than going head-to-head with those companies. But the entrepreneur is still challenging the established order.

These two sides to entrepreneurship – the encouragement to build, the empowerment to destroy – show up throughout American history. The colonies began as commercial enterprises, with London-based investors serving as venture capitalists. Yet many of the early colonists were dissenters, not just religious but also cultural. The U.S. Constitution put in place checks and balances to mediate this ongoing tension through the institutions of government. The result was a persistent tension between a desire for stability and investment on the one hand, and an implicit culture of disruption on the other. From the colonial period through the current day, this balancing act between rewarding builders and enabling challengers, often the same people, has been at the heart of the American entrepreneurial economy. It has been our internal combustion engine of progress.

These dual aspects are easy to see on college campuses today. Many of the most successful start-ups have emerged out of universities, particularly those receiving government grants to support research and promote innovation. These institutions provide stability and access to resources critical to building a company and are often openhanded in allowing students and professors to commercialize their work. But many of these campuses also have a strong undercurrent of anti-authoritarianism, such as MIT with its strong hacker culture, and Stanford with its legacy of freewheeling culture from the 1960s.

This tension, and how it developed over time, is the topic of this book. We show how the American political economy evolved to manage the dynamic between upstarts and incumbents and to balance the various competing forces at play. Just as it is difficult to maintain democratic government over long periods of time, it is hard to sustain an economy that favors both disruptive competition and stable property rights. But the United States has pulled it off, and the ensuing creative destruction has yielded astounding gains in living standards and material prosperity. While daring entrepreneurs and the country's entrepreneurial spirit deserve most of the credit, the political, legal, and institutional systems are not far behind.

Too often we see American history in extremes, either as a deeply flawed, exploitative project, or as a consensus-based march of progress to ever-increasing liberty, participation, and growth. But the genius of America's political economy has been its ability work through competing interests without falling into chaos. We had deep-seated conflict from the beginning, but just enough consensus to keep from disintegrating altogether (except in the 1860s), and the political system worked to channel those conflicts in a way that balanced property rights and openness. People think wise administrators and leaders can achieve the perfect system, but in practice that often leads to cronyism or stagnation, as many countries have found. In both the political and economic spheres, the adversarial process worked well, as long as it stayed in bounds. America's entrepreneurial economy is often messy and inconsistent, but it retains enough openness and stability to motivate daring entrepreneurs to risk their fortunes.

Entrepreneurship is a core American value, and its virtue is one of the limited number of things that almost all Americans agree upon. For conservatives, entrepreneurship reflects important values such as hard work, individual effort, and reward for success. For progressives, the inherently rebellious nature of entrepreneurship represents a check against power and vested interests. While people might differ on who, precisely, is an entrepreneur and what characteristics should be most prized, the debates – which go back as far as Hamilton and Jefferson – take place within a broad consensus of support.

Multiple perspectives have informed our work on this project. The first is practical experience. One of the authors (Howard Wolk) spent three decades as an entrepreneur, corporate executive, and investor in start-up enterprises. He helped to start and build several technology-enabled ventures, and he has made numerous early-stage investments directly in start-ups and through leading venture capital firms globally. This includes experience as an early investor and board member in what is now the largest auto rental company in China.

More pointedly, along with his father and brother and talented teams over many years, he helped build one of the largest privately held firms in Massachusetts, a classic story of a small business that grew into an industry leader and worked hard to maintain its position. The company began in 1972 as Cross Country Motor Club, selling individual memberships, but it pioneered private-label versions of roadside service for automobile companies and insurance carriers in the 1980s and '90s. As the company grew, it took on incumbent players AAA and GE (which had a motor club for many years), ultimately succeeding by customizing its services in ways that the larger firms would not or could not. Later, once the organization's flagship company (renamed Agero) became the industry leader, it had to fend off challenges from a new generation of upstarts. It acquired a firm in San Francisco and embarked on aggressive digital transformation in order to stay ahead. While no successful incumbent likes competition, many at the company would grudgingly admit that the challenge has kept the company sharper and at the forefront.

The second perspective comes from the academic world, including economic history, law, and public policy. John Landry earned a PhD in American economic history at Brown University and has worked in the business publishing world for close to three decades, including years as an editor at the *Harvard Business Review*. There he came to appreciate the messiness and vitality of how companies and economies actually work. Howard Wolk has degrees in history, economics, law, and public policy, and also served in the Clinton Administration as a lawyer and a member of the National Performance Review, a project that sought to "reinvent government" and make it work more effectively; the latter helped inform his perspective on both the possibilities and inherent limitations of political institutions.

Both of us have witnessed the recent explosion of interest in entrepreneurship, even as the understanding of it in the broader context is still new.[1] Business schools offer more classes on the topic each year, and economic policymakers aim to create "the next Silicon Valley." Governments around the world track their progress in fostering innovation and industrial clusters. Still, those governments and policymakers and other interested parties often have little appreciation of the forces that enable a sustained entrepreneurial economy, particularly the legal, political, and institutional factors. At a time of general rethinking of capitalism and the role of government in regulating business, we have written this book to describe how these factors have operated through American history and how they can be maintained, leveraged, and improved going forward.[2]

Summary of the Book

Chapter 1 lays out the basic argument: that the United States developed a dynamic entrepreneurial economy because it balanced the right to compete with property rights. It contrasts the American propensity to allow creative destruction with other countries that take a conservative approach and are much more likely to protect existing corporate, market, and social arrangements.

Chapter 2 delves into entrepreneurial competition and the differences between start-ups seeking to enter markets and incumbents erecting barriers to that entry. Each side has strengths and weaknesses, and a vibrant economy allows both to prosper. Indeed, most successful firms progress from start-up to incumbent.

Chapter 3 is the first of six tracing the entrepreneurial balancing act from its roots in early modern Europe to the present. Unlike their traditionalist neighbors, such as Catholic Spain, the Netherlands and England challenged imperial restrictions and respected merchants and others outside the traditional gentry. They favored personal discipline, risk-taking, and the mobilization and capital for productive purposes, and distinguished the enterprises of individuals from those of the crown. They carried their commercial bent, egalitarianism, and tolerance to the European colonies of North America, which lacked the highly marketable natural resources of the Caribbean and Spanish colonies and thus had to develop sophisticated policies to encourage development. The colonies' desperate need for settlers created an unprecedented egalitarianism and pragmatism that overwhelmed efforts to reproduce Old World hierarchies.

Chapter 4 describes the process of gaining independence from Britain and establishing a federal constitution. The founders decentralized power but established a strong central foundation to protect essential economic rights. Many of the tensions that proved important to the entrepreneurial economy – tensions that other countries would find intolerable – were accepted in the final document. The result was a revolution in political and economic participation, unleashing a wave of ambition. It remains the core of the American entrepreneurial political economy.

Chapter 5 explores the building of the entrepreneurial nation in the early United States. The ongoing debate between Hamiltonians and Jeffersonians illustrates the emerging balancing act as the country's economy gained strength and achieved a degree of national integration. While policymakers pivoted from neo-mercantilist principles to laissez-faire, the courts favored entrepreneurial competition over the narrow view of property rights behind government monopolies and traditional activities.

Chapter 6 starts with the end of the Civil War, which opened the frontier to a new wave of entrepreneurship while ushering in legal and institutional mechanisms such as substantive due process, national infrastructure development, and the broader and larger stock market. The new scale of markets, connected through railroads and telegraphs, promoted massive private organizations that put new pressures on the balancing act. While these new entrepreneurial efforts brought efficiency and productivity, they eventually became too powerful and the dislocation too great. In the early 20th century, the Progressive movement emerged and argued for federal policies to check this power and curb abuses, including antitrust interventions. A rough consensus emerged on the eve of World War I: big business was to be tolerated but watched carefully.

Chapter 7 describes the results with the rise and then (relative) decline of large corporations over most of the 20th century. The pressures of the Great Depression, World War II, and the Cold War led governments to give extraordinary support to these enterprises, and for decades the results were satisfactory to most people. Giant incumbents did much to develop and promote powerful new technologies and business practices. But increasingly they settled into stagnant oligopolies that hindered economic growth. External factors such as the Vietnam War, the oil shock, and foreign competition, as well as new technologies, eventually forced governments to withdraw much of their regulatory oversight and protection.

Chapter 8 describes the revival of the upstarts from the 1980s to the present. In response to economic malaise, the federal government deregulated much of the economy. A heady wave of start-ups, raised in the anti-establishment fervor of the 1960s and '70s and empowered by optimism after the fall of the Berlin Wall, grabbed the opportunities. Financial innovation, especially junk bonds and venture capital, provided crucial new resources, while the personal computer, internet, and other open systems made it easier for upstarts to build products and attract customers. "Blue-chip" incumbents such as AT&T and IBM lost much of their market value and dominance, but the government (except during the financial crisis of 2008) declined to protect them. Government itself faced disruption from "social entrepreneurs" in education and other areas. By the 2010s, one-time start-ups had become "Big Tech" and were pioneering advances around the world.

Chapter 9 tackles the current popular sense that something has fundamentally changed in the balancing act between upstarts and incumbents. There's widespread fear that the latter now have the decisive upper hand due to "winner-take-all" network effects, lax antitrust enforcement, and the rising power of corporate lobbying and electioneering. Worker displacement, lower wage growth, and the prospect of continued automation, outsourcing, and artificial intelligence raise concerns about reduced opportunity for individuals, while encouraging some to look at Europe for answers. Finally, the rise of China and more authoritarian capitalist states stokes concerns about America's global competitiveness over the next century.

A deeper look, however, shows the balancing act is still resilient overall. While some aspects of the current situation are concerning, in particular the dramatic rise in economic inequality and continued lack of inclusion in important areas, the United States has endured greater pressures on the balancing act in the past, and still thrived. Some adjustments to policy may be in order, but any fundamental changes that throw the pendulum far in either direction will likely cause more trouble than benefit.

Chapter 10 concludes with principles and high-level recommendations to bear in mind as we try to improve the current system while maintaining the attributes that have made us successful. If we build on these principles and successes, as an effective complement to government, we may even be able to expand our entrepreneurialism to solve deep-seated problems such as climate change and inequality. The power of individuals as citizens, consumers, and shareholders should not be underestimated.

By understanding the balancing act between upstarts and incumbents in all its complexity, including the cultural, political, legal, and institutional mechanisms that enable it, citizens and policymakers can better appreciate what it takes to keep it going and, indeed, improve it. The system does not require superior wisdom to work; only an open structure that allows competing interests and the voice of the consumer to be heard, as well as an understanding of the fundamental issues. But insights into the dynamic can help us avoid any fundamental changes to the system that could jeopardize entrepreneurship, innovation, growth, and opportunity, while allowing us to leverage its great energy and creativity for an even better future.

Endnotes

1. Some of this explosion of interest is going into giving some long overdue attention to the role of people of color, and women of all ethnicities, in the development of America's entrepreneurial economy. We hope in a future edition of this book to say more about their part in this story.
2. Several histories of American capitalism have appeared in the past decade, but none offers an in-depth assessment of the country's extraordinarily vital entrepreneurship and its link to the country's democracy. Most of them have provided interesting narrative but less analysis. Michael Lind's *Land of Promise: An Economic History of the United States* (New York: Harper, 2012) argued that Alexander Hamilton's nationalist vision of development economics drove the country's progress, despite recurring bouts of Jeffersonian "producerism" that mostly entrenched local elites and prejudices. We suggest that both leaders' visions helped build the entrepreneurial balancing act. Jonathan Levy's *Ages of American Capitalism: A History of the United States* (New York: Random House, 2021) largely took entrepreneurship for granted and instead emphasized where political leaders fell short in stabilizing and broadening prosperity. By contrast, *Capitalism in America* (New York: Penguin, 2018), by Alan Greenspan and Adrian Wooldridge, celebrated entrepreneurship and creative destruction, but explained the bounty with a more libertarian approach than we offer. Bhu Srinivasan's *Americana* (New York: Penguin, 2017) surveyed entrepreneurs over the 400 years of American development and suggested that Americans' commercial drive was so innately powerful that it overwhelmed political, moral, and social structures. Willie Robertson's *American Entrepreneur: How 400 Years of Risk-Takers, Innovators, and Business Visionaries Built the U.S.A.* (New York: William Morrow, 2018) praised innovators and small businesses with less attention to political economy.

Acknowledgments

Several people helped and supported this work. Davis Dyer at the Winthrop Group played an instrumental role in guiding the authors throughout, while Fred Dalzell of that firm assisted greatly with research. Much of the book germinated at Harvard Kennedy School's Mossavar-Rahmani Center for Business and Government, where Howard Wolk served as a senior fellow from 2012 to 2014. He led a study group on entrepreneurship entitled "Bigger, Better, Faster, Cheaper." Thanks go to Richard Cavanagh, John Haigh, Richard Zeckhauser, Scott Leland, and Jennifer Nash, all of whom provided tremendous support during and after that period, as well as numerous colleagues and students who provided feedback and support during the project's early days.

John Landry thanks his professors from the Department of History at Brown University, especially his dissertation advisor, Naomi Lamoreaux.

Many other people were extremely generous with their time in reading portions of the manuscript, often early on when the text was quite rough. We would like to thank Bill Aulet, Alex Berger, Jeffrey Blecher, Robert Brennan, Jeffrey Bussgang, Jonathan Chang, David Cowen, Justin Fox, Jeffrey Gordon, Michael Greeley, Michael Horowitz, Thomas Jones, Jeffrey Kushner, Vikram Mansharamani, Jeffrey Rayport, Mitch Roberts, Stephen Rosen, Devjani Roy, Gabe Scheffler, John Sinclair, Austin Slaymaker, Alex Slawsby, Gabe Smallman, Michael Vorenberg, and Jeffrey Wolk for their heavy lifting and thoughtful critiques.

We also thank the team at Wiley, including Bill Falloon, Purvi Patel, Samantha Wu, Priyadharshini Arumugam, Ranjith Kumar Thanigasalam, Samantha Enders, and Amy Handy, as well as Silvana Bouhlal and Peggy Wright for assistance with many early drafts.

Howard would like to make a special acknowledgment to his father, Sidney, an entrepreneur and company builder whose spirit of optimism and respect for people is a continual source of inspiration and admiration, and to the many, many associates at all levels within the Cross Country organization over the years who have worked together to make it a shared success.

Finally, we thank our families, especially our wives, Candice Wolk and Rochelle Rosen. A project of this sort takes enormous amounts of time and can become an emotional and intellectual distraction. We could not have completed it without their support and enthusiasm at each stage.

About the Authors

Howard Wolk is an experienced entrepreneur, company builder, and investor. He is co-president of The Cross Country Group, a privately held business group, and a former senior fellow at the Harvard Kennedy School's Mossavar-Rahmani Center for Business and Government. He received a BA from the University of Pennsylvania and a BS from the Wharton School. He also holds a law degree from Columbia and a master's degree in public policy from Harvard. He lives in the Boston area with his wife and two children.

John Landry is an independent business historian and writer. He has written or co-authored histories of several companies, including Mylan Inc. and the New England Electric System. He earned a BA from the University of Chicago and a PhD in history from Brown University. Formerly an editor at the *Harvard Business Review*, he lives in Providence with his wife along with two sons away at college.

1

Bigger, Better, Faster, Cheaper

The streets of San Francisco may be tough, but they were not tough enough to deter Travis Kalanick, the pugnacious co-founder and early CEO of Uber. In fact, the street part was a lot easier than the politics. When the ridesharing website UberCab appeared in 2010, it was an immediate hit. But after its official launch a year later, the company was forced to change its name to Uber after taxicab drivers, who had spent thousands of dollars for their government-issued medallions and had to comply with municipal regulations, complained about the competition.

That was just the first of many battles. As Uber expanded into multiple cities in the United States and morphed from a "black car" limousine ridesharing service into one that set up ride-hailing with independent operators, the fights continued, with the aggressive company continuing to skirt the edges of established regulation. Local municipalities and their taxicab interests pushed back, but Uber generally prevailed, as consumers enjoyed the easy-to-use service. When state legislatures got involved, as California's did in 2019 by requiring platforms to treat "gig economy" workers like employees, Uber took to the streets politically, leading and winning a ballot initiative that created a ridesharing exemption the following year. In other cases where resistance was strong, the company argued that it was simply a technology platform, not a service, and thus exempt from other regulations and restrictions. And it was not afraid to take aim at crosstown rival Lyft at any time.

1

In fact, Kalanick and the company almost seemed to relish the battles with regulators, adopting an approach that was purportedly called "Travis's Law": *Our product is so superior to the status quo that if we give people the opportunity to see it or try it, in any place in the world where government has to be at least somewhat responsive to the people, they will demand it and defend its right to exist.*[1]

Kalanick himself was controversial, and he was forced to step down in 2017 after a series of revelations of inappropriate behavior at the company under his leadership. Nevertheless, with a combination of quick consumer adoption of its innovative app and substantial sums of venture capital, Uber rocketed to success in the United States and expanded globally.

Outside the United States, by contrast, the company's entrepreneurial disruption met determined opposition. In London, where taxicab drivers must adhere to strict licensing and conduct codes, the company discontinued its car operations in 2017 and did not resume operations until four years later when a British Supreme Court decision allowed it back in. Meanwhile, local European companies tried to build up operations in their home countries or other locations where Uber was not yet strong. Hailo made early progress in London by partnering with taxi operators but ultimately merged with a German company to form what today is FREE NOW. BlaBlaCar in France had some early success but stayed focused on the ridesharing and struggled. The Estonian company Bolt, founded in 2013, expanded to 300 cities and 45 countries, but it was late to the game. These companies gained traction, but continued regulatory challenges in many of their markets and limited capital kept them from expanding aggressively. At the end of 2021, FREE NOW had a market valuation at around $1 billion, BlaBlaCar at roughly $2 billion, and Bolt at $5 billion. Uber, in contrast, was worth $85 billion, while its rival Lyft reached $15 billion.

China was another story. In 2012 Didi Dache emerged, backed by powerhouse Tencent Holdings, and quickly achieved market leadership. Kuaidi Dache, with lead investor Alibaba, soon followed. In 2015, the two firms merged, creating the dominant player – rebranded Didi Chuxing – with over 80% market share in what would soon be the world's largest ride-hailing market. For all their relentlessness, Kalanick and Uber did not stand a chance against the government favorite, and it sold its UberChina division to Didi in 2016 in exchange for roughly an 18% interest in Didi.[2]

While Uber ceded the Chinese market to the domestic player, it is unclear who will win the global game. In June 2021, Didi went public on the New York Stock Exchange with an initial market value of $70 billion, and appeared to be poised to overtake Uber. But a few weeks later the Chinese government ordered the company to shut down certain of its services out of concerns about data privacy, and the company's app was removed from the major app stores. The restrictions were part of a broader crackdown on technology firms under the country's anti-monopoly laws, an effort by Premier Xi Jinping to assert control over the emerging private-sector giants. By Spring 2022, Didi's market value had dropped to $10 billion — less than half the IPO valuation — and the company announced plans to delist from the NYSE and move to the Hong Kong stock exchange.

Birthing Unicorns

Entrepreneurship goes back to ancient times, but the velocity and scale of start-up activity worldwide has expanded substantially in the past decade. This trend is in large measure due to the success of Silicon Valley technology firms, the ease of idea-sharing around the world, and the low-cost access to technology and markets facilitated by the smartphone and the internet. Alongside these success stories, enabling their efforts, venture capital and other sources of funding have grown to unprecedented levels in virtually every major country. The result is a frenzy of start-up activity across the globe.

Yet the story of Uber and its peers highlights some critical differences in entrepreneurship worldwide. These differences often reflect not just challenges or opportunities related to specific companies or markets, but also systemic differences across countries. These variations indicate deeper and longer-standing cultural, economic, or political factors, often described by academics who study "varieties of capitalism." While most of these analyses look at broad factors in the economy, many of the differences are most pronounced when it comes to entrepreneurship and the fate of start-ups across various regions.[3]

Despite the buzz of entrepreneurial activity around the world, America still stands out. This leadership includes the country's historic and current ability not just to create new companies at high rates but to empower the most successful of them to grow. As the case of taxis illustrates, the dynamics of competition, access to the market, the ability to raise capital, the power of competitors and other constituencies to resist, and broad political and institutional forces all affect the ultimate success of a venture. When one looks at the results, it is clear that America excels not just in enabling start-ups but in supporting them to achieve scale. And as one looks at the dynamics at work underneath, the reasons become clear.

The year 2021 was remarkable in terms of start-up activity, with an astounding $330 billion invested globally – almost double the amount the previous year. And while many countries reached record levels, the United States still represented the dominant share, with nearly half of all the investment going to companies.[4]

While the creation of large companies is not the only barometer of successful entrepreneurship, the United States continued to lead the world in "unicorns" – privately held ventures that reach the billion-dollar valuation level – at 400. Most other nations lag by a wide margin: India counts 38, the United Kingdom 31, Germany 18, Israel 18, France 17, Canada 14, Brazil 13, and South Korea 10.[5] Moreover, as of the end of 2021, the U.S. has given rise to 8 of the 11 companies worldwide with market valuations above $1 trillion.

Certainly, some of this is changing, as countries and investors are awakening to opportunities to build exciting businesses in markets around the globe. But it is not clear how these companies will fare over time and whether the enterprises that emerge in this frenzy will unleash a continual cycle of innovation and entrepreneurship in their countries that will endure beyond those firms, or simply devolve into stagnant industry incumbents once they reach the top.

It is particularly interesting to consider these statistics in light of China's rise. At 158 unicorns, China is the only nation that comes close to the United States and may soon overtake it – albeit with four times the population. However, recent issues such as the crackdown on the large technology firms, the temporary detention of Ant Group founder Jack Ma, the restrictions on civil liberties in Hong Kong, and the Evergrande financial crisis all raise questions about the long-term future off China's entrepreneurial economy and whether authoritarian capitalism and entrepreneurship can coexist over time.

While the long-term success of entrepreneurship in other parts of the world remains an open question, American leadership in this area is clear and has been an important pillar of its development since inception. How do we understand America's remarkable support and encouragement of entrepreneurship?

Historians and other experts have laid out several contributing factors. The country's open frontiers, with virgin land and other natural resources, invited growth and created a culture of expansion.[6] Moreover, from the very beginning, the country desperately needed people to work the land and later to help build out its infrastructure. As a result, the nation developed a culture the that offered people opportunities and welcomed a steady flow of talented immigrants, restless enough to leave their own countries and willing to take on new opportunities.[7] Substantial public investment in infrastructure, research institutions, and fundamental science likewise have been essential to developing many new industries.[8]

Yet these factors alone do not suffice to explain the wave after wave of entrepreneurial activity in the history of American capitalism. After all, the United States is not the only large, immigrant-frontier country with a public-minded and growth-oriented government. But it stands out for the intensity, breadth, and duration of its entrepreneurial verve. Something else is needed to explain how the country has been able to empower people to chase after bold dreams, risking financial resources and tackling a myriad of other challenges, rather than apply their talents toward contented lives in comfortable settings.

That something else may best be described, ironically, as safety. Or at least safety in taking risks and investing the time, talent, and energy in pursuit of dreams. In most other countries, entrepreneurs often face major challenges, impediments, and barriers to entry when it comes to starting businesses. They must overcome stiff or capricious licensing requirements, burdensome regulation, and a weak transportation and financial infrastructure (including access to capital). And should these entrepreneurs falter, they have to deal with devastating liability or even social disgrace.

More significantly, America's cultural, legal, and political systems give entrepreneurs the room to succeed and grow, even if that means pushing up against strong, established foes. In many countries, new enterprises, especially innovative or disruptive ones, often face powerful forces of resistance or co-optation, whether at the national or local level. In some countries, this includes the possibility that government authorities might prevent or deter the new competitive enterprise or even expropriate successful ones. In other countries, especially in more developed ones, the resistance is subtle. Since innovative firms often upset the apple cart, a range of actors including large established firms, small businesses, workers, suppliers, and even customers may object, and these forces of resistance create deterrents through the political and institutional system.[9] Aspiring innovators often have little recourse.[10]

An important corollary to America's pro-start-up culture is its inherent opposition to cronyism and monopoly. As discussed later, America has a strong tradition against protectionism at both the local and national levels. While companies no doubt can be effective in garnering and using political influence, citizen-consumer interests have largely prevailed over time, giving innovators and competitors access to the marketplace at any level while also creating a larger market overall. The result has been greater innovation, productivity, and efficiency, as well as a sustained and continuous cycle of new enterprise.

Would-be crony capitalists are not the only ones vulnerable to new companies and emerging innovations; here, as elsewhere, other constituents and interest groups, including workers and small business, often resist entrepreneurs. While these groups are sometimes quite powerful and effective in using the political process to deter change, they are usually unable to stop new companies or innovations from finding their way into the market, especially if consumers are directly impacted. Among all the many potential forces of resistance, the relative paucity of protection for incumbents is perhaps the most noteworthy difference between America's dynamic entrepreneurial economy and nearly all other competitive economies.

Slaying Dragons

It may seem ironic that even as America spawns more unicorns than other countries, it also is more lenient in allowing large and successful firms to fail. But this underside – the "destruction" component in Joseph Schumpeter's famous formulation – is actually an essential part of the equation. Not only does the hypercompetitive market economy of the United States allow upstarts to challenge incumbents and sometimes win, but the intensity of the competition, and the relatively few ways for incumbents to seek protection, forces those large companies to "stay on their toes."[11] Part of what drives unicorns is the recognition that they may themselves be vulnerable.

It is not a coincidence that while the United States saw more unicorns emerge in the last several years, it also witnessed significant failures of some of its largest and most powerful companies. Even General Electric, a mainstay on the Dow Jones Industrial Average for a century, fell from the index in 2018, preceded by such giants as AT&T, Sears, and General Motors. A study of publicly traded firms on the Standard and Poor's 500 index found that the average "corporate lifespan" is at an all-time low and continues to decline.[12] Amidst the growth of powerful new companies, America's "churn rate" among large firms is higher than elsewhere.

As will be discussed later in the book, there are many reasons why large and powerful incumbents decline. New disruptive technologies might change the underlying economics of a product or market, and established firms have difficulty identifying or adopting to the change. In other cases, corporate bureaucracy, incentive systems, or plain bad luck exact a toll. But the key feature of the American business environment is that, in general, we do not prop up faltering companies and we allow even the largest and most powerful firms to fail.

The difference between the United States and most of the world is striking in this regard. In much of the developing world, inefficient or corrupt governments, along with conservative cultural norms and unclear property rights, stifle entrepreneurship, whether the small business variety or innovative start-ups.[13] In some countries, authoritarian regimes offer stability, but with greater risk of confiscation or favoritism – especially for companies with big ambitions. Successful firms often become aligned with the state. Even in fast-growing "entrepreneurial nations," the state often promotes "national champions," frequently at the expense of true dynamism. China and India have witnessed an explosion of start-ups and the emergence of large, powerful companies, but most of the success stories are tied to the political power base. It remains unclear whether newer entities in these countries will be able to challenge incumbents or, just as important, whether these rising firms will stagnate due to the lack of serious challengers as they obtain and protect a leading market position.[14]

Even the most liberal, Westernized countries have failed to support the level of dynamism seen in America. Germany and Japan are thriving, but they tend to encourage static consortiums of firms and supporting business networks, often as part of concerted national policies. Their leading companies have typically existed for decades and are aligned with the government, major banks, and employee unions. Supplier networks are vibrant and competitive (the German *Mittelstand* firms and members of Japanese *keiretsu* come to mind), but without the winner-take-all dynamism that encourages risk-taking in the United States. France has wrestled with liberalizing, but many incumbents remain entrenched and small business incumbents are politically powerful. The United Kingdom's economy is also largely static and facing challenges to its leadership role in capital markets due to Brexit. To be sure, many European cities have recently seen a high level of entrepreneurial activity – Berlin, Stockholm, London, and Paris have particularly active start-up scenes – but none have yet demonstrated the U.S.'s relentless cycle of start-ups challenging incumbents over decades.

The closest comparison to the United States in this regard is Israel, a small country with an impressive level of innovation from many venture-backed firms. As noted in a top-selling book on the topic, this "start-up nation's" dynamic and assertive culture has been perhaps its most powerful asset. But Israel's export-intensive high-tech economy means it avoids confronting dominant incumbents as new firms develop. As a result, while it is intensely competitive, it doesn't face the opposition of established domestic rivals typical in most large developed countries. Israel is the exception that proves the rule.[15] (See Figure 1.1, Venture Capital as a % of GDP by Country.)

Challenging and Limiting Authority

Underlying the balancing act between upstarts and incumbents is the seldom appreciated tension between two central principles in American political economy: the right to property and the right to compete. While often at odds, these principles emerged together centuries ago out of a general mistrust of powerful authority, especially monarchy. Both principles check the possibility of government overreach, which is how they became embedded in the U.S. constitution at the nation's founding.

The American adoption of these principles emerged from long-running traditions dating back to the feudal system, most notably in England. Early property rights were recognized in 1215 in the Magna Carta, which protected the interests of the nobility from monarchical invasion. This concept of secured interest and limited royal prerogative carried over later to firming up property rights related to the issuance of royal grants and charters during the age of exploration.[16] Wealthy gentry worried that central authorities would confiscate personal property, while venturers sought certainty before investing time and resources to risky endeavors. Over time, these protections expanded to other enablers of commercial activity such as contracts, insurance, and financial instruments, as well as patents for inventions.[17]

Compared with classic property rights, the right to compete is a nebulous concept, but it too has deep roots. The modern sense of economic competition as a positive social force emerged in the early modern period of European history, long after widespread recognition of property rights. The right to compete took shape initially from the questioning of scientific and religious authority during the Scientific Revolution and the Enlightenment, and soon broadened into commerce.[18] The development of guilds also led to early issues regarding the ability or right to conduct trade. The controversy over the enclosure

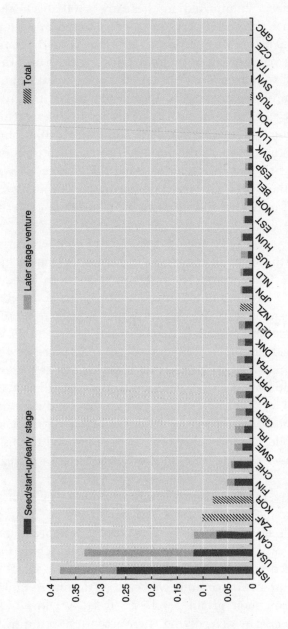

Figure 1.1 Venture capital as a percentage of gross domestic product by country.

Source: OECD Capital Series, "Entrepreneurship at a Glance, 2016."

movement in the 16th century, pitting landowners fencing in their lands against peasants who traditionally had grazed livestock there, is one example where property interests were both asserted and challenged. These developments culminated in the early 1600s backlash against Queen Elizabeth I, whose reliance on patents limited opportunity and fostered resentment among aspiring gentlemen and commoners. Building on this resentment, both John Locke and Adam Smith proclaimed the right to pursue a trade as an inherent, natural right.

The assertion of property rights (specifically the limit on royal confiscation) and the right to compete (especially against overreaching royal grants) gained momentum with England's Glorious Revolution of 1688. Besides limiting the power of the monarch to confiscate property, the revolution brought a Bill of Rights. Among the changes was a radical restructuring of the British East India Company, the dominant commercial enterprise of its day, to end its domestic (though not international) monopoly rights.[19]

Both property rights and the nascent right to compete carried over to America, and the scope of these two rights and principles have continued to evolve. Classic property rights such as those related to the ownership of land have expanded into questions such as the ability of a company to determine retail prices, a software company to bundle products, a smartphone or automobile manufacturer to determine who can make repairs, or a technology company to parlay data into new services. The right to compete has been asserted in areas such as market access and "fair" competition, in some cases arguing the exact flipside of classic property rights. How the right to compete evolved and developed, not just as a complement to property rights but as a challenge to it, and how the American political and legal systems have responded to this tension, is essential to understanding how the American economy actually generates progress.

The interplay of these rights altered not just the political and economic landscape but also the social order, where "new money" often pitted itself against "old money." At times, entrepreneurs threatened the wealth or standing of individuals with far-reaching influence. Schumpeter noted how creative destruction upsets the social pecking order, with entrepreneurs continually taking on dominant interests and knocking them off their proud perches.[20] Today, wealthy individuals can manage this risk by diversifying their activities, so the dynamic is not quite the same zero-sum game it may have been in the past. And often entrepreneurs supersede rather than disrupt, raising the bar and keeping incumbents fresh and vigilant rather than dismantling them.

The striving and success of entrepreneurs can thus have far-reaching effects well beyond just the economic sphere, including politics.

A Political Economy of Competing Interests

In the 1950s, political scientist Louis Hartz noted that the United States features a long-standing tradition of limited government involvement in the lives of its citizens. Hartz and others identified the key attributes of this tradition as a strong orientation toward individualism, the absence of an embedded aristocratic class, and an egalitarian approach toward social and political life. Personal liberty and rational self-interest constitute the essence of the American culture.[21]

This liberal tradition plays out in economic life as well, and the political and economic system embodied by the Constitution largely allowed "private ordering" in the area of economic affairs. It also allowed – some might say even encouraged – a competition of interests. Both the entrepreneurial economy and the political system involve balancing acts. In politics, the country aims to avoid both the extremes of popular democracy, which infringes on the rights of minority groups of all kinds, and the extremes of rule by elites, which suppresses the interests of the populace. Economically, we likewise avoid favoritism toward upstarts, which would undercut the property and other rights of established firms, and favoritism toward incumbents, which would hinder upstarts from mounting challenges. It achieves this balance not through benevolent rulers or even an explicit consensus but through an adversarial and competitive process. As in the realm of politics, the economic system allows competing interests to be heard, with the ultimate goal of stimulating growth and productivity gains. The result is more dynamism, innovation, and social mobility.

These political and economic systems have reinforced each other over time. The democratic political structure balances power and protects individual rights, thereby enabling competing factions to play themselves out. It self-corrects its excesses, if not immediately then over time. Similarly, in the economic realm, the balance between upstarts and incumbents may break down for brief periods, but neither incumbents nor upstarts have succeeded in capturing political (and in most cases economic) power over a sustained period. In fact, James Madison's *Federalist No. 10,* written in support of the Constitution and often cited in support of competing political interests, explicitly applied the concept to the economic sphere.[22]

Critics will accurately point to glaring exceptions when the balance of competing interest fell out of whack, but history shows that even the most powerful firms have eventually petered out, most often due to new firms or innovations that undercut their market position. In rare cases when companies maintain their position within an industry for decades, new industries emerge to supersede them, and the once dominant firms still exist but in a secondary segment of the economy. The stubborn dominance of oil companies is one example of persistent incumbency, with entrepreneurial energy now moving the economy toward green energy alternatives.

Over the last several years, the role of big firms in the political process has gained a lot of attention. The *Citizens United* decision gave corporate entities additional rights in the area of campaign finance, and large technology firms have assembled "armies" of lobbyists. More recently, some large companies have become active in pushing for voting rights in certain states, to cheers in some quarters and legislation in others calling for limits on "woke corporations." While many people equate special interests and lobbying with large firms, in fact trade groups such as those for real estate brokers and car dealers are among the most active business lobbyists, at both the national and local levels.[23]

In truth, the political influence of business interests has been less potent in the United States than in other countries, a fact noted long ago by Mancur Olson, a pioneer in studying interest group politics.[24] Olson warned of the risk that powerful interests pose to both democracy and the economy, while noting that this has largely been avoided in the United States. Most special-interest pressures have worked in niche areas such as administrative rulemaking and regulation. Broad co-optation of government is difficult in an economy so large and diverse. Ultimately, the best way to keep money out of politics is to keep politics out of money, so to speak. But if some intersection between the two is inevitable, the process of competing interests will remain essential both to democratic resilience as well as economic dynamism.

The link between political and economic systems is familiar to scholars of political economy and the field of institutional economics, which argues that the "rules of the game" defined by governments and institutional agreements shape the nature and contours of economic development.[25] But the specific connection between entrepreneurial dynamism and those rules has not been articulated. A recent best-selling book about economic development across nations and history, which distinguished between "inclusive" and "exclusive" forms of government and economic activity, suggested some of the broad themes described here.[26] Several policy books have identified differences among political economies and have made recommendations keep American competitive and to assist countries that seek to replicate our success.[27] Yet a detailed understanding of America's specific institutional dynamics, its historical context, and the nature of entrepreneurial competition will make those recommendations more effective.

The great feat of the American entrepreneurial political economy is in remaining stable and secure enough to attract investment and risk-taking, while welcoming new approaches that challenge existing companies both big and small. Entrepreneurs from Cornelius Vanderbilt to Jeff Bezos can enter an industry and take customers away from the established firms, and those firms (usually) have little recourse outside of business competition. Those emerging entrepreneurs can go on to build large companies and direct enormous investments, with little fear that governments will confiscate or undermine their gains. They can leverage those gains into powerful market positions, subject to certain limitations. They need only fear other major competitors or the inevitable upstarts trying to repeat the process. Or, in many cases, their own inability to adapt. America's system is seldom straightforward, as market conditions change, information is often imperfect, political compromises are frequently required, and legal cases rarely tee up issues in a perfect or timely manner. The balanced government framework means that the various branches rarely move in lockstep, but the messy process generally works issues out over time.[28]

Other countries have enjoyed golden eras in which vibrant economic activity flourished for periods up to several decades or even a century. But what's remarkable about America's story is the relentless series of upstarts, disruption, and renewal, even as large companies emerged and succeeded. These upstarts often came up against vested interests, whether large powerful companies, small local businesses, or workers, who sought political and legal mechanisms to defend their turf. Yet enough of the upstarts prevailed to keep the waves of economic renewal flowing. And, perhaps ironically, large companies and even some small ones were still able to thrive by staying on their toes. Behind all of these changes has been a legal, political, and institutional system that adapted to and even encouraged this dynamism.

Key Features of the American Entrepreneurial Economy

This freedom to invest, grow, and ultimately become an incumbent – but not becoming so entrenched as to impede the next generation of innovators – is essential to American capitalism. How did our political economy balance the right of upstarts to compete with the right of established firms to protect their property, when other countries have fallen into business anarchy or a stultifying favoritism toward incumbents? This book explains the persistence of the upstart-incumbent balancing act and unique American triumph of entrepreneurship by identifying the distinct features of American life and democratic institutions:

The cultural bias: America began as a commercial venture as much as a religious refuge, and the spirit of enterprise has persisted throughout its history. It proved critical to its anti-establishment founding and to its western expansion. We prize the self-made individual and his or her success. Our strong anti-royalist tradition soon manifested itself as both a distrust of government and an opposition to monopoly, which eventually evolved into a suspicion of powerful corporations. And political and administrative mechanisms have valued innovation and progress over stability and other worthy causes. We favor dynamism, whether in the scrappy little firm or the large corporation, while also respecting hard-earned gains.

The political foundations: Sustained entrepreneurship has depended not just on democratic freedoms but on the country's specific institutional framework. The constitution separated federal powers and created an independent judiciary. Patent protections, prohibitions on titles of nobility, restraints on government confiscation without due compensation, and term limits for presidents all fostered openness while safeguarding property rights. The federalist system of government, which kept state and federal government in tension, made cronyism harder to sustain at both the local and national levels, while enabling the development of national markets. The Bill of Rights and individual freedoms encouraged people to pursue their dreams and assert their independence. And the common law system empowered action better than the more restrictive top-down civil code regimes.

Decentralized, risk-enabling finance and corporate governance: Compared to most other affluent countries, the United States has had a fragmented system of channeling savings into investment. Instead of a strong central bank complemented by a few nationwide commercial and investment institutions, the country features a hodge-podge of local, state, and national banks, though the number of small banks has been declining. Stock exchanges began early, first in Philadelphia and then in New York. Equity finance was particularly important, as was the ability of large fiduciary investors to take risks. Innovations in the corporate law and the establishment of the "prudent man" rule for investment pools in the 19th century, the creation of venture capital and high-yield "junk" bonds in the 20th century, and other supporting mechanisms fueled an ongoing stream of new enterprises. The legal system also evolved to facilitate these ventures. Contract law and open general incorporation statutes enabled private exchange and supported risk capital. Limits on interlocking directorates led by large banks, and the Anglo-Saxon investor-driven board model (so different from the Continental European dual board framework, including worker councils) have kept firms more nimble. More recently, America's focus on shareholder capitalism has forced companies to move aggressively and avoid complacency. Even in the area of environmental, social, and governance (ESG) oversight, American companies are driven by shareholder action more than by government directive.

Support of market access for innovation: While generally allowing companies to use their property as they see fit, Americans have drawn the line at certain attempts to prevent rivals or new entrants from gaining access to markets. Courts have struck down discriminatory freight pricing (railroads), proprietary parts and service agreements (appliances), discriminatory software tie-ins (Microsoft and Google), and tiered access (telecom's net neutrality). Policymakers have encouraged new platforms to emerge that disrupt even the largest players, with railroads replacing canals, and highways in turn replacing them, from telegraph to telephone to internet, and from radio to broadcast television to cable to streaming. Once the new platforms dominate, the cycle continues.

Consumers over interest groups: Battles between upstarts and incumbents involve business entities. But in resolving disputes over potentially disruptive innovation or business combinations, the voice of the consumer has weighed heavily. Other countries typically focus on other companies or on workers in areas involving competition. This tends to preserve the status quo even if it means consumers pay more for goods and services. By looking at the diffuse body of consumers, rather than at specific groups, the American approach is much less susceptible to cronyism and more likely to promote productivity gains over the long term.

Tolerating Collateral Damage

The true magic of American entrepreneurial capitalism and political economy, then, is how it fosters continuing cycles of upstarts and incumbents. The system encourages start-up ventures to enter or create markets by promising to respect the wealth that these entities create, free from government confiscation, even as the most successful of them become quite large and profitable. It also limits the ability of these companies to protect their position against the next wave of upstart challengers. By striking this unique balance, America has enjoyed sustained economic growth, productivity improvements, and innovation throughout most of its history. This support of innovation, risk-taking, and development spurred entrepreneurship from the country's very beginning, reinforcing a culture of entrepreneurship and what has been termed the continuous "release of creative human energy."[29]

But the American system is neither perfect nor easy to maintain. By its nature, it creates an ongoing cycle of losers as well as winners. While promoting innovation, productivity, and economic and social mobility, this dynamism yields significant social costs. Many constituencies depend on established companies for employment, for business as suppliers and customers, for tax revenues and other supports to communities, and for general stability and philanthropy.

The disruption can affect both large companies and small businesses, and sometimes both. For instance, in its early days selling books (and still today), Amazon competed against both large chain Barnes & Noble (itself once an upstart) and local shops. Whether it is large firms offshoring production or laying off employees to stay competitive, or small businesses shutting down storefronts, entrepreneurship causes real harm.

Muddying the waters further is how upstarts typically morph into incumbents as they grow. Many Silicon Valley firms adopt David-versus-Goliath rhetoric on their way up, only to go Goliath as they mature, erecting barriers, squeezing out rivals, and hiring lawyers and lobbyists to protect their interests. The paradox is acute when government policy is involved, such as when upstarts that benefitted from public research, infrastructure, or legal decisions later complain about intrusive government oversight. There is irony, if not outright hypocrisy, when an enterprise like Google touts "Don't Be Evil" as its dictum during the early years and then goes on to hire corporate lobbyists to protect its interests. Yet this is a common part of the journey from upstart to incumbent.

Perhaps the most difficult challenge associated with the American entrepreneurial economy is the impact on workers. For sure, new enterprises add employment, and the largest and most successful can create tens of thousands of jobs, many with employee stock ownership. In addition, a number of the new companies, especially the controversial "platforms" that disrupt the foundations of industries, can spawn a whole range of new satellite entities that master new tools and technologies. Today, thousands of companies have been enabled by platforms such as eBay, the Apple Store, or Amazon marketplace, gaining access to a large market in ways unimaginable 20 years ago. At the individual level, the "gig economy" is creating jobs with flexibility and a new worker paradigm that changes employment for many. But the costs are real, whether from large company layoffs, small business shutdowns, or "technological unemployment," and the effect is uneven and often unfair. Well-educated workers in select metropolitan areas are more likely to benefit from the opportunities, while many others are left out. And even some of those who are working within the successful new firms or platforms are pushing for a larger share of the pie, as shown in recent efforts to unionize at Amazon and Starbucks.

Compared with other developed economies, the United States focuses on productivity gains more than on the social safety net. While this may translate into more innovation and often lower costs at the consumer level, it does lead to increased displacement and inequality. This is most pronounced in areas such as health care, unemployment insurance, and education. According to one formulation, Europe suffers from being "too cuddly," while the United States is "too cutthroat."[30]

America's record in sharing its prosperity with all of its citizens is also at best mixed. Without question, the country has an enviable and deserved reputation for providing unlimited opportunity, most often articulated in the American Dream. Upstarts do indeed reach the pinnacles of business at rates much higher than in other countries, and small business has also largely thrived. The success of immigrants is particularly admirable. But America's inclusivity is less enviable when it comes to other groups, particularly women, some minorities, and residents of geographies outside the mainstream of economic life. As protests in 2020 following the killing of George Floyd showed, shortcomings in social and racial justice continue to haunt the country. Finally, as in many other countries, the United States is starting to grapple with climate change and sustainability.[31]

In addressing these challenges, the biggest issue will be doing so in a way consistent with the liberal tradition of limited government and keeping the country from falling prey to the interest groups and protectionism that prevail elsewhere. Within the increasing global consensus about "softening" capitalism to address issues of sustainability and inequality, countries can take different paths to get there. In the United States, enlisting the help and tradition of entrepreneurship, including social entrepreneurship and "green" entrepreneurship, may produce better outcomes than the government-directed mandates typical in other countries.

Understanding the features of the American entrepreneurial economy and how it operates is relevant both within and outside the United States. Within the U.S., recognizing the factors enabling entrepreneurial growth will be essential to preserving it while addressing the social challenges. The rise of technological behemoths, and the increasing political role of major corporations, generate headlines daily, as do broader issues around inequality, inclusivity, and climate change. Addressing these issues without killing the goose that laid the golden egg will be the ultimate challenge, while applying our entrepreneurial strengths to solve these problems offers our greatest opportunity.

Beyond America, many countries around the globe are now looking to establish "the next Silicon Valley." Many take the initial steps to lure entrepreneurial talent and even build successful new companies. They are reproducing the immediate ingredients of a technology cluster with government seed funding, research universities, and perhaps even venture capital. But to succeed over time they must also figure out how to internalize the distinctive economic and political principles at the heart of entrepreneurial dynamism, and understand how the model of the U.S. evolved over the past two centuries.

Endnotes

1. Brad Stone, *The Upstarts: How Uber, Airbnb and the Killer Companies of Silicon Valley Are Changing the World* (New York: Little, Brown & Co., 2017), 195.
2. Stone, *The Upstarts*. See also Rebecca Fanin, *The Tech Titans of China: How China's Tech Sector is Challenging the World by Innovating Faster, Working Harder & Going Global* (London: Nicholas Brealey Publishing, 2019).
3. William J. Baumol, Robert E. Litan, and Carl J. Schramm, *Good Capitalism, Bad Capitalism and the Economics of Growth and Prosperity* (New Haven: Yale University Press, 2007). The authors characterize four types of capitalism: state-guided, oligarchic, big-firm, and entrepreneurial.
4. CB Insights, State of Venture, January 2022. America's share of venture capital investment was approximately 85% in 2004.
5. CB Insights, The Complete List of Unicorn Companies, December 2021.
6. See, e.g., Richard Kluger, *Seizing Destiny: The Relentless Expansion of American Territory* (New York: Alfred A. Knopf, 2007).

7. Dane Stangler and Jason Wiens, "The Economic Case for Welcoming Immigrant Entrepreneurs," Ewing Marian Kaufmann Foundation, September 8, 2015. See also David McClelland, *The Achieving Society* (Princeton:Van Nostrand, 1961).

8. See, e.g., Steven Keppler, *Experimental Capitalism: The Nanoeconomics of American High-Tech Industries* (Princeton: Princeton University Press, 2016); Josh Lerner, *Boulevard of Broken Dreams:Why Efforts to Boost Entrepreneurship and Venture Capital Have Failed and What to Do About It* (Princeton: Princeton University Press, 2009), and Michael Lind, *Land of Promise: An Economic History of the United States* (New York: HarperCollins, 2012).

9. Calestous Juma, *Innovation and Its Enemies:Why People Resist New Technology* (New York: Oxford University Press, 2016).

10. A striking example of an entrepreneur's ability to push through resistance came in 2014, when an immigrant from South Africa, Elon Musk, sued the U.S. Air Force in federal court for refusing to consider a bid from his Space Exploration Technologies company. The Air Force had been content to work with the incumbent consortium of Lockheed Martin and Boeing. The Air Force actually backed down, whereas in other countries it would likely have simply blackballed the presumptuous start-up. Space X went on to win numerous other contracts for its innovative rockets. It also forced incumbents to reduce their costs. See Christian Davenport, *The Space Barons: Elon Musk, Jeff Bezos, and the Quest to Colonize the Cosmos* (New York: Public Affairs, 2018).

11. See Baumol, Litan, and Schramm, *Good Capitalism, Bad Capitalism*: "entrepreneurship is an act of dissent," 85–92; and entrepreneurship constantly churns the pecking order, 115–119 ("Keeping Winners on Their Toes: Playing the Red Queen Game").

12. Innosight, 2021 Corporate Longevity Forecast.

13. For a review of certain basic challenges involving property rights in the developing world, see Hernando de Soto, *The Mystery of Capital: Why Capitalism Triumphs in the West and Fails Everywhere Else* (New York: Basic Books, 2000).

14. See Tarun Khanna, *Billions of Entrepreneurs:How China and India are Reshaping Their Futures and Yours* (Cambridge, MA: Harvard Business Review Press, 2007); de Soto, *The Mystery of Capital*; and Baumol, Litan, and Schramm, *Good Capitalism, Bad Capitalism*.

15. Dan Senor and Saul Singer, *Start-up Nation: The Story of Israel's Economic Miracle* (New York: Hachette Book Group, 2009).

16. See Joyce Appleby, *The Relentless Revolution: A History of Capitalism* (New York: W.W. Norton & Company, 2010), 117–118; Niall Ferguson, *Civilization: The West and The Rest* (New York: Penguin Press, 2011), Chapter 3, "Property," 96–139; David Landes, *The Wealth and Poverty of Nations: Why Some Are so Rich and Some Are so Poor* (New York: W.W. Norton, 1999), 32–35 (property rights in Greece, Rome, and the Bible);

and Nathan Rosenberg and L.E. Birdzell, Jr., *How the West Grew Rich: The Economic Transformation of the Industrial World* (New York: Basic Books, 1986), 113–126.

17. William Rosen, *The Most Powerful Idea in the World: A Story of Industry and Invention* (New York: Random House, 2010).

18. See, e.g., Rosenberg and Birdzell, *How the West Grew Rich,* 28; and also Joel Mokyr, "Culture, Institutions, and Modern Growth," in Sebastian Galiani and Itai Sened, *Institutions, Property Rights and Economic Growth* (New York: Cambridge University Press, 2014), 182–190.

19. Steven Pincus and James Robinson, "What Really Happened During the Glorious Revolution?" in Galiani and Sened, *Institutions, Property Rights and Economic Growth,* 113–126, 195–196 (new rules and institutions solved the "commitment problem").

20. Joseph Schumpeter, *The Theory of Economic Development* (London: Transaction Publishers, 1934), 155–156 (the entrepreneur changes the social strata and there is a "loss of caste" for others; noting the American expression of "three generations from overalls to overalls" and that, like a hotel, people at the top are changing forever).

21. Louis Hartz, *The Liberal Tradition in America* (New York: Harcourt, Brace & Company, 1955).

22. "But the most common and durable source of factions has been the various and unequal distribution of property. Those who hold and those who are without property have ever formed distinct interests in society. Those who are creditors, and those who are debtors, fall under a like discrimination. A landed interest, a mercantile interest, a moneyed interest, with many lesser interests, grow up of necessity in civilized nations, and divide them into different classes, activated by different sentiments and views. The regulation of those various and interfacing interests forms the principal task of modern legislation and involves the spirit of part and faction in the necessary and ordinary operations of government," Federalist Papers, No. 10.

23. Robert D. Atkinson and Michael Lind, *Big Is Beautiful: Debunking the Myth of Small Business* (Cambridge, MA: MIT University Press, 2018).

24. Mancur Olson, *The Logic of Collective Action* (Cambridge, MA: Harvard University Press, 1965) and Olson, *The Rise and Decline of Nations* (New Haven: Yale University Press, 1982). See also Luigi Zingales, *A Capitalism for the People: Recapturing the Lost Genius of American Prosperity* (New York: Basic Books, 2012), 75–78 (discussing "Tullock's Paradox").

25. See, e.g., Douglass C. North, *Institutions, Institutional Change and Economic Growth* (Cambridge, MA: Cambridge University Press, 1971), 48–52.

26. Daron Acemoglu and James Robinson, *Why Nations Fail: The Origins of Power, Prosperity, and Poverty* (New York: Crown Publishers, 2012).

27. Baumol, Litan, and Schramm, *Good Capitalism, Bad Capitalism.* Branko Milanovic, *Capitalism Alone* (Cambridge, MA: Harvard University Press, 2019).

28. Both Vanderbilt and Bezos benefitted from at least implicit government sanction that encouraged innovation. Vanderbilt broke into the steamboat business with the help of a U.S. Supreme Court decision discussed later, and Bezos launched Amazon in part due to a favorable Court decision on sales tax. Both later also benefitted as large incumbents from policies that encouraged infrastructure development in transportation and communications.

29. James Willard Hurst, *Law and the Conditions of Freedom in the Nineteenth Century United States* (Chicago: Northwestern University, 1956), 5–6. Larry Schweikart and Lynne Pierson Doti, *American Entrepreneur: Fascinating Stories of the People Who Defined Business in the United States* (New York: AMACOM, 1999), 86.

30. Philippe Aghion, Celine Antonin, and Simon Bunel, *The Power of Creative Destruction: Economic Upheaval and the Wealth of Nations* (Cambridge, MA: Belknap Press, 2021).

31. See, e.g., Irving Kristol, *Two Cheers for Capitalism* (New York: Basic Books, 1978).

2

Gorillas and Guerillas

One hundred years ago, John Hartford and his brother George sat atop one of the largest empires in the world, and certainly the largest in the Eastern United States. The Great Atlantic and Pacific Tea Company (A&P), founded in 1859 and largely taken over by their father, George, in the late 1870s, had by 1919 become one of the five largest companies in the world, with sales topping an astounding $1 billion. With over 15,000 stores (the most of any company in history until 1990), its own manufacturing capacity, and private brands, the company dwarfed its competitors in the grocery business. Its largest competitors, West Coast–based Safeway and midwestern Kroger's, were less than half its size. And the Hartfords, who still controlled most of the company stock, were among the richest men in the world.

A&P had achieved its success with an aggressive strategy that emphasized increasing volume and reducing costs and prices, upsetting the norms and practices of the local provisions retailers. The company focused on high-volume items, cut out expensive middlemen and wholesalers to source items directly, and developed its own in-house brands in areas such as coffee and baked goods. A&P used its powerful distribution network to speed inventory turnover, add efficiency to the supply chain, and enhance its marketing clout by relying less on promotional trading stamps and expensive national brands. The company also capitalized on demographic trends – increasing numbers of immigrants were moving into the cities, where A&P had most of its stores – as well as the adoption of technologies such as "scientific management" and market research.

Not surprisingly, by the 1920s A&P confronted a backlash. The most obvious critics consisted of small independent grocers who simply could not compete with A&P's low prices. While the company had intentionally jettisoned industry practices by not providing service or offering credit, these benefits were not enough to dissuade consumers at a time when food costs were a large part of household budgets. But local grocery firms were not the only parties who deemed themselves victimized in the rise of A&P. Wholesalers had occupied a profitable position as intermediaries between suppliers and grocery retailers but they were largely cut out of the A&P supply chain and under increasing pressure from their remaining customers to cut costs. And companies like Coca-Cola and Campbell's with national brands often found themselves at odds with A&P.

A&P's critics attempted to rally public support through the political process. The first salvos came at the state level, with various legislatures passing "anti–chain store" acts designed to limit the practices of A&P and other multistore chains to set prices below levels that could sustain small independent retailers; by 1937, there were at least 225 anti–chain store bills in effect or under consideration in 42 states, supported not just by the independent grocers but also their networks of local vendors, bankers, and other constituencies. At the federal level, the Robinson-Patman Act (1936) restricted the ability of large firms to negotiate favorable prices and terms based on volume, and set limits to advertising and discounts. The local incumbents persisted, and by the mid-1940s, the Federal Trade Commission brought an antitrust action under the Sherman Act, seeking to break up the company into several smaller retail groups and spin off its manufacturing operation. The case was eventually settled with A&P agreeing to divest its produce brokerage unit. The company also faced government pressure to accommodate worker unions. Despite the populist nature of the outcry, however, two-thirds of the population supported A&P, and consumers in general voted with their feet. The company continued to thrive by offering low cost and value to its customer base.

But A&P soon faced a more potent rival, a new form of retailer dubbed the "supermarket." Started by a few small entrepreneurs across several states in the early 1930s, larger-format stores offering a range of national consumer brands and more convenience began to take off during World War II. As with A&P's growth decades earlier, supermarkets benefitted from changes in demographics, especially the growth of the suburbs, as well as new technologies – refrigeration, radio and television, even the shopping cart. The supermarket chains also began to offer a broader range of goods, allowing them to use some grocery products as loss leaders and providing concessions to third parties to sell additional goods in their stores. A&P, finding itself with many of its stores "in the wrong locations with the wrong format" and its proprietary brands and manufacturing capacity less important, was at a crossroads. Just as importantly, its new competitors (and even some traditional ones that were able to pivot into the new category more quickly) were fast developing know-how and expertise in new areas such as customer segmentation.

To its credit, A&P took courageous action and pivoted sharply. First trying out supermarkets in 1938, it ultimately made the hard and painful decision to close its older and outdated stores. The company reduced the number of outlets from 15,000 smaller stores to 4,000 in the new format and laid off many long-standing employees. The company was successful, at least in the short term. In 1950, A&P was still the second largest company in the United States (behind General Motors), with over $3.2 billion in revenue. But this apparent victory proved short-lived. The Hartford brothers died in the 1950s, and after going public later in the decade the company began to pay out dividends and reinvest less. Under conservative leadership, the company moved less aggressively into the suburbs, often missing out on what proved to be choice locations, and it proved slow to adopt newer brands and merchandise. Meanwhile, the new supermarkets continued to leverage their strengths in those areas. By 1970 A&P's competitive advantages had disappeared, and in 1979 a German firm acquired controlling interest in A&P for $200 million.[1]

It may seem counterintuitive, but the best way to understand entrepreneurship in the United States is by looking at the large incumbent companies that entrepreneurs often try to unseat, either directly or by creating new industries and ways of doing business that alter the playing field. While considering the behaviors and vulnerabilities of big incumbents may not be immediately relevant in the developing world, where so much of the economic challenge is related to basic building blocks and attracting investment, it is crucial to understanding how America developed into a nation that has sustained entrepreneurial innovation and energy for nearly 250 years. And it might also provide insights into how developing economies that have stagnated may need to evolve.

The story of A&P is both one of continued entrepreneurial growth and innovation, as well as one of almost inevitable decline. Understanding the strengths and weaknesses of large enterprises, including the natural limitations and the approaches they use to protect their positions throughout the "corporate life cycle," highlights both the possibilities for entrepreneurship as well as the forces of resistance. And because the incumbents in the United States are so large, the possibilities for startups are correspondingly greater.

Studying large incumbents also makes it easier to spot the openings that often exist for entrepreneurial innovation. Just as large incumbents have certain advantages, so too do start-ups. We need to recognize and understand the strategies and behaviors of start-ups and large corporations and the interplay between those two very different types of companies. Policymakers and regulators should also recognize how these competing interests work in the marketplace to facilitate harnessing their energy for long-term economic and social benefit. With this context, we can see how the features of American entrepreneurial capitalism described in Chapter 1 serve to encourage innovation and productivity in both new enterprises and established ones.

Understanding Incumbents

Start-up firms tend to garner the most attention and inspire the popular imagination, often positioning themselves as underdog Davids fighting against lumbering Goliaths. But incumbents are often underappreciated. Large companies contribute in many important ways to the economy as whole, and to the entrepreneurial ecosystem specifically. Most critically, these firms define the market and create the fundamental boundaries and traditional economic positions of customers, distributors, and suppliers in any industry. They establish the basic economic and financial parameters against which start-ups innovate and compete.

Most successful large incumbents think a lot about continuing improvement of their operational performance, including incorporating "sustaining" innovation. Big, well-run companies possess organizational competencies and managerial talents that become critical components of productivity, efficiency, and competitiveness. Global logistics, efficient manufacturing, brand marketing, distribution, and supplier management have evolved into sophisticated professional capacities, originally nurtured in large corporations and subsequently instrumental in capitalizing any number of upstart ventures. Many important innovations would not have reached scale and impact without the involvement of large incumbents, either as innovators or as prime supporters in some way or other. From society's point of view, moreover, these competencies in large-scale management can be essential to global competitiveness and security – potential benefits demonstrated by the importance of large corporate firms in rationalizing railroads, assisting with two world wars, and commercializing science. Going forward, one can anticipate the role large corporate entities might play in areas such as climate change, data security, supply chain protection, and other key issues. The performance of companies such as Target, Walmart, Roche, and others during the COVID crisis, for instance, highlights this.[2]

Moreover, many incumbents are growth-oriented, and they are often looking to expand into new markets or redefine the boundaries and definitions of their firms. This natural desire to grow also helps create a rich environment for would-be entrepreneurs who can develop these adjacent markets and perhaps partner with larger companies. Incumbents are vitally important as "anchor" customers, particularly when a new venture needs large accounts to achieve scale and establish credibility in the market. Many consumer products companies, for instance, have located offices near Bentonville, Arkansas, simply to be near Walmart headquarters. For other companies, mastering the Google search process or selling on eBay or through Amazon can be a defining core competency. And, for many entrepreneurs, the goal is to sell their company to a bigger firm.

Large corporations are also underappreciated when it comes to innovation itself. While many like to point to the failings of corporate research and development efforts (R&D), the amount spent by large companies on an annual basis is substantial and, in many cases, effective and significant. Despite the headline gaffes and missed opportunities, large incumbents often serve as leading actors in the effective commercialization of innovation developed by themselves or others. The importance of standard-setting and ubiquity is one such area.[3] For example, IBM in the 1980s proved instrumental in the design of the personal computer platform (including Microsoft's operating system) as well as in its distribution to households and businesses around the world, much as the online platforms and "app stores" run by Google and Apple today remain essential in channeling start-up apps and new innovations to market. And even when incumbents fail to turn their ideas into viable commercial endeavors, the work they do remains quite important and can lead to breakthroughs. Established companies, for example, may generate the initial research that supports later innovation – as Xerox famously did with graphical user interfaces and point-and-click computing. And large corporate R&D is still essential to the progress of a wide range of industries, even if departing employees or venture-backed enterprises may prove more adept at commercializing the findings.[4]

But large incumbent firms also have significant shortcomings and limitations, some of them structural or fundamental in nature, however competent their management. It is hard for large firms to stay ahead of innovation or to chase numerous small opportunities in the hope of finding the one that will ultimately gain traction. Even when companies are on high alert for potential innovative threats and major technological platform shifts, it is no simple matter to identify and execute the required transformation in a timely manner. And sometimes seemingly innocuous upstarts find room to operate in small or otherwise apparently unattractive market segments, and from there grow into meaningful threats, either via a deliberate market entry and migration strategy or simply as a result of the natural tendency of successful new ventures to grow and become more profitable. In the technology field, the natural pace of improvement is a critical factor – early crude technologies often improve faster than the underlying market requirements. As a result, innovations that initially appear unappealing and unfit for mainstream use often move along trajectories that bring them into established markets over time, as Clay Christensen noted in his classic, *The Innovator's Dilemma*. Thus may intrinsic strategic shortcomings of incumbents open windows of opportunity for new entrants or industry disruptors.[5]

In many cases, it is precisely the prudent decision making and focused discipline of incumbent management that creates windows of opportunity for upstarts in the first place. Experts in corporate strategy have actively encouraged focus and discipline among incumbents. Large firms are advised to concentrate on core markets – a strategic imperative that usually generates excellent performance in a short or medium time period but that also leaves untended niches and voids in markets for other parties to fill.[6] Focus is essential, of course, if big companies hope to harness resources and align their organizations, and financial discipline is also critical as firms grow, especially if they are public companies. In such situations, effective strategy becomes the art of choosing both *what* to do and *what not* to do. Nevertheless, a focused strategy cannot prevent disruptions that occur in spite of, or even as a direct result of, intelligent decisions by managers at larger companies that open entrepreneurial opportunities. The ability of entrepreneurial ventures to "fill in the blanks" left by larger rivals becomes critical within evolving industrial ecosystems.

As companies grow bigger, external constraints may also influence strategic options. Important but inherently short-term requirements that banks or regulators impose, for example, may limit available choices for companies. Similarly, Wall Street expectations often influence the options open to corporate strategists. Institutional investors and analysts may assess a public company in ways that discourage risk-taking or volatility, or preempt any investments beyond those that enhance the current core business or achieve particular financial hurdles in the near term. In recent years, pressure from shareholder activists has made these influences pronounced, even paramount. Likewise, companies "taken private" by private equity firms face the pressures of servicing substantially increased debt loads, often limiting the availability of resources for research and development, innovation, or other strategic options.

Firms also face a natural set of organizational challenges as they become bigger and older. The difficulties range from organizational and communications bottlenecks to the difficulties in developing new competencies, altering performance metrics, or recruiting new talent. This latter challenge makes itself felt acutely in the technology field, where modern work environments, new technologies (offering a chance to work with new tools rather than contend with the legacy systems and "technical debt" of older firms), and the potential financial rewards, especially stock options associated with fast-growing companies, tend to drain talent from incumbents and shift it toward smaller upstart ventures. Organizational culture, compensation systems, and internal prestige all complicate this problem. Some companies also cope with the pitfall of past achievement and the natural tendency of successful enterprises to keep doing what they have been doing well, to a fault.[7] Examples include the missteps companies take by focusing narrowly, venturing far afield, becoming disconnected from the market, or pursuing many priorities as they get bigger. In addition, incumbents often suffer the "curse of the installed base," the inertia associated with a legacy business and the difficulty of trying something new that might somehow undercut it.

Finally, incumbents face the "normal" problems that plague even well-run companies. These include downturns in the economy, strategic miscalculations, and the simple failure to respond well or in a timely fashion to adversity or threats.[8] External economic factors, such as interest rates, currency fluctuations, or other forces outside an industry, can roil the business. Many of these factors also affect upstarts, but incumbents cope less easily, more awkwardly, or less quickly. They feel pressures more acutely, with greater repercussions, particularly if they carry debt (which most large well-run firms do). Facing such pressures and failing to respond effectively opens doors to upstart challengers.

For all the negative headlines that have been generated about large, powerful incumbent companies over the past two centuries, the fact remains that many of them – from the British East India Company, Cornelius Vanderbilt's ocean liners and railroads, and A&P's chain stores to U.S. Steel, Pan American Airlines, RCA, Woolworth, and even Sears and GE – have either disappeared or become shadows of their former selves. This remarkable fact attests to both the natural life cycle of corporations and the sometimes life-and-death battle at the heart of American entrepreneurial capitalism.

Erecting Barriers to Entry

While established companies bring strengths and weaknesses to bear as they seek to capitalize on opportunities, they also possess valuable tools and resources to protect and even enhance their market position. How effectively they deploy these capabilities generally determines how they fare in contests against upstart challengers. Understanding the various tools and how they are deployed, as well as appreciating the contours of the battle between upstarts and incumbents, is important in determining the appropriate "rules of the game."

Incumbents typically operate according to accepted principles of corporate and competitive strategy. In his classic study, Michael Porter emphasized "five forces" that determine how competitors – especially incumbents in established industries – can secure their market position. These are the strength of competitive rivalry in a particular market, barriers that keep potential new entrants from joining the fray, the potential for substitute offerings to take business away, and the relative bargaining power of a company's suppliers and customers. Such structural analysis explains why some industries are more profitable than others, as well as how particular competitors are advantaged or disadvantaged. The analysis also identifies how industry dynamics and corporate life cycle factor in and suggests where an incumbent may be vulnerable to upstart competition. In important respects, the core of competitive corporate strategy is to erect "barriers to entry" that obstruct easy market entry for start-ups.[9]

Incumbents possess more weapons than competitive strategy. They may acquire emerging ventures, for example, especially as these become more successful or threatening. In most cases, the goal is not to kill a nascent competitor but to add new competencies to an organization. These can include bringing new skills or intellectual property into a company, helping to transition to a new technology platform, or reaching new geographic or demographic segments. Increasingly, policymakers and regulators are scrutinizing acquisitions of nascent competitors, especially if the acquirer's motivation is to dampen innovation. But in the majority of cases the goal of the incumbent is to stay competitive. Ironically, while acquisitions can be an important tool for growth, it often has the powerful side effect of encouraging even more venture capital into an industry, as entrepreneurs and investors see the opportunity for natural exits from strategic acquirers concerned about the upstarts' innovations.

The most controversial problems arise when effective corporate strategy clashes with public policy goals. In their pursuit of commercial excellence, for instance, incumbents may strive to preserve competitive advantage by attempting to block innovations and defend against new entrants that leverage these. Common approaches include bolstering proprietary distribution channels and securing unique supply arrangements. Such approaches come with obvious political risks: as highlighted in several later chapters, antitrust policy focuses on actions that may create unusually high barriers to entry, such as vertical integration, illegal tying or bundling, price discrimination, or other schemes to impede market access. In many cases, legitimate business strategies that extend the bounds of property rights far into the market, such as enhancing installed software in ways that preempt the features of potential new competitors or requiring original manufacturer parts in order to maintain warranties, also test the limits of a market entrant's right to compete.[10]

Finally, incumbents large and small may resort to outright protectionist strategies involving legislation, courts, or the political process, as local grocers did with A&P. If an incumbent has long-standing ties with regulators, for example, it may lead to "regulatory capture," a time-honored tactic to draw regulators to protect an incumbent's position, as occurred over many decades in the railroad and telephone industries, for example. Using the media to stoke the fears of consumers or employees is another common tactic.[11] Even historic adversaries such as unions or small businesses may be enlisted in the defense against innovative new market entrants. Understanding the tools incumbents use helps distinguish legitimate corporate efforts to compete from those that simply attempt to box out new competitors or postpone market access for innovation. It is crucial to helping policymakers to balance property rights – or at least the pursuit of proprietary advantage – and the right to compete.

Start-ups and Market Entry

What opportunities do start-ups pursue and what are they good at? How are entrepreneurs motivated and how do their strategies evolve? Answers to these and other questions are essential to fostering and harnessing entrepreneurial dynamism.

In many parts of the world, opportunities tend to be "greenfield" and the focus is on basic economic development. But in more advanced economies, new ventures reinvigorate the economy broadly. New firms are involved at many levels of the economy and have been responsible for countless innovations ranging from incremental or "sustaining" types to paradigm-shifting "disruptive" breakthroughs that transform industries or create new ones entirely. Upstart ventures bring unique perspectives, distinctive strengths, and a clean slate to the field, raising the possibilities of breakthrough advances. Such ventures tend to be small, young, nimble, and able to address opportunities that bigger rivals either do not perceive or choose not to pursue. Unencumbered by legacy systems and processes, upstarts tend to leverage new tools, technologies, and platforms more readily and rapidly. They often start with a low-cost infrastructure, enabling them to exploit early cost advantages in certain markets before economies of scale become important, or to serve niches that may be too small for larger firms to notice or serve effectively. In many cases, new ventures start with more intuitive understandings of emerging demand: they pick up on market shifts, for example, enabling them to reach new or untapped audiences or consumers. Finally, young firms with exciting promise often entice potential talent with equity stakes, such as stock options that, while risky, often prove extremely appealing. Such incentives preserve cash flows while offering huge upside rewards.

Entrepreneurs and young ventures competing or innovating in a given industry tend to follow similar "market entry" strategies, even if they may not be conscious of it. Many advice manuals for start-ups begin with specific reference to existing markets, aligning value propositions within existing norms and economics. For example, one framework distinguishes "pioneering," "imitative," and "adaptive" categories in considering the nature of new ventures. With respect to market entry specifically, another defines four strategies including "intellectual property," "disruptive," "value chain," and "architectural" approaches to the market, each reflecting the potential role of a new entrant vis-à-vis the established industry. Entrepreneurs, another advisor counsels, should choose which specific approach to pursue against incumbents, making either "frontal," "side," or "guerilla" attacks.[12] The list of potential strategies is long, but in many cases the path is simply to get started and get better.

Many good ideas simply present themselves to would-be entrepreneurs based on their experience with established firms. Whether it is by rational intent or blind spots and organizational constraints, large companies often leave opportunities "on the table." A study of entrepreneurs found that 70% of new businesses were started by people whose plans had taken shape during previous employment.[13] This is more evidence of the symbiotic relationship between upstarts and incumbents and the role of new ventures in finding and creating opportunities to create value that might be ignored in larger entities.

What about small business? Whether it is Amazon challenging Walmart, or JetBlue and Tesla competing in mature industries, American business history teems with examples of the new supplanting or replacing the old, only to find themselves contending with another new upstart in the fray. Yet while fast-growing disrupters garner most of the headlines, effective challenges to industry incumbents do not just arise from venture capital–funded start-ups. Over the course of American history, most of the great companies started as small businesses, and that continues today. The Four Seasons Hotel chain, for example, began as a lower-cost motel operator before evolving into a premier global luxury brand, while Comcast grew from an upstart cable operator into a multi-industry behemoth. Starbucks began with a single coffee shop, and Dunkin Donuts with a truck. Many small businesses get traction through forward or backward integration, or by migrating into adjacent markets and sectors, or simply by grinding away. And, some argue, the future of opportunity may lie in the advantages of the small.[14]

Despite arguments that point to the inefficiency of small business, the potential for innovation in this segment is significant. Israel Kirzner, like Schumpeter an economist from the Austrian tradition, wrote extensively about how entrepreneurs push the bounds of established markets.[15] Whereas economists from the supply-meets-demand "equilibrium" school might see markets and market structures as relatively fixed, he and like-minded colleagues perceived how entrepreneurs' decisions and actions can alter the definition of goods and services. In this view, the entrepreneur is the economic actor who, "alert" to opportunity, pushes to "get ahead" and so embodies an innately competitive force and acts as a nimble agent of disruption. As entrepreneurs compete, they change the marketplace itself, particularly when they find ways to differentiate their offerings from those of the competition by creating unique features or improving how they are sold. Even something as seemingly mundane as offering and promoting free parking can upset a marketplace, and these kinds of contributions energize the competitive and innovative process.

Many small businesses stay comfortably inside their niche. But the natural inclination of many small business owners is to grow. For some, this means expanding into new markets, while for others there is the chance to vertically integrate or offer new products and services to existing customers. Studies of successful high-growth midsize companies show how even in mature or stable markets certain companies can outperform competitors by deploying "guerilla strategies" or by "edging out" into new areas. These include continually innovating, creating and serving niches, and building on core strengths to outmaneuver competition.[16]

Of course, start-ups have challenges and weaknesses of their own. New teams might be inexperienced and have difficulty scaling up. The clean slate that new ventures enjoy often means they must start processes from scratch, thus missing years of institutional learning. And a chronic shortage of capital and other resources can plague young, unproven ventures. The high failure rate of venture-backed start-ups, even in this golden age of upstarts, shows the risks and uncertainties entrepreneurship entails. Many venture capital firms fail to generate an adequate return and even lose money, while small business failure rates are significant. For every Steve Jobs, as for every Thomas Edison in earlier times, as for every Benjamin Franklin in still earlier times, vast numbers of entrepreneurs fall short.

Upstarts, Incumbents, and Innovation in an Entrepreneurial Economy

The importance of innovation to productive economies has been recognized for a long time, extending back to early commentaries on modern capitalism. Adam Smith clearly articulated the concepts of specialization, and these have remained foundations of economic differentiation and business strategy ever since. As the economy grew and large corporations came to the fore throughout the 19th and 20th centuries, these concepts developed further, resulting in greater understanding for how such entities organize and operate, as well as an appreciation of upstarts as sources of innovation.

More recently, economists have studied why some societies foster technological innovation better than others. In many cases, it is relatively easy for countries to play catch up, simply by investing government resources into research or by promoting "national champions" to compete globally. Sustained innovation often requires more, especially if countries want to stay ahead over longer periods of time and operate at the "technological frontier." Often, this requires strong "domestic rivalry" between firms, as well as the catalyst of new entrants forcing change. In fact, this dynamism is a key aspect of competitive advantage.[17]

Joseph Schumpeter is widely acknowledged as the first to identify the role of entrepreneurs in economic development: as catalysts of "creative destruction," a force that "incessantly revolutionizes the economic structure *from within,* incessantly destroying the old one, incessantly creating a new one."[18] While some of this dynamism could be attributable to external events such as wars or business cycles, innovators play a central role. He noted that "the fundamental impulse that sets and keeps the capitalist engine in motion comes from the new consumers' goods, the new methods of production or transportation, the new markets, the new forms of industrial organization that capitalist enterprises create."[19]

Schumpeter grappled with the relative merits of large firms and upstarts in the process of innovation. In his "Mark I" view, he celebrated individual entrepreneurs as heroes or "wild spirits" (*Unternehmergeist* or "entrepreneurial spirit"). In this line of thinking, the inherent bias among established firms toward maintaining the status quo makes it hard for them to lead change. "It is not owners of stagecoaches who build railways," he observed.[20] Schumpeter eventually expanded his views as he saw the potential for large corporations with sizeable research and development budgets and strong distribution networks to commercialize innovation from upstarts, his "Mark II."[21] Schumpeter also began to worry that large companies, coupled with government oversight, might dominate the economy in ways that could be problematic.[22]

Corporate strategists have also seized on the strengths and weaknesses of large corporations compared with upstarts in helping to identify the best catalysts for innovation. Peter Drucker, viewed by many as the father of corporate strategy, recognized that established firms might neglect or be unable to exploit opportunities, creating windows for smaller or less entrenched firms. Writing a generation after Schumpeter, Drucker focused on the strengths and limitations of big companies, which seemed to him the most dynamic agents of research, development, and commercialization.[23] He understood that established companies might not always identify or seize significant opportunities.

Drucker classified the "sources" of opportunity that recurred regularly across time and industry as a way to define innovation prospects. Some of these might arise from external trends and events. Evolving demographics – increases in the number of retirees, changes in education levels and the growth of the professional workplace, migration patterns, and other factors – for example, could generate new opportunities for economic actors to pursue. "New knowledge" could spawn entirely new industries like computing and life sciences. Most often, Drucker observed, new industries emerged in response to multiple, often disparate developments. Air travel and transportation, for example, hinged on contemporaneous advances in both engine technology and aerodynamics.

The most interesting sources of opportunity Drucker identified involved those emerging "within" existing markets: "unexpected" occurrences, such as when appliances and white goods became available and a few mass retailers like Sears, Roebuck used them to build market share and increase consumer loyalty; "incongruities," such as container- ized shipping, which caught many traditional freight companies by surprise but massively benefitted a few early movers; and "process need," opportunities to make significant productivity gains in operations through automation or the use of new materials. To Drucker, the opportunities "within" underscored the inherent potential for entrepre- neurship even in established industries. But it raises the question as to whether (and under what circumstances) incumbents or upstarts are more effective in bringing them to fruition.

As the growth in start-up activity and its impact on established industries became pronounced in the 1980s and 1990s, companies and management strategists grappled with how to respond. For some, the solution was the creation of in-house venture capital firms, while others adopted aggressive strategies to acquire new firms before they became threats, or to spin out their own homegrown innovations so they could move more quickly. Most were on the lookout for the technology shifts that would redefine their industries, and companies made important and in some cases existential wagers as to what might come next. Some suc- ceeded and others failed, but interplay between upstarts and incumbents was intense. Schumpeter's concept of "industrial mutation . . . *from within*," Drucker's list of sources of opportunity, and the work of Christensen and others noted earlier indicate that innovation is inherent in developed economies. Both upstarts and incumbents play important roles in the process of developing and commercializing innovation. It is therefore vitally important to leverage the strengths and not protect the weaknesses of each to ensure that the dynamic tension between them is preserved and stimulates overall economic growth.[24]

Corporate Strategy 2.0: Ecosystems, Platforms, and Networks

Marshalling, then, these strengths, weaknesses, strategies, and opportuni- ties, incumbents and upstarts contend with each other in a complex, never-ending tug-of-war. The playing field for this tug-of-war, however, can shift over time. In the first decades of the American republic, securing transportation routes, water access, or government charters was seen as the key source of competition advantage. Later, economic efficiency, "economies of scale," and vertically integrated distribution and supply channels became important competitive factors. Moreover, the playing field can shift not just over historic time periods but within industry life cycles.

Consider vertical integration. As an enterprise achieves control over all facets of a product, from proprietary supply through to proprietary distribution, it can erect powerful barriers to new competitors. Many great companies, ranging from early merchants and railroads to chain stores and photography companies, have sought to secure these advantages. Yet this approach may lead to ossification. Developments such as interoperable parts in the 19th century and "outsourcing" and "open networks" in the present day have demonstrated offsetting advantages for firms that are adept at managing third-party partners to reduce cost and speed innovation.

The most significant change over the last several decades has been the move beyond "economies of scale" to "network effects" as a potent and enduring source of competitive advantage. In the past, increasing size led to reduced costs and provided market leaders with an inherent advantage, particularly within the technology industry. Network effects confer a similar kind of scale advantage to firms that have the most users and high levels of engagement.[25] Part of this line of strategy stems from "path dependence," which highlights the power of the past – for good or bad – as a constraint affecting future choices. The classic illustration is the QWERTY keyboard, developed in a context much different from its current use as an intermediary between humans and their electronic devices. The keyboard in the 1870s enabled fast typing on mechanical typewriters without jamming the key levers of common letter pairings like "s" and "t." Yet the QWERTY keyboard remains dominant nearly 150 years later because so many people have learned to use it and the costs of switching them to another layout remains prohibitive. The past abides with us, shaping our options, and big companies understand that branching too far afield poses big challenges.

As a result of network effects and "open networks," the nature of competitive advantage has been transformed, and with it the ways that incumbents seek to protect or enhance their market position. In the past, low costs, price discrimination, and proprietary service or distribution arrangements, as with A&P, were the competitive mechanisms of choice. More recently, effective competitive advantage is being generated by data gathering, analytics, customer engagement, as well as organizational speed and adaptability. With the emergence of new data sources and analytical tools, the competitive playing field is shifting even further in favor of firms that can best understand and anticipate consumer needs. Competitive "lock-in" is being established both by developing holistic relationships with customers as well as by securing proprietary advantages with the supply chain. Recent scrutiny of the so-called FAANG companies (the acronym of Facebook, Apple, Amazon, Netflix, and Google that is a proxy for dominant technology platform companies), for instance, reflects the concern that competition policy should address privacy and use of information and the unique advantages it creates for incumbents. The ability of customers to control their data and how it is used will become increasingly important in counteracting these new sources of competitive advantage.

Despite the recent outcry over "Big Tech" and the power of new platforms to dominate industries, several recent books have highlighted that not all these new enterprises are invincible. One recent book, for example, notes that, despite the outcry of the inevitable domination of digital platform companies, there are significant differences between network effects and more sustainable forces of competitive advantage.[26] Similarly, in looking back at failures of many new would-be unicorns since the creation of the internet economy, one can see that companies with powerful network effects can quickly lose their audiences by failing to preserve their important roles in areas such as trust.[27] The recent controversies surrounding Facebook (now Meta), which some argue is starting to face declining engagement by younger audiences, and Apple, which recently loosened restrictions on third-party billing in its App Store, highlight potential vulnerabilities. While government intervention may still be needed in this area – and indeed the threat of same has been a catalyst for change in the area of Big Tech – as in the case of A&P, the natural forces of creative destruction may ultimately prove to be the most effective way to curb incumbent power.

Finally, the dynamism between upstarts and incumbents in the modern era has benefitted from supporting networks of advisors and services. Incumbents, for example, rely on the advice of large law firms, accounting firms, and consultancies, not to mention big banks and providers of financial services. These actors have material interests in reinforcing an incumbent's position and defending it from threats. Similarly, upstarts benefit from specialized service providers – venture capitalists and law firms, marketing agencies, and consultancies focused on early-stage ventures – that nurture and protect their interests. Often overlooked, the sophisticated services available to both sets of enterprises are an essential part of America's balancing act.

No country has enabled and empowered entrepreneurs as effectively as the United States, which has spawned world-changing technologies, empowered the creation of market-leading companies, and maintained long-term, above-average economic growth – all this despite a constantly changing world. For nearly 250 years, the United States has enabled the most vital and vibrant start-up and entrepreneurial ecosystem in history, while also supporting both small businesses and the development of dominant global corporations. This is no accident, as entrepreneurship has roots that trace back to the beginnings of European colonization in North America. As the next several chapters reveal, American political and legal institutions formed and evolved in ways that encouraged and maintained the dynamism among these various types of enterprises, striking an imperfect yet essential balance that has proven critical to sustaining the nation's long-term economic vitality.

Endnotes

1. See Richard Tedlow, *New and Improved: The Story of Mass Marketing in America* (New York: Basic Books, 1990). See also Marc Levinson, *The Great A&P and the Struggle for Small Business in America* (New York: Farrar, Straus and Giroux, 2011).
2. Robert D. Atkinson and Michael Lind, *Big Is Beautiful: Debunking the Myth of Small Business* (Cambridge, MA: MIT Press, 2018) (large firms create more jobs and exports and also lead in environmental protection, cybersecurity, worker safety, diversity, and other important areas).
3. Cornelia Dean, "Determined to Reinspire a Culture of Innovation," *New York Times*, July 10, 2007 (discussion of innovation with computer scientist William Wulf).
4. See, e.g., Samuel Kortun and Josh Lerner, "Assessing the Impact of Venture Capital to Innovation," *RAND Journal of Economics* 31, no.4 (Winter 2000). For a broader discussion of innovation, see Joel Mokyr, *The Lever of Riches: Technological Creativity and Economic Progress* (New York: Oxford University Press, 1990), 162–163, 284–286 (citing the work of Paul David, Joseph Schumpeter, and others). See also Steven Johnson, *Where Good Ideas Come From: The Natural History of Innovation* (New York: Penguin Book, 2010).
5. Richard Foster, *Innovation: The Attacker's Advantage* (New York: Simon & Schuster, 1986); and Clay Christensen, *The Innovator's Dilemma: When New Technologies Cause Great Firms to Fail* (Cambridge, MA: Harvard Business Review Press, 1997).

6. Michael Treacy and Fred Wiersema, *The Discipline of Market Leaders: Choose You Customers, Narrow Your Focus, Dominate Your Market* (Cambridge, MA: Harvard Business Press, 1997) (suggesting three distinct and mutual exclusive alternatives: operational excellence, product leadership, customer intimacy). See also Walter Kiechel, *The Lords of Strategy: The Secret Intellectual History of the New Corporate World* (Cambridge, MA: Harvard Business School Publishing, 2010).

7. Danny Miller, *The Icarus Paradox: How Exceptional Companies Bring About Their Own Downfall* (New York: Harper Business, 1990). See also Ichak Adizes, *Corporate Lifecycles: How and Why Corporations Grow and Die and What to Do About It* (Hoboken, NJ: Prentice Hall, 1988).

8. David K. Clifford Jr. and Richard Cavanagh, *The Winning Performance: How America's High-Growth Midsize Companies Succeed* (New York: Bantam Dell Publishing Group, 1991), Chapter VI: "When Bad Things Happen to Good Companies."

9. Michael Porter, *Competitive Strategy* (New York: Free Press, 1980). See also Todd Hewlin and Scott Snyder, *Goliath's Revenge: How Established Companies Turn the Tables on Digital Disruptors* (Hoboken, NJ: John Wiley & Sons, 2019).

10. See, e.g., Gary Reback, *Free the Market! Why Only Government Can Keep the Marketplace Competitive* (New York: Portfolio, 2009); Barry C. Lynn, *Cornered: The New Monopoly Capitalism and the Economics of Destruction* (Hoboken, NJ: John Wiley & Sons, 2010); and Alex Moazed and Nicholas L. Johnson, *Modern Monopolies: What It Takes to Dominate the 21st-Century Economy* (New York: St. Martin's Press, 2016).

11. See, e.g., Calestous Juma, *Innovation and Its Enemies: Why People Resist New Technologies* (New York: Oxford University Press, 2014). See also Lucio Cassia, Michael Fattore, and Stefano Paleari, *Entrepreneurial Strategy: Emerging Business in Declining Industries* (Cheltenham, UK: Edward Elgar Publishing Limited, 2006).

12. See, e.g., Bill Aulet, *Disciplined Entrepreneurship* (Hoboken, NJ: John Wiley & Sons, 2013); Gregory D. Dess, G.T. Lumpkin, and Alan B. Eisner, *Strategic Management* (New York: McGraw Hill Education, 2012); Karl Vesper, *New Venture Strategies* (1990); Howard Stevenson and J. Carlos Jarillo, "A Paradigm of Entrepreneurship," *Strategic Management Journal* (1990); Howard Stevenson, Michael Roberts, and Harold Grousbeck, *New Business Ventures and the Entrepreneur* (Homewood, IL: Richard D. Irwin Publishing, 1989); Gideon Markman and Phillip Phan, *The Competitive Dynamics of Entrepreneurial Market Entry* (Cheltenham, UK: Edward Elgar Publications, 2011); Larry Keeley, *Ten Types of Innovation* (Hoboken, NJ: John Wiley & Sons, 2013); and Joshua S. Gans, Scott Stern, and Jane Wu, "Foundations of Entrepreneurial Strategy," *Strategic Management Journal* (2019).

13. Amar Bhide, "How Entrepreneurs Craft Strategies That Work" (1994), reprinted in *Harvard Business Review* Series on Entrepreneurship, 60.

14. Nicco Melle, *The End of Big* (London: Picador, 2014). See also Peter Thiel with Blake Masters, *Zero to One: Notes on Startups, or How to Build the Future* (New York: Crown Business Press, 2014).
15. Israel M. Kirzner, *Competition and Entrepreneurship* (Chicago: University of Chicago Press, 1973), 144.
16. Donald K. Clifford Jr. and Richard E. Cavanagh, *The Winning Performance* (New York: Bantam Books, 1988).
17. See Philippe Aghion, Celine Antonin, and Simon Bunel, *The Power of Creative Destruction: Economic Upheaval and the Wealth of Nations* (Cambridge, MA: Harvard University Press, 2021); Philippe Aghion and Peter Howitt, *Endogenous Growth Theory* (Cambridge, MA: MIT Press, 1998); and Michael E. Porter, *The Competitive Advantage of Nations* (New York: Free Press, 1990), (entrepreneurship and domestic rivalry as key sources of national competitive advantage).
18. Joseph A. Schumpeter, *Capitalism, Socialism and Democracy* (New York: Harper, 1942), 82–83. See also Thomas K. McCraw, *Prophet of Innovation: Joseph Schumpeter and Creative Destruction* (Cambridge, MA: Harvard University Press, 2007), 42–54 (comparison of Classical, German, and Austrian economic traditions), 70–75 (reviewing *The Theory of Economic Development* and the role of entrepreneurs in undermining existing structures; the five types of innovation: new goods, new methods of production, opening of new markets, new sources of supply, new organization), 148–150 (importance of private property and a framework for the rule of law), 159–162 (the significance of different types of business with the industrial order, e.g., "between a tycoon and medium factory owner"), 181 (incumbent market leaders tend to resist change; examples of Michelin and Toyota as disruptive outsiders), 252–270 (business cycles and the role of entrepreneurs in industries such as textiles, railroads, the automobile, steel, and electricity), 351–359 ("creative destruction" coined in *Capitalism, Socialism and Democracy*), 495–506.
19. Joseph A. Schumpeter, *Capitalism, Socialism and Democracy* (New York: Harper, 1942), 82.
20. Joseph A. Schumpeter, "The Creative Response in Economic History," *Journal of Economic History* 7 (1947): 149–159. Reprinted in Joseph A. Schumpeter, *Essays on Entrepreneurs, Innovations, Business Cycles, and the Evolution of Capitalism* (2002), Ed. Richard V. Clemence (2008), 221. See also Joseph A. Schumpeter, *The Theory of Economic Development* (New York: Oxford University Press, 1974), 66, 81–93; and David McClelland, *The Achieving Society* (New York: Free Press, 1961).
21. Schumpeter, *Capitalism, Socialism and Democracy*, 82 ("large concerns account for much of the progress") and "The Theory of Economic Development," 24, footnote 49 (citing "The Instability of Capitalism," *Econ. Journal* (1929) ("in later stages, innovation becomes the business of wealthy, established enterprises rather than new industrial soldiers of fortune").

See also Jonathan Baker, "Beyond Schumpeter vs. Arrow: How Antitrust Fosters Innovation," *Antitrust Law Journal* 74 (2007).

22. Schumpeter, *Capitalism, Socialism and Democracy*, 82 ("large concerns account for much of the progress"), and "The Theory of Economic Development," 24, footnote 49 (citing "The Instability of Capitalism," *Econ. Journal*, 1929, "in later stages, innovation becomes the business of wealthy, established enterprises rather than new industrial soldiers of fortune").

23. Peter F. Drucker, *Innovation and Entrepreneurship* (New York: Butterworth-Heinemann, 1985).

24. See James F. Moore, "Predators and Prey: A New Ecology of Competition," *Harvard Business Review* (May–June 1993), ("As a society, we must find ways of helping members of dying ecosystems get into more vital ones while avoiding the temptation of propping up the failed ecosystems themselves.")

25. Carl Shapiro and Hal Varian, *Information Rules: A Strategic Guide to the Networked Economy* (Cambridge MA: Harvard Business School Press, 1999). See also Paul A. David, "Clio and the Economics of QWERTY," *American Economic Review* 75 (May 1985), 332–337, and Brian Arthur, "Competing Technologies, Increasing Returns, and Lock-in by Historical Events," *Economic Journal* 99 (March 1989), 116–131.

26. Jonathan A. Knee, *The Platform Delusion: Who Wins and Who Loses in the Age of Tech Titans* (New York: Portfolio/Penguin, 2021).

27. Alex Moazed and Nicholas L. Johnson, *Modern Monopolies: What It Takes to Dominate the 21st Century Economy* (New York: St. Martin's Press, 2016).

3

European and Colonial Foundations

R oyal grants had been around for hundreds of years, and monarchies across Europe had used proprietary charters to accomplish a variety of purposes. But Elizabeth I had gone too far. She had already issued hundreds of patents to generate revenue and reward favorites, even if the recipient had no experience in the designated field. When the queen allowed the grants to be challenged in court in 1601, the lawyers lined up.[1]

Three years earlier, she had issued a patent for the manufacture and distribution of playing cards to Edward Darcy, a "Groom" in her Privy Council. Elizabeth claimed that playing cards were promoting idleness and needed to be limited with a monopoly charter. But the choice of Darcy was clearly a reward for loyalty, as he lacked expertise in the area.

When a London merchant named Thomas Allein flouted the grant and imported his own cards, Darcy sued. Allein himself was a member of the Worshipful Company of Haberdashers, an early guild that engaged in its own restraint on competition. But to many observers a merchant-driven trade guild differed fundamentally from a royally issued monopoly. Allein won the case, an early victory in the long struggle to free commerce from government direction.

Edward Coke, a renowned barrister, was then England's attorney general, having previously served as Speaker of the House of Commons, and he litigated the case on behalf of the state. Yet he had a long history supporting artisans and guild members, and many felt his true sentiments lay with the defendant. In reporting the decision, he called Darcy's patent an "odious monopoly." This was not about laissez-faire, as Coke had actually represented Allein's guild in its previous efforts to squeeze out new competitors.[2]

Likewise, Chief Justice John Popham, who decided for Allein, had himself benefitted from royal charters as a leading investor in the Plymouth Company and its settlement of what is now part of Maine (known in the 17th century as the Popham Colony). He was also deeply enmeshed in the power politics of the era, sentencing rival venturer Sir Walter Raleigh, who had helped settle Virginia, to torture and imprisonment.

Still, *Darcy v Allein* served as a foundation for challenges to the monarch's ability to confer broad privileges without criteria or limitations. Elizabeth and then her successor, James I, continued to issue hundreds of grants, but then Parliament put its foot down. In 1623 it passed the Statute on Monopolies, which explicitly restricted patents to 14 years maximum. It also required some novelty and mastery in the recipient (the "first and true inventor"), and some degree of public purpose. Coke helped to draft the legislation and advocate its passage in Parliament. It was an important early step in promoting a right to compete.

Both the case and the statute proved to be catalysts for invention and the democratization of innovation that would help unleash the Industrial Revolution. Entrepreneurs of all kinds, seeing that protections were now open to merit rather than connections, saw their opportunity. By 1800 the Crown was registering dozens of patents a year, with critical new technologies building on one another as never before. That same spirit spread throughout the world, most notably to the colonies that would become the United States. Writing 200 years after the statute, Abraham Lincoln, the only U.S. president to hold a patent, said it had "added the *fuel* of interest to the *fire* of genius in the discovery of new and useful things."[3]

More broadly, the case and the statute helped usher in England's political, religious, and economic upheaval, culminating in the Glorious Revolution of 1688. The tumult transformed the legal and institutional framework, altering both the political and the economic landscapes and empowering merchants, inventors, and nascent manufacturers. American entrepreneurship took root in this fertile ground.[4]

Old World Meets New Opportunities

It was a remarkable era, full of burgeoning ideas, political upheaval, new technologies, and considerable energy. By 1600, the economy in Europe – especially England and the Netherlands – was bustling. The population was growing, and rising literacy encouraged new generations to rise above their station. The spread of Protestantism likewise went along with many challenges to orthodoxy and traditional social structures. Scientific thinking sparked not only fundamental ways of understanding the world but also mundane mechanical inventiveness and tinkering. New technologies such as transoceanic ships and better tools for navigation were creating opportunities in far-off and unexplored parts of the world.[5] This soon extended to political and economic liberties, challenging the unquestioned authority and power of monarchies and large landowners.[6]

Other parts of Europe, however enlightened, were slow to encourage entrepreneurs. French kings actually discouraged aristocrats from engaging in trade, taking titles from those who did. Their system of tolls and seigneurial or hereditary privileges checked the development of a nationwide market, even as the economy was among the wealthiest in Europe. The monarchy eventually sought to catch up in technological development in the mid-1700s, but even then it focused on standards and state-sponsored prizes rather than democratized patents. In Germany, the farsighted Frederick the Great sought to enact reforms, but his military state limited the ability of real transformation.[7]

The New World initially promised more of the same. Monarchs across Europe saw the Americas as a chance to enrich their kingdoms, dispense favors, or solve problems, relying on traditional notions of power and authority. The theory of "mercantilism" – using colonies and the new merchant class to expand the country's coffers – took hold. Monarchs stepped up their issue of charters and other privileges in order to generate investment in these emerging opportunities.

The Entrepreneurial Breakthrough

English and Dutch rulers were certainly eager to build up colonial bases to rival those of larger rivals, but their fragile geopolitical position induced them to make substantial accommodations to do so. They issued charters that gave settlers a remarkable degree of freedom from royal control.

To sustain the faltering settlement of Virginia, England gave "headright" grants to non-gentry settlers, a change that has been characterized as "the start of democracy in the U.S."[8] The extreme version was Rhode Island, whose 1663 charter from the newly restored King Charles II granted what was practically self-rule with full freedom of religion – and which fostered an intense spirit of entrepreneurship.[9] Other colonies, such as Massachusetts and Pennsylvania, arose in part from the need to find an outlet for religious dissenters, which further encouraged ordinary people to settle and make their way in the world.

The English and Dutch also brought their cultural, political, and legal innovations, all fostering this remarkable commercial orientation. The relative poverty of their northern colonial lands induced them to pay more respect to the needs of merchants, and these charters enabled settlers to largely control their destinies. English monarchs were relatively weak, and the independent Dutch Republic, newly separated from Spain, was a commercial state at its core (it did not even name a monarch until after 1800). Protestant churches were likewise weaker there than in Catholic Spain and Portugal.

That commercial orientation included contract law and insurance, legal mechanisms that empowered private economic activity while protecting property and limiting risk. With these innovations, wealth shifted from inflexible land-based assets to more fluid, marketable forms – capital. Joint stock companies, stock exchanges, and other financial institutions turned wealth from a personal, family-based quality to something easily traded and directed to better and more profitable uses. The economy shifted from communitarian manorialism, epitomized by traditional pasturing rights, to market-based capitalism.

The Dutch led the way in most of these developments, partly because their situation was precarious well into the 1600s. They also lacked the historical cohesion that would have enabled a strong monarch to dominate. Small in both area and population, with few natural resources, they maximized the one asset they had: people. To preserve their independence against the Spanish, they developed a highly egalitarian republic that welcomed immigrants of diverse religions. As one English commentator noted in 1658, "the Dutch behave as if all men were created equal."[10] It was an era of intellectual ferment, ranging from legal theorist Grotius to religious renegade Spinoza (the son of a merchant who bristled under monopoly charters). The university in Leiden attracted foreigners with new ideas, including René Descartes, John Locke, and certain English Puritans.[11] Even their aesthetics rejected many of the European conventions, as seen in the experimental, exquisite paintings of the Dutch "Golden Age" that focused on individuals and everyday themes rather than the royal or religious.[12]

Economically, the key institution was the VOC, or Dutch East India Company, essentially a state-chartered group of merchants with monopoly trading rights to Asia. This legally sanctioned cartel started in 1602 and continued for almost 200 years, becoming an incumbent force powerful enough to create markets at home and abroad. It employed over a million people and deployed 4,700 ships over that period. Yet this was no simple crony-driven institution: limited liability and the creation of one of the first stock exchanges resulted in the VOC having over 1,000 individual investors. The tradability of interests also enabled the company to be permanent in nature, rather than tied to a specific expedition. Even within the company outposts, political governance included protections for individual rights.

That dominance couldn't last. The VOC became ever closer to the Dutch government, which gave it extraordinary powers to build forts, wage war, and execute prisoners – a mini-state in the future Indonesia, the West Indies, and New Amsterdam (later New York). As the company took on these obligations, it eventually collapsed of its own weight. In response, the wealthy Dutch stockholders redeployed their capital elsewhere abroad, rather than innovate internally – they became financiers rather than builders.[13] When the republic gave way to monarchy at the end of the 18th century, the Golden Era was largely over.[14]

The English looked on admiringly and eventually caught up. The British East India Company, which Elizabeth chartered in 1600, soon overtook its rival. Learning from the VOC's success, she also allowed limited liability shares to be traded, which led to financial markets, including the London Stock Exchange.[15] Shakespeare's play *The Merchant of Venice*, written in the 1590s, responded more to emerging English entrepreneurship than to Italian commerce.

While the English developed economic institutions on par with the Dutch, it was in the political sphere that things changed the most. Debates over patents were only part of a broad conflict that led to civil war between royalists, led by landed gentry and the Anglican Church, and Parliamentarians, dominated by merchants.[16] While the latter eventually agreed to restore the monarchy in 1660, the merchants gained most of what they wanted.

The Glorious Revolution of 1688 sealed Parliament's triumph. It replaced King James II, who had absolutist tendencies, with a merchant-friendly ruler, the Dutch head of state William of Orange. It firmly established constitutional monarchy under a Bill of Rights, preventing the king from suspending laws, levying taxes, appointing ministers, and maintaining a peacetime army. Soon thereafter the government established the privately funded Bank of England, which shored up royal finances, but whose independence further weakened the monarch. Parliament also took away the East India Company's exclusive right to the domestic trade, though it allowed it to keep its overseas monopoly.[17] The "Honourable Company" went on to eclipse its Dutch counterpart and become a central driver of the emerging British empire – but it also eventually struggled under its own weight.[18]

An Economic Theory for Entrepreneurs

While economic forces put pressure on monarchs, intellectuals provided the rationale for a new set of rights. Until the 18th century, most thinkers were mercantilists who saw economic activity as largely statist and static. France's Jean-Baptiste Colbert, a finance minister in the Court of Louis XIV and leading proponent, argued that a nation's wealth depended on its supply of land, precious metal, and balance of trade – all to be controlled by the crown. The only way to boost wealth was to expand these supplies through empire and restrictions on imports. (Today we hear about "High-Tech Colbertism" as a kind of state-focused industrial policy.) Even the English and Dutch still closely linked their commercial institutions with the state. Thomas Mun, the leading advocate of mercantilism in England in the early 1600s, was an East India Company director.

As people saw opportunities for private initiative and the cost of government control, these views softened. John Locke, who argued broadly for natural rights in his *Two Treatises of Government* in 1690, was particularly concerned with protecting real property from government usurpation. He never explicitly identified a corresponding right to compete, but he noted how individual labor created value, which gave it a kind of sanctity itself.[19] Locke's work influenced English developments in intellectual property such as the Copyright Law of 1710 and the Engraver's Act of 1735.

Locke's concept of natural rights cast a long shadow over the century that followed, including many of the Founding Fathers in the colonies and the Scottish Adam Smith. Writing in the 1770s, Smith explicitly acknowledged this basic individual right in *The Wealth of Nations*, noting "the property which every man has in his own labor . . . is the original foundation of all other property, so it is sacred and inviolable."[20] Thomas Jefferson and other colonists were swayed by the broadened conception of property that can be traced to Locke's work.[21]

Even many French thinkers came on board and took the idea a step further. Perhaps the most important of these was Charles-Louis de Secondat, also known as the Baron de Montesquieu, whose *Spirit of the Laws* (1748) was one of the most widely read books among the educated leaders in the colonies. Montesquieu not only articulated the separation of powers as a safeguard of political liberties, but also saw *"les gens d'industrie"* as economic agents of change and the civilizing virtues of "gentle commerce."[22]

Also challenging mercantilist orthodoxy were the Physiocrats, who were the first to see economic development as the prime creator of national wealth. Most of the Physiocrats focused on agriculture and took markets for granted, but Richard Cantillon, in his *Essay on the Nature of Commerce* (1730), identified the *entrepreneur* as a critical economic agent between landowners and laborers. By risking their resources to buy low and sell high, entrepreneurs made markets work. They helped the state by increasing the circulation of goods and services, and helped landowners by adding value to their produce.[23] Cantillon's entrepreneur was no simple administrator, but a dynamic and disruptive force, and an agent for mobilizing capital.[24] Another Physiocrat, Vincent du Gornay, in protesting mercantilist policies, was apparently the first to use the term *laissez-faire, laissez-passer* (let do, let go).

Cantillon and other Physiocrats believed that individual actors could do much to develop the marketplace, boost productivity through specialization and scale, and even create new products or markets. They also drew the link, implicitly or explicitly, between robust economic activity and a more open political system. While they had little immediate influence on France, whose absolutist rulers continued to follow mercantilism, they gave conceptual heft to the budding calls for respecting the efforts of entrepreneurs.[25] Their arguments for dynamism paved the way for Adam Smith and then Jean-Baptiste Say.

Meanwhile Sir William Blackstone, an Oxford legal scholar, published his four-volume *Commentaries on the Laws of England* (1765–1769). The work codified a commercial sensibility in the common law, and made law more accessible and consistent in the American colonies as well as England. Most of the leaders of the new United States, including John Adams, Alexander Hamilton, John Marshall, and James Kent, were trained with Blackstone's treatise.

Common law was not just consistent across the colonies and the new states, but it also brought with it distinct benefits as a legal system.

Its bottom-up approach to resolving issues as they arose allowed people to act first rather than seek permission ("dispute-resolving" rather than "policy-implementing"). It put the individual, rather than the state, as the central actor, especially in economic matters – in direct contrast to the top-down, government-directed civil code regimes in most of Europe. Common law also gave judges more autonomy and flexibility to adjust laws.[26] This English heritage fostered the development of the American entrepreneurial economy in the first half of the 19th century.

Colonial Openness

While entrepreneurship gained traction in economic theory, its success was hardly guaranteed in the American colonies. Early investors in colonial settlements may have complained about monarchical encroachment at home, but few promoted competition per se in the New World. They saw elite control as essential to the operation of any good society.

Unlike the silver-rich Spanish and Portuguese possessions south of the Rio Grande, or the "sugar islands" of the Caribbean, the American colonies lacked high-value natural resources. Tobacco was the only major cash crop, and its price fluctuated a great deal, leaving many planters with heavy debts. Most colonists depended on mundane exports such as timber and grain to pay off the investors who had secured their passage. With crop prices too low to justify slave labor, especially north of the Chesapeake, they relied mainly on ordinary immigrants to settle the land and build up the economy. And since most immigrants insisted on owning land, the result was a far more egalitarian arrangement than existed in the Spanish colonies.

In every case, colony after colony, the elitist visions of the proprietors proved unrealistic and unworkable. Meanwhile, disease decimated the local native population, giving the settlers a degree of security that made them less willing to grant strong powers to local rulers. Nonconformist religion also played into the mix, breaking down certain institutions of centralized power and laying the foundation for an entrepreneurial culture.

Massachusetts was the clearest example. The colony was dominated by dissenters from the Anglican Church, yet most of them also came with a strong commercial spirit. The Puritan ideology emphasized both religious faith and worldly success, a juxtaposition that may appear paradoxical but that in practice meshed well. As Max Weber famously noted, the sober Protestant temperament encouraged devotion to business and a calm acceptance of risk. Rather than depend on a great lord to assign one's place in the economy, individual colonists had ambitions to build something themselves.[27] Even the son of the founder of the Puritan "City on a Hill" in Boston, John Winthrop, had such a strong commercial spirit that he helped develop the Saugus Iron Works.[28]

By the 1650s, upstart citizens were developing markets in the Caribbean for New England lumber, barrels, beef, butter, and dried fish. Over time they expanded into the slave trade and the rum trade, as well as shipbuilding. These ambitions tested traditional political and religious authority, as seen in the multiple royal charters issued and reissued throughout the 1600s. Merchants successfully fought restrictions imposed by the local theocracy, especially as most colonists were not church members.

Along the way, these merchants also challenged English imperial restrictions. The mercantilist Navigation Acts of 1650 and 1660, which forbade colonists from trading outside of the empire, rubbed up against the emerging belief in the right to compete.[29] Merchants also increasingly saw themselves as a powerful group with interests opposed to landowners.[30] Likewise farmers pushed for land banks to broaden property ownership and issue paper money, even as critics denounced them for "leveling" the social classes.[31]

Unlike the monolithic governments in Spanish America, the English colonies benefitted from a diversity of rule. Rhode Island and Connecticut, founded by disaffected leaders from Massachusetts, were especially open and liberal. Roger Williams founded Providence Plantations with freedom of religion, after Massachusetts expelled him in 1636. Thomas Hooker's Hartford Sermon of 1638, and the Fundamental Orders of Connecticut of 1639, were particularly bold in asserting rights that individuals would have enjoyed if they were in England or Holland.[32] Liberality in one colony encouraged openness elsewhere.

New Amsterdam, which Henry Hudson founded in 1624 under Dutch sponsorship, had a mixed approach. To encourage settlement, the colonists had secured a Charter of Freedoms and Exemptions. Yet the company tightly controlled the settlement's government. The charter also allowed for "patroonships," large estates that gave the owners substantial political power provided they settled at least 50 people.[33] Both the charter liberties and Dutch commercial traditions safeguarded patroon property interests to a point, while also encouraging profit-sharing with their tenant farmers. When the English captured the colony in 1664, the Articles of Capitulation included assurances on property rights (including the patroonships, not to be dissolved until New York State passed primogeniture laws in the early 1800s).

As with Massachusetts, the English monarchs saw Pennsylvania as a solution to the problem of religious dissenters. William Penn's Quaker colony granted individuals increasingly broad political and economic rights, as well as religious freedom. Penn's regime initially favored large landholdings, but the liberal charters and fertile lands quickly attracted ambitious settlers. The colony was known as the "best poor man's country," and Philadelphia eventually became the most cosmopolitan city in colonial North America. As in New England and New York, merchant activity was robust, and brought with it the dynamism and upstart ethos that was becoming uniquely American in nature.[34] By the end of the colonial period, the Penn family's control was effectively diminished.

Maryland also arose to alleviate religious tensions, with Lord Baltimore (Cecil Calvert) receiving a grant for a haven for English Catholics. While Anglican Protestants eventually took over control of the state, its largest landowner, a Catholic named Charles Carroll, helped advocate for religious freedom after the revolution.

The first colonial charter, in Virginia, started out elitist, but eventually granted headrights of 50 acres along with civil control over government.[35] While the colony was more top-down than most, egalitarian structures spread even here by the mid-18th century.[36]

The Carolina colonies were perhaps the most traditionalist and elitist (ironically, John Locke helped write the colony's founding charter, which codified slavery), but even they moved toward equality of ownership and smaller parcels rather than large, very wealthy interests. Georgia's founding Oglethorpe Plan actually limited the amount of land an individual could acquire, in order to avoid the creation of large plantations seen elsewhere.

Development Without Entrenched Incumbents

As the colonists gained both economic freedom and prosperity, tensions developed between hierarchy and equality. These would set the foundation for the evolution of the two entrepreneurial principles noted earlier, the right of property and the right to compete. Most of the colonies had granted special privileges to attract settlers, but then gradually reduced these benefits as the territories developed, which created friction. But with much of the land still unexploited, venturers of all kinds self-selected to immigrate, creating an economy not just more commercial but also more competitive and open than in Europe. Traditional deference to incumbents fell, even to the wealthiest in society.

Thomas Hancock came as close as any colonist to the status of merchant prince. Originally a bookseller in Boston in the early 1700s, he branched out to cloth, tea, salt, and other dry goods. Soon he was gathering cargoes of New England commodities to send to Newfoundland and the Caribbean. From there he bought cargoes bound for London and other European ports, which then yielded him wares that he sold in Boston. He eventually expanded into whaling and the manufacture of potash. He even pioneered vertical integration by opening shops for his goods with incentives to retain capable managers at each outlet. By the mid-1700s he had amassed a substantial fortune and positioned himself to take advantage of lucrative contracts supplying the British army during the French and Indian War. By the time he died in 1764, Thomas Hancock had made himself into the richest man in Boston. His nephew and scion, John Hancock, carried on the flourishing business.[37]

Yet neither of them was ever free from constant, vigorous competition. Merchants of all sizes and scales of operation rose and fell continually in America. Like everyone else, the Hancocks had to reenter the competitive arena with every new cargo. Rather than control large ventures, they took shares in numerous ships and shared risks with other Boston merchants. Their circumstances may have grown comfortable, but their risky ventures meant they could never become complacent. Shifting imperial restrictions could quickly end a lucrative trading route. In Providence, the prominent Brown family consolidated a comparable commercial position, but never stopped hustling, venturing, dealing, and diversifying.[38] In New York, and especially in Philadelphia, the competition and dynamism proved even more intense.[39]

The Southern colonies, with their economies based on agriculture, were more stable, but even tobacco-based Virginia never established a full aristocracy akin to what still prevailed in England. Robert "King" Carter, at the apex of the social pyramid, amassed an enormous estate with hundreds of slaves. He used his commensurate political power to manipulate the surveying and settlement of western lands in which he invested. Here seemingly was the stuff of formidable incumbency. Yet Carter's land speculation still proved risky, and the prices received for tobacco fluctuated widely in world markets.[40]

Carter and other elites jostled with a swarm of smaller landholders, who also called themselves "planters" and fiercely guarded their own access to political influence. George Washington, for example, worked hard to expand his Mount Vernon farm into a plantation to be reckoned with, seeking to emulate his mentor Lord Fairfax. In the West Indies, the dominant sugar planters earned fortunes substantial enough for them to retire, return to England, and buy positions in the aristocracy. Not so their counterparts in Virginia, who complained that the rest of society was showing them less deference. Carter retired rather than adjust to what he called "the new system of politics."[41]

Incumbents often gained the upper hand in the colonies, but they still had to contend with challenges from upstarts, not to mention pressures from London. To outsiders the environment looked unstable and often chaotic. Americans came to see it as a normal state of affairs.

Franklin and the Self-Made Man

No figure better embodies the colonies' emerging entrepreneurial spirit – and those lingering temptations of aristocracy – as Benjamin Franklin. Born in 1706, Franklin's life spanned not only the entire century but also the journey from the vestiges of Boston's Puritan theocracy to the bustling cosmopolitan city of Philadelphia. Franklin came from a line of anti-authoritarian freethinkers, and he combined the Puritan mix of faith and business with an appreciation for Enlightenment writers such as Locke.[42]

In business he was clearly an upstart. Leaving his brother's printing shop (where he secretly wrote the satirical, anti-establishment Silence Dogood column), Franklin moved to Philadelphia and aggressively competed with incumbents. With his newspapers he created a leading media company in the colonies, specializing in sex, crime, and gossip. The enterprise went so well that he could retire in 1748 at the age of 42.

Yet his entrepreneurial commitments continued. A leading scientist, Franklin became known worldwide for his discoveries and accomplishments. He founded the University of Pennsylvania in 1749 as the first nonsectarian institution of higher learning in the country; it encouraged aspiring young men to obtain practical business skills such as accounting, rather than study Latin or Greek. Nine years later he penned The Way to Wealth, a bible of sorts to entrepreneurial Americans for generations to come. And in 1764, he led a group of merchants challenging the continuing control of William Penn's descendants in the colony.

Like many successful entrepreneurs before and after, Franklin worked assiduously to gain entrance into elite society, covering up his artisanal origins. Upon his retirement, he commissioned a foppish portrait of himself to confirm his position as a gentleman. His investments marked him more as a would-be incumbent than a hungry upstart, to the point of serving as an imperial agent supporting the Stamp Act (he did try to convince Parliament to rescind it). He suffered for a time from his association with English rule, and only his later role in the revolution resuscitated his reputation.

Franklin eventually set the paradigm of the self-made man in America. In the 19th century, his *Autobiography* became a bestseller and inspired many to understand the possibilities the country would offer. Aside from providing lessons and values that became embedded in American culture, he articulated what many were already seeing – that hardworking upstarts could find room to succeed in the new nation.

Resisting Imperial Incumbency

Before they could create a true republic of their own, the American colonists had to confront the most powerful of all incumbents: their British imperial masters. Like incumbents before and since, it was becoming both bloated and aggressive – leading to heavy taxes to pay for the French and Indian War (1754–1763). Besides raising taxes, it looked to restrict the colonies to the subservient mercantilist role of supplying natural resources.[43]

Parliament's Proclamation of 1763 also imposed strict limits on settlement beyond the Allegheny and Appalachian Mountains. The move angered a great many would-be entrepreneurs, including Washington, who had just cofounded the Mississippi Land Company and was looking to build his own fortune.[44]

Newly tightened and enforced Navigation Acts forced colonists to send and receive goods only on British- or colonial-owned ships, and all foreign trade had to first go through London. Similarly, the Sugar Act of 1764 increased enforcement of the steep tax on molasses from the French and Dutch West Indies in order to boost high-priced sugar from the British West Indies. New Englanders had built a thriving rum industry by evading the tax and selling lumber and fish in exchange.

But it was the Stamp Act of 1765 that created the largest controversy. The act covered legal documents, newspapers, and other printed material (including playing cards) and it had to be paid in scarce British currency. While the merchants did not support the tax, it was broader popular opposition – including boycotts and demands on merchants for nonimportation – that ultimately forced its repeal less than two years later. The populist outcry was so strong that many merchants and some

landowners worried as much about the emergence of radicals (and
the risk it posed for their property interests) as about the actions of the
mother country.[45]

The Stamp Act crisis unleashed a new force within the colonies –
consumers. Colonists had enjoyed an increasing reliance on and appreciation of consumer goods in the years preceding the crisis, but their
willingness to boycott those niceties awakened them as a political – and
eventually national – class.[46]

Undaunted, the British passed the Townshend Duties a year later,
in 1767. These, too, met with resistance, leading to the burning of
John Hancock's *Liberty* by the British in 1768 (due to accusations
of smuggling), the Boston Massacre in 1770, and Rhode Islanders
destroying the customs collector *Gaspee* in 1772.

Then came the crisis over tea. It began with one of the least appreciated consumer price cuts of all time. In 1770, the Crown eliminated
essentially all of the Townshend Duties except for a tax on tea. Yet colonists continued to object, smuggling three-quarters of all their tea from
the Dutch, despite its inferior quality.

With the British East India Company's tea piling up unsold,
Parliament agreed to an idea apparently proposed by, among others,
colonial agent Benjamin Franklin. The government eliminated the
export duty from London while keeping the Townshend tax in place, a
victory of sorts for imperial principle that simultaneously undercut the
smugglers. The plan also required direct shipment of tea into select colonial parts via a few designated consignees. The result would be lower
costs for consumers, a rescue of the company, and a rebuke of the independent merchants.[47]

It still wasn't enough. Those independent merchants denounced the
designated consignees as politically favored appointees.[48] Rallying people around "no taxation without representation" and inciting the mob
against the company's agents, the Sons of Liberty disguised themselves as
Indians and threw the cargo overboard. Even many consumers who had
little to gain from the upheaval, and would have paid less money for better tea, supported the cause.[49]

Despite the aggressive tactics, many of the Sons of Liberty were
establishment figures in the colonial society, particularly merchants. John
Hancock, John Brown of Providence, Christopher Gadsen of Charleston,
and Charles Wilson Peale and Benjamin Rush of Philadelphia, among
others, were all prominent local economic elite who supported resistance. But other leaders behind the movement, such as Samuel Adams
and Patrick Henry, were upstarts from the lower classes, working to

disrupt not just imperial rule but also the social pecking order. While making common cause against the British, these divergent interests revealed tensions in the political and economic framework that emerged following the revolution.

Entrepreneurial Rebels

On the eve of the American Revolution, many of the enablers of American entrepreneurial capitalism were in place. The first was cultural. The colonists as a people had been ambitious enough to undertake risky immigration in search of opportunity, resulting in a population imbued with self-reliance and risk-taking. They were supported by religious and social forces that encouraged material achievement, an emerging consumer consciousness, and an increasing suspicion of large and distant political institutions. They also benefitted from a developing bias against political and economic incumbency.

The legacy of English law was profound. Most of the colonists identified as British subjects, and they sought independence under their rights as Englishmen. The legal and political and economic principles – especially those from Coke and Locke and the Glorious Revolution – created values and politics favoring both property rights and the right to compete. Besides the common law, the newly independent states drew heavily on British political and economic institutions.

But how to combine this culture and these institutions in a new nation was still uncertain. Rebellion was one thing, but actually running independent states was something else. Without a final authority in London, important questions emerged as to how diverse consumers, merchants, mechanics, large landowners, farmers, bondholders, and others would coexist, much less cooperate, in a new political context and with entrepreneurial opportunity everywhere.

Endnotes

1. Elizabeth did refuse some patents she believed to be destabilizing. In 1589, she famously declined to issue protection to William Lee, who invented the "stocking frame" for knitting.
2. Aside from reporting out *Darcy*, also known as the Case of Monopolies, Coke was the Chief Justice of the Court of Common Pleas in 1610, when it decided *Bonham's Case,* a landmark in the concept of judicial review (and often seen as a precursor to *Marbury vs. Madison,* the early U.S. Supreme

Court case that established judicial review and the separation of powers). Coke was an active member of Parliament when the Petition of Right was passed in 1628.

3. Lincoln's patent was for inflatable bellows that would lift boats over shoals in a river.

4. William Rosen, *The Most Powerful Ideas in the World* (Chicago: University of Chicago Press, 2010), 44–53, 323 (*Darcy* was "the lawsuit that marks the ideological transformation that would decades hence create the Industrial Revolution"). See also John Butman and Simon Targett, *New World, Inc.: The Making of America by England's Merchant Adventurers* (New York: Hachette Book Group, 2018); Stephen Alford, *London's Triumph: Merchant Adventurers and the Tudor City* (New York: Bloomsbury, 2017); and Craig Allen Nard and Andrew P. Morris, "Constitutionalizing Patents: From Venice to Philadelphia" Case Western University Faculty Publication 587, *Review of Law and Economics* (2005) (removing the patent process from executive or legislative discretion reduces patronage and adds to the durability and general welfare created by patents).

5. Joel Mokyr, *A Culture of Growth: The Origins of the Modern Economy* (Princeton, NJ: Princeton University Press, 2018).

6. See, e.g., David Landes, *The Wealth and Poverty of Nations: Why Some Are So Rich and Some So Poor* (New York: W.W. Norton, 1995).

7. See Joyce Appleby, *The Relentless Revolution: A History of Capitalism* (New York: W.W. Norton, 2010), 46–55, 84; Niall Ferguson, *The Ascent of Money: A Financial History of the World* (New York: Penguin Press, 2009); Niall Ferguson, *Civilization: The West and the Rest* (New York: Penguin Group, 2011), 71–85, 87–120; and Nathan Rosenberg and L.E. Birdzell, Jr., *How the West Grew Rich: The Economic Transformation of the Industrial World* (New York: Basic Books, 1986).

8. See, e.g., Daron Acemoglou and James A. Robinson, *Why Nations Fail: The Origins of Power, Prosperity, and Poverty* (New York: Crown Publishing Group, 2012), 19–28; Ferguson, *Civilization*, 103–115.

9. Rockwell Strand, *Newport: A Lively Experiment, 1639–1969* (Newport, RI: Redwood Library & Athenaeum, 2007).

10. K.W. Swart, "The Miracle of the Dutch Republic as Seen in the Seventeenth Century," Lecture at University College, London, November 6, 1967. See also Douglass C. North, *Institutions, Institutional Change and Economic Performance* (Cambridge, UK: Cambridge University Press, 1990), 130 (innovations and institutions in Amsterdam).

11. Russell Shorto, *Amsterdam: A History of the World's Most Liberal City* (New York: Random House, 2013).

12. On the art of the Dutch in the 17th century, see especially Simon Schama, *The Embarrassment of Riches: An Interpretation of Dutch Culture in the Golden Age* (New York: Alfred A. Knopf, 1987).

13. Appleby, *The Relentless Revolution*, 40 (The Dutch grew fat and happy and complacent without following the English path toward progressive

improvements), and 50 (The Dutch became financiers rather than producers and began to ossify).

14. Mike Wallace and Edwin G. Burrow, *Gotham: A History of New York City to 1898* (Oxford, UK: Oxford University Press, 1998). See also Nick Robins, *The Corporation That Changed the World: How the East India Company Shaped the Modern Multinational* (London: Pluto Press, 2012), 41–42.

15 See John Keay, *The Honourable Company: A History of the English East India Company* (New York: HarperCollins, 1991).

16. Rosenberg and Birdzell, *How the West Grew Rich*, 122 (the Glorious Revolution came mainly from merchants).

17. See Landes, *The Wealth and Poverty of Nations*, 234 (Navigation Acts of 1650); Acemoglu and Robinson, *Why Nations Fail*, 187–195 (the Glorious Revolution resulted in Declaration of Rights/Bill of Rights of 1689, breakdown of overseas monopolies, pro-manufacturing tax policies, reform of finance, and independent Bank of England in 1694); Pincus and Robinson, "What Really Happened During the Glorious Revolution?" in Sebastian Galiani and Itai Sened, Institutions, Property Rights and Economic Growth (New York: Cambridge University Press, 2014); and North, *Institutions, Institutional Change and Economic Performance*, 138–140 (the Glorious Revolution led to enforceable contracts and the development of the capital markets, the Bank of England, securities/financial instruments, and property rights).

18. Like the VOC, the EIC eventually lost its vigor. Its competitiveness particularly suffered in the late 1700s and early 1800s as its large ships and costly infrastructure became an inflexible burden. See John Keay, *The Honourable Company*, 174–184 (describing the challenge of Sir Thomas Child and the formation of the New Company in 1698); Nick Robins, *The Corporation that Changed the World*, 24–35, 39, 50–58 (permanent entity in 1657, rival company in 1698, London Stock Exchange in 1773, governance and control vs. Dutch VOC); and James R. Fichter, *So Great a Proffit: How the East Indies Trade Transformed Anglo-American Capitalism* (Cambridge, MA: Harvard University Press, 2010).

19. John Locke, *Two Treatises of Government* (1690), Book II, Chapter 5. See Niall Ferguson, *Civilization* (citing Locke, "Freedom as ability to dispense, and order, as he lists, his Person, Actions, Possessions, and his whole property, within the Allowance of those laws"), 109. See also Rosen, *The Most Powerful Idea in the World*, 65.

20. Adam Smith, *An Inquiry into the Nature and Causes of The Wealth of Nations* (London: J.M. Dent & Sons, 1776), Vol 1, Chapter 10, Part 2.

21. See Paul Johnson, *A History of the American People* (New York: Harper Collins, 1998), 145–146; Stuart Bruchey, *Enterprise: The Dynamic Economy of a Free People* (Cambridge, MA: Harvard University Press, 1990), 127 (citing Hamilton: "Adieu to the security of property, adieu to the security of liberty" in Defense of the Funding System, July 1795).

22. See David Caritthers, editor, *Charles-Louis de Secondat, Baron de Montesquieu* (Routledge, 2009), 506.

23. Richard Cantillon, *An Essay on Economic Theory* (1730), transl. by Chantal Saucier (Auburn, AL: Ludwig von Mises Institute, 2010).
24. Cantillon's remarkable personal history added to his credibility. The son of an Irish landowner, he became a French citizen in his 20s. He cultivated business connections and became a successful banker, specializing in money transfers between Paris and London. But most of his fortune came from well-timed speculation in American land, selling out of John Law's ill-fated Mississippi Company before it crashed. He was also politically active, supporting Lord Bolingbroke and other opponents of the entrenched political order in England.
25. Joyce Appleby, *The Relentless Revolution,* 156 ("In France, arcane laws bogged down would-be entrepreneurs. Laborers and peasants had privileges that frustrated economic development" along with a moribund French monarchy).
26. This is the Legal Origins theory of development, which will be discussed further in Chapter 4.
27. Max Weber, *The Protestant Ethic and the Spirit of Capitalism* (New York: Penguin Books, 2002). See John Steele Gordon, *Empire of Wealth: The Epic History of American Economic Power* (New York: HarperCollins Publishers, 2004).
28. John Steele Gordon, *An Empire of Wealth,* 32–36.
29. James Truslow Adams, *The Founding of New England* (Boston: Atlantic Monthly Press, 1921), 326, 376. See also Bernard Bailyn, *New England Merchants of the Seventeenth Century* (Cambridge, MA: Harvard University Press, 1979).
30. Edwin J. Perkins, *The Economy of Colonial America* (New York: Columbia University Press, 1988), 137. Carla Gardina Pestana and Sharon V. Salinger, *Inequality in Early America* (Lebanon, NH: University Press of New England, 1999), 48.
31. Gardina Pestana and Salinger, *Inequality in Early America,* 46, 51, 55.
32. Adams, *The Founding of New England,* 215 (Adams viewed the more liberal policies developed in Connecticut and Rhode Island during this period as the foundation of America's institutional success).
33. Burrows and Wallace, *Gotham,* 16, 21, 30, 37, 47.
34. Jonathan Hughes, *The Vital Few: The Entrepreneur and American Economic Progress* (New York: Oxford University Press, 1986), 40, 50, 58 (Hughes cites many who view Penn as the foundation of America's institutional success; King Charles II gave him proprietorship of the vast lands of Pennsylvania, but he gave most of it away). See also James Lemon, *The Best Poor Man's Country: Early Southeastern Pennsylvania* (Baltimore: Johns Hopkins University Press, 2002), and Thomas Doerflinger, *A Vigorous Spirit of Enterprise: Merchants and Economic Development in Revolutionary Philadelphia* (Chapel Hill, NC: University of North Carolina Press, 1986).
35. Bacon's Rebellion in 1675–1676 pitted rebel land seeker Nathaniel Bacon against Colonial Governor William Berkeley, one of the initial proprietors.

36. Richard Kluger, *Seizing Destiny: The Relentless Expansion of American Territory* (New York: Random House, 2007), 4–83; Rhys Isaac, *The Transformation of Virginia, 1740–1790* (Chapel Hill, NC: University of North Carolina Press, 1982).

37. William T. Baxter, *The House of Hancock* (Cambridge, MA: Harvard University Press, 1945); and Harlow Giles Unger, *John Hancock: Merchant Prince and American Patriot* (Hoboken, NJ: John Wiley & Sons, 2000).

38. James B. Hedges, *The Browns of Providence Plantation: Colonial Years* (Cambridge, MA: Harvard University Press, 1952).

39. Doerflinger, *A Vigorous Spirit of Enterprise,* 11–66.

40. Gordon Wood, *The Radicalism of the American Revolution* (New York: Knopf, 1992), citing Louis Morton's *Robert Carter of Nomini Hall*, Colonial Williamsburg, 1941.

41. Wood, *Radicalism,* 142–143.

42. Walter Isaacson, *Benjamin Franklin: An American Life* (New York: Simon & Schuster, 2004), 6, 14. See also Walter Isaacson, *The Innovators: How a Group of Hackers, Geniuses, and Geeks Created the Digital Revolution* (New York: Simon & Schuster, 2014), 146, 150, 156.

43. Stuart Bruchey, *Enterprise,* 106–108 (including the Staple Act, 1663; Woolen Act, 1699; Hat Act, 1722; Iron Act, 1750; Sugar Act, 1764; etc.).

44. Joseph Ellis, *His Excellency George Washington* (New York: Vintage House, 2005), 53–58. Ferguson, *Civilization,* 115–117 ("British government attempts to limit settlement to the West of the Appalachians struck at the hard of colonists' expansion plans"). See also Edward Lengel, *First Entrepreneur: How George Washington Built His – and the Nation's – Prosperity* (Boston: Da Capo Press, 2016) and Cyrus Ansary, *George Washington Dealmaker-in-Chief: The Story of How the Father of Our Country Unleashed the Entrepreneurial Spirit* (Lambert Publications, 2019).

45. Arthur M. Schlesinger, *The Colonial Merchants and the American Revolution* (London: P.S. King & Son, Ltd., 1918).

46. T.H. Breen, *The Marketplace of Revolution: How Consumer Politics Shaped American Independence* (New York: Oxford University Press, 2004).

47. It is also worth noting the argument that the British East India Company ships and port infrastructure were bloated and becoming inefficient around this period, evidence of incumbency seeking protectionism. See James R. Fichter, *So Great a Proffit,* 27 (American trade would prove to be faster and cheaper than the B.E.I.C. in the China trade).

48. The group included Governor Thomas Hutchinson's brother-in-law and son, as well as John Singleton Copley's son-in-law.

49. See Benjamin L. Carp, *Defiance of the Patriots: The Boston Tea Party and the Making of America* (New Haven: Yale University Press, 2010); Benjamin Woods Labaree, *The Boston Tea Party* (Boston: Northeastern University Press, 1979); and T.H. Green, *The Marketplace of Revolution: How Consumer Politics Shaped American Independence* (New York: Oxford University Press, 2004).

4

Upstart Nation

E ven for John Adams, who had come to Philadelphia to push for independence, the pamphlet went too far. Later calling it a "crapulous mass," Adams was so exercised by Thomas Paine's *Common Sense*, appearing in January 1776, that he published a counterargument a few months later. But Paine's simply written piece was a stunning success, selling over 100,000 copies in a few months and eventually topping half a million.[1]

Paine's argument for radical democracy, including waiving the requirement of property ownership in order to vote, and providing a simple unicameral legislature (a cause for upheaval in the Netherlands at the time), pointed to the tensions beneath the widespread complaint against the British empire. Some delegates to the Continental Congress were still loyal to the Crown, and their favored political and economic position would be threatened by any change. At the other extreme were people like Paine and Adam's cousin Samuel, who sought fundamental political, social, and economic upheaval.

Most, however, were ambivalent or at least conservative in framing what might come after. Many merchants and landowners hesitated to declare full independence at first, and came around only later as events unfolded. As successful colonial incumbents, they were eager to maintain their position in the world that followed, so they were a ready counter against Paine and others who asserted rights against the mother country. Adams and others in the middle worked to manage these tensions.[2]

The speedy efforts to create state constitutions showed some of the dynamics at work. George Mason drafted the Virginia Declaration of

Rights in June of 1776, asserting that "all men are by nature equally free and independent and have certain inherent rights, of which, when they enter into a state of society, they cannot, by any compact, deprive or divest their posterity; namely the enjoyment of life and liberty, with the means of acquiring and possessing property, and pursuing and obtaining happiness and safety." After declaring independence, Virginia's convention approved a state constitution with a bicameral legislature and a property requirement for voting. Mason's constitution separated the legislative and executive powers and included a bill of rights, setting a precedent for the federal constitution that became a condition for its passage years later.

Pennsylvania soon followed with a constitution of its own, considered "more democratic," matching Paine's approach broadening voting to all taxpayers (not just property owners) and calling for a single legislative body. Besides declaring independence, the new state assembly arrested colonial governor John Penn and confiscated his family's proprietary lands, later granting him some compensation. Some Philadelphia merchants such as Robert Morris opposed the change in government, but they quickly took on important roles as the success of the independence movement became clear.

During the war, Paine himself worked with Morris at the behest of George Washington, but it was an uneasy alliance. After the war, Morris worked to modify Pennsylvania's constitution in response to government-imposed price controls, successfully achieving a more "republican" form of government that included a bicameral legislature and veto power for the executive.[3] Paine eventually left for England and later France, where he published *The Rights of Man* (1791), a populist response to Edmund Burke's conservative *Reflections on the Revolution in France* (1790).[4] Samuel Adams would similarly clash with John Hancock, who was elected governor of independent Massachusetts but was unable to become president of the federal union, largely because of his lavish lifestyle and lack of appeal to the common man.

Wartime unity gave way to varied interests, as the thrilling victory at Yorktown was not enough to establish a consensus-driven government administered by virtuous elites. The independent states eventually formed a federal union, but with a decentralized structure that allowed populism and democracy. Yet with both George Washington and John Adams atop the federal government and contentious nation-building imperatives ahead, the tensions would continue.

The Compromise Constitution

The war's aftermath helps explain the foundation of the messy but effective American approach to entrepreneurship. Following the Peace of Paris in 1783, most people assumed political and economic leadership would take place at the state level. In spite of many shortcomings, the Continental Congress had functioned sufficiently during the war. As a result, it yielded to the weak Articles of Confederation, which the 13 states had ratified back in 1781.

Many state-level efforts proved to have a populist bent. As each of the former colonies produced their own state constitutions, some went further than others in altering political and economic rights, including loosening the property qualification for voting, establishing unicameral legislatures to reallocate power, and issuing paper money to alleviate the burden on debtors. The idea of 13 diverse and sovereign states appeared to work, and the transition to self-government proceeded apace.

Despite a postwar recession, the economy was strong in some sectors, including agriculture, which enjoyed high market prices. Mechanics, artisans, and yeoman farmers were especially eager for an egalitarian and open society. Even Benjamin Franklin, who would participate in the making of the new Constitution several years later, noted that many groups in the diverse economy had prospered under the Articles, including the working classes.[5]

Yet the entrepreneurial energy and economic churn following independence carried an anti-authoritarian undertone. Rhetoric decrying "aristocracy" and "monarchy" filled the air, eroding long-standing habits of deference in both the political and economic spheres. Everywhere people asserted the right to challenge, to compete. Upstarts came elbowing in. To would-be entrepreneurs, the mood of the times signified the arrival of openness and expansive opportunity.

Groups with traditional power were naturally concerned. Many feared mob rule, having witnessed it during the revolution. Others centered on specific problems. As state legislatures issued paper money with few restrictions, for example, and the balance between creditors' and debtors' rights tilted in the latter's favor. Many, particularly economic elites, worried about the safety of property rights and investment.

Given Americans' instinctive upstart bias, they would never stand for a permanent aristocracy, much less a monarchy. But many of them also felt a deep need for social and political order. As the new states sought stability, the basic question became whether a de facto economic aristocracy or an egalitarian democracy, even one with shades of the "leveling" principle, would serve as the foundation?[6]

The outbreak of violence in western Massachusetts in 1786 catalyzed action. Known as Shay's Rebellion, it came from farmers opposed to debt collectors (private and state), and war veterans who sought unpaid military wages. While the resurrection was soon put down, by 1787 many leaders agreed that something needed to be done, and they called a constitutional convention.

According to a classic argument, the Constitution emerged from competing economic interests and attitudes playing themselves out. The main ones were creditors (concerned about rampant paper money issuance), holders of wartime public securities (worried about states honoring their obligations), merchants and early manufacturers (who sought protection from foreign competition as well as free trade between the states), and land speculators (who sought certainty over their western holdings). Most of these groups were wealthy, established citizens, yet the convention included some representatives of farmers and workers.[7] Nor were those incumbents of a single mind. Large landowners' powerful local interests made them ambivalent about a strong national government that might interfere with their prerogatives.

Most of the delegates shared the goal of enabling the country to enjoy the fruits of economic development – a point highlighted when they witnessed one of the early launches of a steamboat along the nearby Delaware River, a technological marvel. Through this array of interests, the federal constitution emerged with hard-earned compromises that promoted entrepreneurship.[8]

The Federalist framers were concerned foremost with protecting property rights against local mobs or populist state legislatures. "Property must be secured, or liberty cannot exist," wrote John Adams.[9] "Most of our political evils may be traced to commercial ones," James Madison observed. The states' "pernicious substitution of paper money, for indulgences to debtors," as well as "postponement of taxes," had created an "anarchy of commerce" that threatened to ruin the young nation's economic prospects.[10] So the framers wrested the power to issue currency from the state governments and lodged it firmly with the federal government. They also promoted the integrity of private contracts, against states restricting out-of-state debt collectors.

Still, they sharply limited the new federal powers, because they were concerned about acceptance by the states. As it was, prominent revolutionary leaders, along with rural interests undercut by some provisions, strongly opposed the ratification. Anti-Federalists warned that lodging vigorous powers in a central government would vest economic decisions in the hands of an aristocratic and potentially tyrannical political elite, creating an economic incumbency and *rentier* class in charge of the new government. Yet among those opposed to a strengthened federal system were not just Sons of Liberty firebrands such as Samuel Adams and Patrick Henry, but even landowners Thomas Jefferson, Richard Henry Lee, and George Clinton, who feared the loss of local power. Should the new country maintain certain economic privileges, and, if so, who should control them?

Origins of American Political Economy

Amidst this turbulence, James Madison and Alexander Hamilton emerged as leaders who understood not just the immediate political and economic forces but also the broader issues. Like most other elites, they focused on establishing the credit of the new country and distrusted popular sovereignty. Secure property rights and political stability, they believed, would foster long-term development. The only way to guarantee that result, they argued, was through a supreme national government. Madison in particular pushed hard for a national executive elected directly by the people, so as to gain full authority. He dismissed the state governments as mere "local authorities" that would remain in force "as far as they can be subordinately useful." To keep them in line, he even wanted the national executive to have full veto power over their legislatures, just as King George had.

As primary drafter of the Constitution, and influenced by thinkers such as Montesquieu and Locke, Madison also sought the separation of powers as a check on central government excess. He understood that limiting this power through checks and balances among the various branches would also create countervailing forces. These forces, while messy on the outside, would enable private economic activity to flourish and a mixed economy of diverse interests to take hold.[11]

Madison combined both the common suspicion of monarchy and fear of popular sovereignty, especially at the local level. Here, too, a mixed economy of differentiated interests, including landowners, creditors, farmers, artisans, mechanics, and others would help offset extreme political swings. Madison's *Federalist No. 10*, often cited as a justification for the distribution of political power through representative (as opposed to direct) democracy, also suggests that "factions" can be economic as well as political and are often linked.[12] As with political power, those economic factions would prevent any single group from gaining too much economic power over the others – which is essentially what happened.

Those messy, drawn-out debates over ratification thus served a vital purpose. Anti-Federalist opposition was crucial in curbing the more elitist measures of the Federalists, not just federal supremacy over the states but also the inclusion of a Bill of Rights to protect individual liberties. The new federal government thus emerged with a balanced political and economic system that supported private enterprise as a whole, while embedding within it a natural dynamism. The Constitution limited both populism, which threatened all property rights, as well as the power of federal and local elites, which might have endangered these rights as well as the right to compete.[13] It established the federal power to tax, open up interstate commerce, and enact tariffs against foreign competition, while addressing specific issues such currency, patents, eminent domain, and contracts.[14]

More broadly, the political framework opened the door to an entrepreneurially driven economic system. Throughout American history, new innovations and new entrants would find mechanisms to counter attempts by protectionists or *rentiers* to squash their development, while the system still preserved property rights to encourage investment. By working through one or more of the three branches of the federal government or by using the dynamic tension between the national and state governments, a faction seeking market entry would most often find a way to succeed.

The Entrepreneurial Constitution

In looking at the structure and certain provisions of the U.S. Constitution, we can see how America's pro-entrepreneur political economy took shape. Scholars in the field of institutional economics study how the "rules of the game" in a country affect economic performance, and America's entrepreneurial growth stems largely from its foundational document.[15] Relative to other countries' much simpler approaches, the Constitution had several main attributes that have kept the American economy liberal (in the sense of limited government intervention), inclusive (in promoting market access to at least some groups), open, and supportive of economic growth and productivity.

First is the separation of powers, which increases the likelihood of considering trade-offs as well as avoiding a concentration of power. The second is the relationship between the federal government and the states, which results in a give-and-take between national and local interests. In that give-and-take, tensions between upstarts and incumbents, and the rights of property versus competition, have often played out. Third is the Bill of Rights, which codifies individual liberties, along with various specific economic provisions. Fourth is a general deference to private economic activity, including the state-level common law (especially its decentralized finance and corporate mechanisms) that enabled this activity.

The separation of powers effectively disperses control and respects competing interests, so different from the unified or at least more centralized governments in many other parts of the world.[16] The bicameral legislative structure balances the highly localized interests of representatives with the broad constituencies of senators, and this often has ramifications when it comes to issues involving market access, protectionism, and other matters. An independent judiciary, with jurisdiction over the other two branches as well as the ability to protect individual liberties at the state level, has proven particularly significant. Even with this decentralized system, the early justices succeeded in maintaining the overall supremacy of the rule of law.[17] Here they and the framers drew on the principles of limited authority dating back to Britain's 1688 Glorious Revolution, as described in the previous chapter.[18]

As for the federal structure, it has yielded a sometimes competitive relationship with the states. Many issues of property protection and the right to compete have played out here. The federal Supreme Court has frequently intervened to limit state activities that would weaken private property (including contracts), grant special privileges or monopolies to select local individuals, exclude new market entrants, restrict the development of a national marketplace, or unduly regulate economic activity. It did so whether these state initiatives came at the behest of local elites or populists. Over time, the power of the federal government expanded and played an essential role in developing the national market and preventing state protectionism. Even today, entrepreneurs use federal supremacy over interstate commerce to pry markets open against local regulations, from taxicab licensing to lodging restrictions.

By the same token, the states have promoted entrepreneurship by supporting local businesses and by luring firms from other states. Competition among the states, free from federal intervention, has led to innovation in areas such as corporate law. New Jersey and Delaware led the way in enabling the formation of enormous firms in the late 19th and early 20th centuries. Despite arguments that this would create a "race to the bottom," this competition has often fostered an environment of productive opportunity.[19] While fragmenting the national market in some cases, state power, especially in banking and insurance, has helped to disperse opportunity.

Individual liberty, as embodied in the Bill of Rights, was an essential underpinning of the constitution, but it took some time to become a powerful factor in support of entrepreneurship. The most important such liberty is freedom of speech, essential in disseminating new ideas and innovative practices; the Supreme Court eventually extended this political right to commercial speech.[20] Similarly, the Fifth Amendment's protection of due process expanded to protect property rights, particularly against government takings without compensation.[21]

The post–Civil War 14th Amendment broadened these liberties substantially. These now extended to the state level, and included economic rights ("substantive due process") that applied to corporate entities, not just individuals. Though controversial, particularly as corporate power has grown, these liberties have encouraged both upstart and incumbent enterprises.[22]

Along with those overall liberties, the Constitution offers numerous specific protections related to economic development, including respect for contracts,[23] federal oversight of interstate commerce and international trade,[24] and patents and copyright for inventions (subject to time limits). How to apply these economic provisions has been at the center of much of the tension associated with entrepreneurial activity, often adjudicated alongside disputes over separation of powers or federalism.[25]

The fourth and perhaps most powerful core attribute of the American political economic system is its support of individual private action at the center of economic activity. This takes place outside of the Constitution but is deeply enabled by it. Unlike most countries, where the government holds the reins on most economic activity, American government generally stands aside, deferring to individual initiative instead. With its checks and balances, its Federalist structure, and its explicit protection of individual liberties, the system has been able to leverage this private activity while still maintaining strong enforcement and decentralized coordination.[26]

A key enabler in this area has been the common law, which (as noted earlier) tends to be more supportive of active commercial activity than the civil code prevalent in most Continental European countries. The common law works to establish a broad-based understanding and application of the rules (thus, the "common" law) rather than one based on administrative-heavy experts. As many entrepreneurs like to say, "It is easier to ask for forgiveness than permission," and common law brings with it an inherent "bottom up" orientation in which activity is generally allowed unless expressly prohibited. Similarly, scholars who study the importance of "legal origins" often claim that common law plays out as more "dispute-resolving" and supportive of private market ordering, rather than the "policy-implementing" for state-desired outcomes as promoted in top-down civil code systems.[27]

Contract law has been especially vital for commercial activity. Written contracts enforced by courts were essential to joint stock companies, patents and prizes, bills of exchange, and insurance, for instance. In the early years of the country, sanctity of contract was critical in securing investment. More recently, proponents of the study of "law and finance" note the role of contracts and other aspects of the law in serving as the foundation for modern finance.[28] Other fields of law, such as property and torts, have similarly supported development, initiative, and growth.[29]

Common law also gives independent judges a flexibility not generally enjoyed by those in civil code regimes, and this flexibility tends to support entrepreneurial innovation. Flexible judicial systems can be more responsive to market-based needs than are courts under state-oriented formalism. The judiciary in common law countries can even serve as a buffer against the state and prevent interference that might misallocate resources or lead to policy-determined outcomes. At the same time, the common law tradition relies on precedent, so changes in the law move gradually even as they evolve. Thus, as with the constitutional system, common law transforms itself to accommodate innovation even as it does so in measured fashion. This flexible and highly independent judiciary may be especially important for upstart firms.[30]

Even as the country works bottom-up in many areas, America has benefitted from an underlying consensus that promotes the rule of law. The checks and balances that work to maintain the political and legal system as a whole also support economic performance. The strong culture of enforcement and the credibility of the legal system are often underappreciated in the economic context.[31]

The orientation toward "private ordering" rather than top-down control also helps explain the rise of sophisticated financial markets that lead to economic growth. Investors and creditors have secured better protections through market-based negotiation rather than depending on state policymaking, which in turn has facilitated more resources to be invested, the development of advanced financial instruments, and a broader dispersion in ownership. These factors also encourage unique features of American corporate governance, with more sources of risk capital, less dependence on large banks, and, most recently, activist shareholders.

In lockstep with these factors, American law opened the corporate form to entrepreneurs earlier than many other countries and allowed the range of corporate activities to expand to meet market needs and opportunities. The broad access to the corporation brought with it limited liability and a mechanism to amass resources. Similarly, deference to private activity supported the development of decentralized financial intermediaries, which takes capital allocation decisions out of the hands of cronies, and encouraged the proliferation of business activity and the mobility of capital far more than in countries with centralized corporate and financial institutions.

Despite this messy division of authority, or perhaps because of it, the most noteworthy aspect of the U.S. Constitution has been its continued authority. The system has won this authority by balancing the inherent tension between stability and dynamism, and thereby supporting innovation, economic progress, and productivity over time. Legal decisions or policies that made sense in one time period could be reversed decades later, yet the system maintained its stability. In terms of sheer longevity, the U.S. Constitution is by far the longest running in the world today. Few other countries have constitutions older than 60 years, and the median age is less than 20 years. The persistence of a two-party system, which yields a natural equilibrium as rival groups oppose each other while supporting overall stability, helped here as well.

America's tolerance of creative destruction may well follow from this equilibrium, as it allows ongoing tensions to create energy that is both disruptive and stable at the same time. With a large, fluid, and diverse economy, it has been hard for special interests to garner or at least maintain privileged positions over long periods, and this has led to a virtuous cycle in which new entrants and innovations can continue to reinvigorate the system. The difficulty interest groups have in dominating the economic sphere over extended periods is at least partly due to the political framework.

The Perils of Central Administration

To understand the stakes in the 1780s and the importance of the resulting institutions, we can look at the experience of France, which threw off its monarchy almost simultaneously with the passage of the U.S. Constitution. While partly inspired by the break with Britain, what followed in France was a populism that went unchecked. Why the difference? Alexis de Tocqueville usefully pointed to five fundamental differences: (1) France was centralized under the monarchy; (2) the French elevated the general will above the law; (3) they attacked religion, while America was more sectarian; (4) they gave more power to intellectuals than to practical men; and (5) they put equality above liberty.[32] Regardless of the reasons, the result was chaos, as successive leaders set up a new authority and then met the guillotine. The country lost an entire generation of entrepreneurs and economic development at a time when the Industrial Revolution was just beginning.

Society didn't stabilize until Napoleon, a war hero, took over in a coup d'état and moved toward an authoritarian model. In certain respects, his leadership was farsighted and effective, and he became what one biographer called "the Enlightenment on horseback." To administer his far-reaching state, he centralized government and set up elite national schools in the arts of commerce, engineering, and government. He favored meritocracy and established a top-down legal system based on clear principles rather than local preferences, all in service to a top-heavy republic rather than a ground-up democracy.[33]

But Napoleon's institutions lacked a mechanism for dynamism, and the result has been a series of empires and republics that failed to achieve either stability or dynamism. Even today, France relies heavily on rule by experts. The result is an orderly, affluent society, with secure property rights. But it comes with a less open and dynamic economy, as elites inevitably favor incumbents over time. This "centralized administration machinery" and "rationalist" (as opposed to "empiricist" or evolutionist approach in England and the U.S.) has held back innovation and productivity.[34]

France's top-down approach continues, as the institutional and cultural traditions remain intact. French president Emmanuel Macron – himself a product of elite schools – is now working hard to promote entrepreneurial openness. But much data suggests that entrenched elites continue to control most of the resources, even those that are privatized.

The Rise of Ordinary Entrepreneurs

In spite of the strong protections of property and the seemingly conservative nature of the Constitution, many of the powerful interests in the economy before the Revolution faltered in the years after it. Why didn't the Founding Fathers or other elites dominate the new

United States? Because the rest of the people, those ordinary farmers, mechanics, and artisans, rose up to turn the war for independence into a true revolution. Rather than exchange their imperial masters for local elites, they sought an utterly new political order, even as property rights remained secure. They eagerly took advantage of that order as it emerged. And if the lower classes did not entirely triumph, new upstarts and varied interests among the existing economic elite kept incumbents from insulating themselves from competition.

We can see their efforts in the macro economy. In the late 1780s and '90s, after the postwar recession, the nascent U.S. economy took off. Productivity rose substantially, and markets grew impressively. All of this was happening before the industrial takeoff of later decades. Textile mills were only just starting to use machines, and practical steamboats and railroads were still years away. It wasn't technology but a basic expansion of human effort that turbocharged what had been, aside from some coastal cities, a slow-moving economy. Turnpikes spread rapidly, connecting remote villages. Farmers were eager to get their harvests to regional markets, rather than consuming it locally. The more buyers they found, the harder they worked to raise crops.

Much of this was the product of a cultural shift. Before the war, most colonists had seen themselves within a great hierarchical order where everyone knew their rank in society. The vast majority of people were "the vulgar," expected to show deference to their betters. Largely stuck in their positions, they sought protection in personal ties, and only *noblesse oblige* from their patrons kept many from falling into utter poverty. The wealthy classes, especially away from the coast, often sought stability over market-oriented efficiency and growth.

After overthrowing the monarchical order, ordinary Americans didn't look for new elites for protection. They realized more than ever before that they could change their station in life. Many farmers took up home manufacturing on the side, hoping to afford the luxuries once deemed appropriate only for gentlemen. Marginal lands fell under the plow. What had been a trickle of migrants going west soon became a flood. Literacy shot up as the masses started taking education seriously for their children.

That new mindset in turn did much to spur the speedy adoption of technologies in later decades. As historians have increasingly appreciated, technology is usually a secondary factor in economic development. Entrepreneurs must do the hard and risky work of developing early advances into something that truly works in the marketplace. Elite-dominated countries can move fast to catch up to pioneers, because they can mobilize capital for basic entrepreneurship. But innovation is a different story, and for that most countries usually need a great many hungry entrepreneurs experimenting on a problem to arrive at a successful adoption.

To the more conservative-minded in the 1780s, the popular tumult was verging on economic anarchy. These leaders hoped the Constitution would restore some measure of stability both politically and economically. Instead, the new government only furthered the transformation, more by unleashing new energies than by explicitly limiting existing elites. Over time, many of the nondemocratic elements of the federal government faded away, while the states phased out all property qualifications for the electorate. An open, democratic system gradually emerged despite the opposition of elites.

Aghast at the rise of partisanship and nakedly self-interested politicians, many of the Founding Fathers felt betrayed. Benjamin Rush, a leader in spreading Enlightenment ideas as well as signer of both the Declaration and the Constitution, bemoaned how the government had fallen "into the hands of the young and ignorant." George Washington lost all hope for democracy at the end of his life. Alexander Hamilton, now celebrated as the epitome of the self-made man, concluded that "this American world was not made for me." Even Thomas Jefferson, the most egalitarian of the Founders, denounced the emerging democracy for falling prey to ignorance and superstition.

Some of the most powerful leaders in the economic realm had difficulty solidifying their incumbency. Hancock left no direct heirs and Robert Morris, the financier of the revolution, ended up in debtors' prison, the result of unsuccessful land speculation after the war.[35] The Constitution allowed the states to abolish some anti-democratic property rights, especially primogeniture and entail, which eventually eliminated the great patroonships in New York and undermined John Penn and his progeny in Pennsylvania.[36] Only the Southern planters largely maintained their incumbency. The opportunities unleashed by independence disrupted power across the board, with new players emerging as opportunities developed. Those who sought to remain on top had to reach a higher bar or find themselves displaced.[37]

The American Revolution itself emerged from a broad upstart-incumbent dynamic, with anti-authoritarian and anti-monopoly principles that have remained at the country's core ever since. The democratic spirit, increased availability of land, and the corresponding shortage of talent created opportunities at all levels, and in turn promoted a culture of openness that empowered upstarts to compete. Yet the resulting legal structures also secured most property rights and provided tools against the excesses of populists. Americans had broken open the most powerful incumbency the world had known, but they were just embarking on a journey of their own in balancing property rights and the right to compete.

Sketched in broad strokes, the Constitution left much to be figured out. Yet by rescuing the fragmented states from the Articles of Confederation, it was a triumph of stability against Europeans expecting the new country to devolve into chaos – without giving incumbents entrenched power. The country unified instead around the ideal of ordinary men rising in their station and achieving economic independence.

Nevertheless, the burgeoning commercial economy, along with those emerging technologies, would both inspire and challenge the young country and its emerging democracy. If upstarts challenging incumbents were the future, how would the courts handle the inevitable disputes in a fast-changing economy? What place did governmental privileges and subsidies, if any, play in a democratic system committed to economic development? These and other issues would need to be resolved as the government and nation itself moved ahead.

Endnotes

1. Letter from John Adams to Thomas Jefferson, June 22, 1819. See also William Hogeland, "How John Adams and Thomas Paine clashed over inequality," Salon.com, March 29, 2011.

2. William Hogeland, "Thomas Paine's Revolutionary Reckoning." *American History* 46, no. 2 (2011): 64–69. Paine is also often credited with authoring the "Entrepreneurs Creed," though some historians have indicated this is incorrect. "I do not choose to be a common man . . . It is my right to be uncommon . . . if I can. I choose opportunity . . . not security; I do not wish to be kept a citizen . . . Humbled and dulled by having the State look after me. I want to take the calculated risk; To dream and to build, To fail and to succeed. I refuse to barter incentive for a dole; I prefer the challenges of life to the guaranteed existence; The thrill of fulfillment to the calm state of Utopia. I will not trade freedom for beneficence . . . Nor my dignity for a handout . . . I will never cower before any master . . . Nor bend to any threat. It is my heritage to stand erect. Proud and unafraid; To think and act for myself . . . To enjoy the benefits of my creations . . . And to face the world boldly and say: This, with God's help, I have done. All this is what it means . . . To be an Entrepreneur."

3. Morris's impressive leadership during the revolution did not translate to special privileges after the war, as he was heavily criticized for supposed special dealings to enrich himself and his cronies. He invested aggressively

in western land and ended up in debtor's prison, until Congress finally ended the practice of jailing bankrupts. Charles Rappleye, *Robert Morris, Financier of the American Revolution* (New York: Simon & Schuster, 2010). See also Gordon Wood, *The Radicalism of the American Revolution* (New York: Random House, 1991).

4. Ironically, Paine was nearly guillotined for running afoul of Robespierre during the Reign of Terror in France, but he was ultimately saved by a combination of good luck and intervention by Gouverneur Morris (no relation to Robert), the American ambassador.

5. Charles Beard, *An Economic Interpretation of the Constitution of the United States* (Princeton, NJ: Princeton University Press, 1913).

6. See Wood, *The Radicalism of the American Revolution*; David Lefer, *The Founding Conservatives: How a Group of Unsung Heroes Saved the American Revolution* (Sentinel, 2013); and Stuart Bruchey, *Enterprise: The Dynamic Economy of a Free People* (Cambridge, MA: Harvard University Press, 1990), 109. See also Arthur M. Schlesinger, *The Colonial Merchants and the American Revolution* (London: P.S. King & Son, Ltd, 1918), 606 ("the mercantile interests became a potent factor in the conservative counterrevolution that led to the establishment of the United States Constitution").

7. See Beard, *An Economic Interpretation of the Constitution*. See also Stuart Bruchey, *Enterprise,* and Forrest McDonald, *We The People: The Economic Origins of the Constitution* (Chicago: University of Chicago Press, 1958).

8. See, e.g., John Steel Gordon, *An Empire of Wealth: The Epic History of American Economic Power* (New York: HarperCollins, 2004), and William Rosen, *The Most Powerful Idea in the World* (Chicago: University of Chicago Press, 2010), 276–78.

9. John Adams [President of the United States of America], "Discourses on Davila," *Gazette of the United States* (1790).

10. Madison to Thomas Jefferson, March 18, 1786. Partly in Cipher: *The James Madison Papers, 1723 to 1850: Series 1, General Correspondence, 1723 to 1850,* Library of Congress. See also Beard, *An Economic Interpretation of the Constitution,* 179–83.

11. The Federalist Papers, No. 51 ("ambition to counteract ambition").

12. The Federalist Papers, No. 10 ("But the most common and durable source of factions has been the various and unequal distribution of property. Those who hold and those who are without property have ever formed distinct interests in society. Those who are creditors, and those who are debtors, fall under a like discrimination. A landed interest, a mercantile interest, a moneyed interest, with many lesser interests, grow up of necessity in civilized nations, and divide them into different classes, activated by different sentiments and views. The regulation of these various and interfacing interests forms the principal task of modern legislation and involves the spirit of party and faction in the necessary and ordinary operations of government").

See also Frederick Hayek, *The Constitution of Liberty* (Chicago: University of Chicago Press, 1960).

13. Larry Schweikart and Lynne Pierson Doti, *American Entrepreneur: The Fascinating Stories of the People Who Defined Business in the United States* (New York: AMACON, 2009), 49–52, (citing also Charles Beard, *An Economic Interpretation of the Constitution*. Forrest McDonald, *We The People*.

14. Rhode Island held out the longest, not ratifying the document until 1790, a year after it went into effect, and only when the new federal government threatened to impose tariffs on all goods it sent to other states – at which point merchant-oriented Providence threatened to secede from the rest of the state. Joseph Ellis, *The Quartet: Orchestrating the Second American Revolution: 1783–1789* (New York: Knopf, 2015).

15. Douglass C. North, *Institutions, Institutional Change and Economic Performance* (Cambridge UK: Cambridge University Press, 1990), 47, 51, 54, 73 (suggesting a hierarchy of institutional rules, including constitutions, statutes, laws, bylaws, and individual contracts, with each having varying degrees of flexibility).

16. Frederick A. Hayek, *The Constitution of Liberty*, 168–187.

17. Kenneth W. Dam, *The Law-Growth Nexus: The Rule of Law and Economic Development* (Washington, D.C.: Brookings Institution Press, 2006). See also Robert D. Cooter and Hans-Bernd Schafer, *Solomon's Knot: How Law Can End the Poverty of Nations* (Princeton, NJ: Princeton University Press, 2012).

18. As noted in the previous chapter, this includes the Bill of Rights of 1689 and the Act of Settlement of 1701(independent judiciary) as well as an independent Bank of England and other features. See Douglass C. North, *Institutions*, 138–139; Douglass C. North, *Structure and Change in Economic History* (New York: W.W. Norton & Company), 155; and Joyce Appleby, *The Relentless Revolution: A History of Capitalism* (New York: W.W. Norton & Company, 2010), 92, 111. See also Dam, *The Law-Growth Nexus*, 78–86; Steven Pincus and James Robinson, "What Really Happened in the Glorious Revolution," *Institutions, Property Rights, and Economic Growth: The Legacy of Douglass C. North* (New York: Cambridge University Press, 2011).

19. See, e.g., Niall Ferguson, *Civilization: The West and The Rest* (New York: Penguin Press, 2011), 41 (the importance of multi-level competition between and within states). See also Nathan Rosenberg and L.E. Birdzell Jr., *How the West Grew Rich: The Economic Transformation of the Industrial World* (New York: Basic Books, 1986), 136–137 (Europe's political divisions as a source of growth).

20. *Virginia State Pharmacy Board v. Virginia Citizens Consumer Council* (1976). See also Narain D. Batra, *The First Freedoms and America's Culture of Innovation* (Lanham, MD: Rowan & Littlefield, 2013).

21. Fifth Amendment: "nor to be deprived of life, liberty or property, without due process of law; nor shall private property to be taken for public use, without just compensation."

22. Adam Winkler, *We the Corporation: How American Business Won Their Civil Rights* (New York: W.W. Norton & Company, Inc. 2018).

23. Art 1, section 10, clause 1: "No State shall [pass] any [law] impairing the obligation of Contracts" [...or grant the title of nobility].

24. Art 1, section 8, clause 3: Power of Congress to regulate commerce and preempt state laws.

25. Many of the important cases will be noted again in the following chapter. There are many important and complex facets of how the constitution was implemented, and a detailed study is beyond the scope of this book. But a few important principles set forth in the first decades stand out. The first of these principles is the notion of independent judiciary and the concept of judicial review, as famously established in *Marbury v. Madison* (1803). The second of these is the supremacy of the United States over the states in the area of taxation and other economic activity, as set forth in *McCulloch v. Maryland* (1819) and other cases. The third of these principles is the sanctity of contract, as seen in *Fletcher v. Peck* (1810) and *Dartmouth College v. Woodward* (1820), which upheld the legitimacy of the corporation and of contract. Finally, the supremacy of Congress to regulate interstate commerce, thereby securing a strong national market, was set forth in *Gibbons vs. Ogden* (1824). For a review of many of these cases, see Jean Edward Smith, *John Marshall: Definer of a Nation* (Henry Holt & Co., 1996), and Stuart Bruchey, *Enterprise*.

26. North, *Legacy*, "The Theory of Decentralized Enforcement," 124–136. ("Constitutional law is at once a body of rules and principles that facilitate private ordering and decentralized coordination on enforcement; a system of public reasoning to explain and extend that system; and an equilibrium that sustains that system").

27. See Dam, *The Law-Growth Nexus*, 3, 5, 26–28, 33, 37; Douglass C. North, *Institutions*, 15; and Hayek, *The Constitution of Liberty*, 16. See also Mahoney "The Common Law and Economic Growth: Hayek Might Be Right," *Journal of Legal Studies* 30 (June 2001).

28. See Rafael La Porta, Florencio Lopez-de-Silanes, Andrei Shleifer, and Robert W. Vishny, "Law and Finance," *Journal of Political Economy* 106, no. 6 (December 1998), and Rafael L. Porta, Florencio Lopez de Silane, and Andrei Schleifer, "The Economic Consequences of Legal Origins," *National Bureau of Economic Research*, November 2007, 5–18. See also Katharina Pistor, "Rethinking the 'Law and Finance' Paradigm," BYU Law Review (2009): 1647.

29. See, e.g., Morton Horwitz, *The Transformation of American Law, 1780-1860* (Cambridge MA: Harvard University Press, 1977); Herbert Hovenkamp, *Enterprise and American Law, 1836–1937* (Cambridge MA: Harvard University Press, 2014); and James Willard Hurst, *Law and the Conditions of Freedom in the Nineteenth Century of the United States* (Wisconsin: University of Wisconsin Press, 1956).

30. Dam, *The Law-Growth Nexus*, 93 (noting the link between a strong, independent judiciary and the growth of smaller firms).
31. Ibid, 5–26 (limited ability to persecute individuals, no secret law, nobody is above the law, access to enforcement is equal).
32. Niall Ferguson, *Civilization*, 153–54. See also David Landes, "French Entrepreneurship and Industrial Growth in the Nineteenth Century," *Journal of Economic History* 9, no. 1 (May 1949): 45–61 (describing cultural biases against entrepreneurship including lack of access to capital, limited use of the corporate form, business suspicion of government, rivalry with nobility and civil servants, and Calvinist vs. Catholic clashes).
33. Andrew Roberts, *Napoleon: A Life* (New York: Penguin Random House, 2014).
34. Hayek, *The Constitution of Liberty*, 55–58, 193–195.
35. Ryan K. Smith, *Robert Morris's Folly: The Architectural and Financial Failures of an American Founder* (New Haven: Yale University Press, 2014).
36. Bruchey, *Enterprise,* 112 (Primogeniture outlawed in Georgia (1777), North Carolina (1784), Virginia (1785), Maryland (1786), New York (1786), South Carolina (1791), Rhode Island (1798).
37. See, e.g., Joyce Appleby, *Inheriting the Revolution: The First Generation of Americans* (Cambridge, MA: Harvard University Press, 2001).

5

Building
the Entrepreneurial
Republic

Alexander Hamilton, the new Secretary of the Treasury, saw better than anyone the need for industrial development. In 1791, while working on the *Report on Manufactures* that he delivered to Congress that same year, he founded the Society for Establishing Useful Manufactures (SEUM) with his colleague Tench Coxe. Thanks to their connections with investors, the first stock subscription sold out immediately, and they worked quickly to develop a waterpower site near the Great Falls of the Passaic River in New Jersey. They envisioned a state-sponsored manufacturing town and called it Paterson, in honor of the sitting governor – who returned the favor by granting the new company a state charter for exclusive access to the falls, as well as a 10-year tax exemption. Soon a cotton spinning mill was up and running, with plans for a major complex churning out a variety of products. Meanwhile, the spies they had sent to Britain collected valuable information that would help in the endeavor. They also hired some immigrants who claimed experience in factory life and operation.

Flush with capital, cozy with the local government, and likely overconfident, the SEUM took on too much too soon, with inadequate oversight. Hamilton hired Pierre L'Enfant, future architect of Washington, D.C., to design the factory town, and the Frenchman embarked on an extravagant, costly plan. Hamilton also packed the board with financiers who lacked industrial expertise, including chairman William Duer, who stole from the coffers when the Panic of 1792 squeezed his other investments. Misappropriation was rife, and underpaid workers resorted to stealing machinery. By 1796, his grand SEUM had collapsed into bankruptcy and all operations ceased.

Meanwhile in Rhode Island, an entrepreneur of a different sort mounted a similar attempt. In 1788, Moses Brown, one of the Brown brothers who led the rebellion against the British and helped build Providence into a flourishing port, was hoping to discover a new area of economic activity. The postwar loss of access to British colonial markets had severely diminished the general shipping trade, and he had already abandoned the slave trade. Rhode Island lacked the natural resources of other colonies, so unemployment was severe; hence its reliance on paper money. Eager to help his fellow citizens and open a new line of business for the next generation of Browns, Moses came out of retirement and tried to set up a textile factory.[1]

He journeyed to New York, looking for skilled mechanics, but got nowhere until receiving a letter from Samuel Slater, an ambitious young Englishman who had worked in Richard Arkwright's pioneering spinning mill in England – and had memorized the designs of those machines. Brown jumped on the news and promised Slater not just a salary but a share in the profits. Slater had already arrived in New York, but Brown's generous offer convinced him to move to Providence. By 1790, Slater had set up a rudimentary spinning mill along the Blackstone River in Pawtucket, a village just north of Providence. The experiment worked well enough to convince Brown to build a bigger, complete factory on the same spot.

Once the mill was running, Moses Brown returned to retirement, leaving the mill to the firm of his son-in-law William Almy and his nephew Smith Brown. Unlike the SEUM, Almy & Brown went into manufacturing with no protections and no illusions. They saw the mill as simply a cheap source of yarn to resell to their commercial contacts, and they gave Slater only just enough capital to keep operating. He worked hard to build up the new mill, innovating in small ways, while Almy & Brown gradually and soberly built up a steady market for the yarn. Eventually the mill in Pawtucket did so well that Slater, tired of sharing profits with Almy & Brown, set off on his own. While still overseeing the Pawtucket mill, he attracted enough capital to build what became a series of textile factories in southern New England. Slater became the "father of the American industrial revolution," while the hit Broadway musical *Hamilton* never mentions Paterson.[2]

The Competing Visions of Hamilton and Jefferson

At the dawn of the new republic, grand visions of how – and by whom – the newly independent economy would be developed jostled in fierce competition. Some, like Hamilton, sought to replace the English mercantile system with a homegrown version, with the federal government working actively to develop infrastructure through grants, charters, and privileges; support nascent manufacturing industries; and use tariffs and the financial system to encourage growth and a national market. But others, most notably Thomas Jefferson, felt that this national government-sponsored development brought with it a risk of cronyism writ large. They feared that a homegrown elite would simply recreate the troubled experience under monarchy.

Hamilton and Jefferson also had differing conceptions of who would drive this growth, with Hamilton believing that innovative national entrepreneurs with a large market would take the lead in pioneering new industries. Jefferson championed classic small business entrepreneurs such as artisans, mechanics, and yeoman farmers.[3]

Adam Smith, whose *An Inquiry into the Nature and Causes of the Wealth of Nations* (1776) was published the same year as the Declaration of Independence and Paine's *Common Sense*, made the case for laissez-faire and the power of the "invisible hand" over government control. He argued in support of the colonies against England's mercantilist policies, and his ideas largely prevailed over time. Yet the basic needs of the new country and the competitive advantage that England had been developing in manufacturing weighed heavily on many, especially Hamilton.

With the Constitution providing only basic principles and a general framework, it fell to the initial Congress and executive to flesh out the new government. Led by George Washington and Hamilton, followed by Adams, the Federalists asserted broad federal powers, while the Democratic-Republicans, under Jefferson and James Madison, promoted a countervailing sovereignty in the states. Federalists aimed to jump-start development through federal intervention, which sparked worries of creating an aristocratic class of government-sponsored incumbents. Democratic-Republicans celebrated the right to compete in open markets free of quasi-monarchical interference – though in doing so, they supported a legal status quo that usually favored local incumbency.

Federalists and Democratic-Republicans agreed on some important institutions and provisions, such as the Patent Office to protect property rights to innovation, an important carryover from England.[4] Similarly,

Congress established a bankruptcy code to support risk-taking, though the first act was only in place for a few years.[5]

Hamilton succeeded in convincing Congress to assume the debts incurred by the states during the Revolution in order to ensure the cardinal virtue of "property & credit." The move both headed off dangerous state-based currency plans, which were damaging creditors and deterring potential investors, and created a reliable market for federal government bonds. Such a market proved essential for channeling European savings into American development.[6]

But Hamilton made less headway in urging the government to foster and fund manufacturing enterprise through tariffs and subsidies. Would-be entrepreneurs faced daunting obstacles, he wrote, including "the strong influence of habit and the spirit of imitation; the fear of want of success in untried enterprises; the intrinsic difficulties incident to first essays toward a competition with those who have already attained to perfection in the business to be attempted [referring to British manufacturers]."[7] Hamilton wanted to protect these daring risk-takers. But concerned about undercutting open markets and creating a privileged incumbency, Congress imposed only a modest tariff.[8]

Even as a select few were able to secure privileges at either the federal or state level, the rising middle class of artisans and small shopkeepers eventually jostled their way into opportunities as well. An important transition occurred in 1800 with the election of Thomas Jefferson to the presidency. Federalist John Adams was supported by the incumbents who had dominated trade with the British and had secured most of the privileges in the first years of union, so the transfer of power helped to prevent those incumbents from entrenching their position.[9]

Rather than undo the early Federalist building blocks for innovation, Jefferson's and subsequent Democratic-Republican administrations concentrated on phasing out privileges at the federal level and shifting power to the states. State legislatures readily issued grants and charters, especially for infrastructure such as banks, turnpikes, and canals that required greater up-front capital.[10] Politically connected entrepreneurs combined pro-development arguments with self-interest, especially the Erie Canal, a state project begun in 1817 by Democratic-Republican governor DeWitt Clinton and completed in 1825.[11]

Jefferson did of course consummate the Louisiana Purchase in 1803, which along with the earlier Northwest Ordinance (1787) had led to rampant speculation and development. Moreover the expansionist policy of national infrastructure regained force under Madison after the War of 1812, with increases in tariffs and a rechartered federal bank. Nevertheless, the tension between national and state-oriented development, as well as questions about the role of government involvement generally, would continue.

The Race to Get Ahead

At the end of the 18th century, opportunities were everywhere. With British restrictions removed, American merchants were free to compete in global trade, particularly in China, and in whaling. The Western frontier beckoned and fortunes such as John Jacob Astor's in fur trading were beginning.[12] A series of regrettable policies removing many Native Americans to lands west of the Mississippi River encouraged settlement.[13] Moreover, new technologies and the harnessing of steam power meant that more innovation and commercial manufacturing possibilities were well underway.[14] Finally, a swelling immigrant population (and expanded slave trading in the South) offered additional resources to help tackle the opportunities, while also themselves constituting a growing market. The country's population more than doubled from 3.9 million in 1790 to 9.6 million in 1820 and 31.5 million by 1860. Gross domestic product grew by a remarkable 3.7% per year from 1800 to 1850.[15]

In Salem, Massachusetts, Elias Derby dispatched ships for India and China and grew by 1800 to become the nation's "first millionaire." But just like the Hancocks before the Revolution, he could not entrench his position. Soon the upstart Crowninshield family had jostled its way into the field, with help from the shifting legal system as well as opening new markets such as the first seagoing pepper trade.[16] Like many, this rivalry also manifested itself in politics and the desire for influence. The Derbys were staunch Federalists, while the Crowninshields had thrown their hat in with the Democratic-Republican party, the northern contingent of Jefferson's supporters.

The rise of new entrepreneurs could be seen in all parts of the economy. In Philadelphia, French immigrant Stephen Girard replaced Robert Morris, whose failed speculation landed him in debtor's prison, as the country's foremost financier. Girard purchased the impressive building of the First Bank of the United States, which was set up with Hamilton's support in 1791, after its 20-year charter expired in 1811. Girard became one of the wealthiest men in the country and was critical in financing the government during the War of 1812. Local banks also sprouted up to support growth.[17]

Americans were also inventing, but amid entrepreneurial currents, even patents were no guarantee of success. The Constitution had clearly provided for the protection of patents and copyrights, but enforcement in the early days of the Republic was difficult and competition abounded. When Eli Whitney registered his cotton gin in 1793, he expected to profit through the gristmill model of charging farmers a percentage of the processed commodity. But Whitney lacked the capital to build enough gins (short for "engines") to meet the enormous demand for this momentous new technology. Nor did he invest in perfecting the device. In the face of Whitney's passivity, patent infringement was inevitable, and the early Republic lacked the enforcement power – or will – to protect Whitney's property by itself. After only four years of operation, his firm went out of business.

Despite Whitney's mixed success, the pace of innovation continued. The country generated the most patents per capita in the world between 1810 and 1845, and much of this activity came from upstarts.[18] According to one study, between 1820 and 1845, fewer than 20% of issued patents were to the children of professional or large landowning families, and about 40% of all patentees had at most a primary school education.[19] The cost of obtaining a patent was lower in the United States than elsewhere.

Ironically, Whitney's failure in commercializing the cotton gin helped spawn another unique American feature, that of interchangeable parts. Such was the entrepreneurial culture that Whitney parlayed his fame as an inventor into a second career as a maker of low-cost muskets, with a federal contract in 1798. This innovation helped speed innovation and efficiency, as incremental changes quickly found their way into the marketplace and economies of scale from specialization could be achieved. Interchangeability also democratized the economy by lowering the capital requirements for new market entrants. The "American System of Manufacturing" was taking root.[20]

All of this activity resulted in significant increases in growth and productivity. It also led to quickened cycles of creative destruction. In transportation, for instance, early chartered companies had built roads, but the newer canals were increasing the range and lowering the cost of transportation. The Erie Canal cut costs by 75% and the time for transport by two-thirds. Steam power similarly increased in use, with over 2,000 engines in operation by 1838, up from a handful in the 1780s.[21] By the 1840s, railroads would be creating yet another set of changes.

Even the most substantial American fortunes could not afford to remain static, as prosperous markets soon became crowded. Capital had to move quickly to support the next big thing. Over the first half of the 19th century, the savviest merchants shifted their wealth from traditional shipping and commerce into manufacturing and railroads. In 1814, Francis Lowell and other Boston merchants built up the country's first integrated textile mill, financed largely by the capital of an earlier generation of sea captains and merchants.[22] The mill took raw cotton through the entire textile process, from spinning and cording all the way to finished cloth, dramatically changing the profitability of that crop. Several decades later, when the market for textiles began to decline, the capital shifted elsewhere, including railroad securities and western development.

A scurry was underway locally and nationally, with incumbents seeking to secure their positions and upstarts trying to capture a share of the fast-developing market. People had to hustle amid the shifting economic landscape, but the booming marketplace gave everyone an opportunity, especially the emerging "middling sort." By 1800, Benjamin Franklin's *Autobiography*, the inspirational story of a resourceful, self-made man that became America's paradigm, had become a bestseller. "Their Revolution told them that people's birth did not limit what they might become," wrote Washington Irving.[23]

Visitors picked up on the entrepreneurial mood. Alexis de Tocqueville, who came from France in 1831, reported that Americans were upstarts to the marrow of their bones. It was "difficult to describe the rapacity with which the American rushes forward to secure this immense booty that fortune proffers to him . . . Before him lies a boundless continent, and he urges onward as if time pressed and he was afraid of finding no room for his exertions." This energy grew out of ambition, but also an innate optimism and spirit of adventure. "The desire of prosperity has become an ardent and restless passion in their minds, which grows by what it gains."[24]

Tocqueville was convinced that the leading cause of this striving was the openness of the government. "The democratic institutions of the United States, joined to the physical constitution of the country," explained "the prodigious commercial activity of the inhabitants. It is not engendered by the laws, but the people learn how to promote it by the experience derived from legislation."[25] That sense of relative equality, or at least no fixed hierarchy, fostered the entrepreneurial spirit.

Not just foreigners recognized something was afoot. Ralph Waldo Emerson touted American individualism and today is often cited – incorrectly – for coining the memorable phrase "build a better mousetrap and the world will beat a path to your door." Emerson's celebration of self-reliance and observations such as "man is born to be rich" made him a patron saint of sorts for American entrepreneurs of the era.[26] His assistant Henry David Thoreau, the son of a Concord pencil maker, was as rebellious as any entrepreneur, but ironically decided to abstain from the commercial frenzy altogether and live in the woods.

Balancing Property and Competition

During this period, the legal and institutional framework proved adept at supporting economic growth. Chief Justice John Marshall was the pivotal figure in establishing the national government's authority in the early era. Marshall was a Virginian and a cousin of Jefferson, though they disliked one another. Appointed by John Adams as the fourth chief justice in the country's history, he fell squarely in the camp of the nationalists, and his decisions reflect a bias toward nation-building, a large nationwide marketplace, and secure property rights, while limiting local roadblocks and populist challenges. America's unicorns owe much to Marshall.

Overall, however, the judicial system maintained the balancing act between property rights and the right to compete. Marshall's Court initially tended to the former in order to promote investment. Meanwhile the more populist states favored both: the right to compete, as seen in laws against primogeniture and liberal rules on debt collection and paper money, and property rights at the local level. Together they worked to encourage a *nouveau riche* class to challenge the social dominance of the older elite.[27] The states still tolerated a great deal of local cronyism, but the trend was now to give ambitious upstarts a chance.

The supremacy of the Constitution was particularly important in securing contracts and safeguarding corporations at the mercy of state governments that tried to take them over or restrict their activities. In *Trustees of Dartmouth College v. Woodward* (1819), the Court ruled that legislatures must respect existing charters, even those granted under colonial rule, a critical step in ensuring stability for investment. Through this and other decisions, the independent federal judiciary promoted contractual rights at the state level, reinforcing private ordering in economic life and limiting local government overrides.

One of the most famous cases of the period solidified federal supremacy over the states for interstate commerce and the development of a national market. In *Gibbons v. Ogden* (1824), the Supreme Court ruled against a New York state-granted monopoly to run a ferry line between New York and New Jersey, concluding that only the federal government could confer privileges over interstate commerce. The decision limited the ability of states to put up roadblocks to economic activity, the corollary of the federal government's exclusive right to regulate in this area; this principle would later become known as the "dormant" commerce clause. But the case also tacitly acknowledged that property rights could be removed under certain circumstances in order to enable competition.

New York had given the monopoly to the well-connected Robert Livingston, who had had the foresight to invest in Robert Fulton's innovative steam technology a decade earlier. But now the monopoly threatened to limit further innovation and was restricting competition in the growing transportation market. With the court's ruling, Livingston's patrician family was forced to compete with a young man of little education or social standing named Cornelius Vanderbilt. Property rights were important, but cronyism would not be permitted, especially if it would stand in the way of innovation, competition, and economic intercourse among the states.[28]

The common law also evolved during this period to help address the changing needs of the rapidly developing economy. In the past, judges resolved tensions within business cases by deciding on the basis of fairness, an approach that was consistent with the traditional judicial role. They might have focused on communal standards of propriety and the interests of the larger society. But instead judges and the common law evolved and adopted an "instrumentalist" approach, allowing the laws to serve economic development. Law was to be a tool to give private parties flexibility in ordering their economic arrangements as they saw fit. Instead of abstract ideas of fairness, judges focused on the intent of contracts. This "will theory" of contracts, seeing the agreements as the meeting of the minds between private parties, added certainty to commercial transactions and opened up sophisticated tools of commerce in areas such as insurance and bills of exchange. Reflecting the popular mood against governmental control over business, judges largely refrained from dictating to individuals how they should run their affairs. It helped that they were working within the flexibilities of common law, which gave discretion to judges, rather than a directive system such as the Napoleonic code.[29]

While adding predictability and certainty, the courts found ways to support economic development and entrepreneurs. For instance, to generate waterpower for mills, entrepreneurs often needed to dam streams — which flooded the land of nearby farmers. Rather than respect property rights absolutely and allow stubborn landowners a veto on the dams, courts supported entrepreneurs and required farmers to accept reasonable compensation for the land. As one historian said, "the law became more about protecting ventures than protecting holdings."[30]

Just as the political climate and legal framework evolved from prizing stability and investment to encouraging innovation, so too did the new field of corporate law. In the first decades following independence, corporations were chartered for specific infrastructure projects such as canals and turnpikes. Most of these charters had strictly defined terms and scope. Corporate charters initially depended on special state legislation and often included unique privileges, as with Hamilton's Paterson works. But starting in 1809 in Massachusetts, the states adopted incorporation statutes that allowed entrepreneurs without political connections to get access to this form of capital formation, thereby expanding opportunity and competition.[31] Instead of conferring privileges, the charters came to be understood simply as quasi-automatic registration for a new business, open to anyone who could make a modest investment.[32] Moreover, rather than limited to specific purposes or time frames, the corporations were allowed broad latitude in their activities and received expansive terms, ultimately becoming "general" in nature and "perpetual" in status. The creation and access to the "general perpetual corporation" supported entrepreneurship at all levels, but was particularly useful in enabling ventures of large scale.

Vanderbilt as the Relentless Mogul

Vanderbilt, the upstart in *Gibbons,* went on to become perhaps the most successful entrepreneur in American history, ultimately obtaining a near-unrivaled position of economic incumbency. As an upstart, Vanderbilt started by working as a ferry hand and then captain on his uncle's boat, plying the waters between Staten Island and Manhattan. He then went to work for wealthy fleet owner Thomas Gibbons, leading the charge in the famous case.

The favorable court decision was just the beginning of his remarkable entrepreneurial run. Going on his own, he assembled a transportation network that improved service, cut costs, and mercilessly undercut rivals. He continued to innovate by implementing new technologies and building bigger and faster boats. He named one of his flagships *Lexington* to signal his anti-authoritarian streak, and his network would come to be known as the "People's Line."

Most significantly, he wouldn't stop. Vanderbilt moved from steamboats to ocean liners, especially after the Gold Rush in 1849, and challenged the powerful Cunard line for transatlantic passengers. Then, while seemingly at his apex, Vanderbilt moved into railroads, mastering the technical engineering issues associated with integrating disparate lines and routes. He also learned the nuances and technicalities related to stock trading and securities, famously battling with Jay Gould and others over control of the Erie Railroad.

Vanderbilt epitomized the model of the relentless innovator. He daringly challenged incumbents, mastered new technologies and platforms, and abandoned old ones as needed. He inspired generations of aspiring entrepreneurs.[33]

Jackson and the Decentralization of Finance

The neo-mercantilist system in the first decades after independence had led to a federal government dominated by elites, but only temporarily. They were gradually challenged, not just by a new generation of entrepreneurs but also by artisans, mechanics, small farmers, and those not included in the developing economy.[34] Demographic changes brought about by opportunity, immigration, and transportation were significant; by 1850 half of the population lived west of the Appalachian mountains.[35] Innovations in transportation, energy, manufacturing, and other areas were creating pressure for openness in many areas and industries. At the same time, the Panic of 1819, the result of a precipitous decline in cotton prices and the first large-scale financial crisis in the country, fueled resentment against the financial elite. The challenge to incumbency reached its breaking point with the election of Andrew Jackson in 1828.

Jackson saw his attack on the privileged few and the promotion of laissez-faire populism as consistent with the assertion of rights in 17th-century England and the 18th-century colonies. He voiced special wrath toward the Second Bank of the United States, calling it a "hydra of corruption" and denouncing it as a monopoly that favored a small commercial and financial elite, particularly its establishment head, Nicholas Biddle. When the charter, due to expire in 1836, came up for extension, Jackson overruled his cabinet and vetoed the legislation. Then for good measure he withdrew federal funds from the bank when it tried to carry on as a purely private institution.[36]

Jackson sought to lessen the federal government's involvement in other areas of the economy as well. In particular, he discontinued the federal government's investment in corporate securities, a position that has largely continued to the present and deeply affected corporate governance (discussed in a later chapter).[37]

The financial retreat proved costly, as it triggered a severe financial crisis and prolonged depression. Jackson shifted federal deposits to "pet" banks across the states, themselves vulnerable to local cronyism and loose lending standards, and many failed in the Panic of 1837. In the ensuing decades, the American economy suffered periodic episodes of volatile financial collapse, as the era of "free banking" helped create many state institutions that lent funds recklessly. Ruinous panics became the price, as it were, of Americans' instinctive aversion to central banking and concerns about undue economic and political power among a certain elite.[38] Yet Jackson's costly transformation served as a vital counterweight against an emerging class of incumbents.

With strong justification, some argue that unstable banking brought about by Jackson created uncertainty that raised the cost of entrepreneurship. But the generally decentralized nature of banking that evolved in the United States has helped spawn small business and local entrepreneurship in the long run. This aversion to large central banks continued, both with the development of the stock market as a funding mechanism for large-scale projects (particularly the railroads, as discussed in the next chapter) and ultimately the development of venture capital.

The relatively reduced power of large banks in the United States, compared with other sources of entrepreneurial financing, can be seen today, as most start-ups and many other enterprises look for growth capital from venture funds or capital markets, rather than large banks. This decentralization is in sharp contrast to the concentration and power of banks in countries such as Germany, France, and England, where large banking institutions often have close ties to major incumbent enterprises and are less apt to fund small, risky, or disruptive entities.[39]

When the Right to Compete Trumped Property Rights

Back in 1785, Massachusetts had granted a monopoly to a company that built and managed a bridge between Boston and Charlestown. The investors included relatives of John Hancock and other wealthy and politically connected families. Forty years later, in response to population growth, long waits, and still-hefty tolls, the state allowed another company to build a second bridge between the two municipalities. The owners of the original bridge sued, claiming infringement on their monopoly, and the case eventually went to the federal Supreme Court in 1837.

Even more than *Gibbons v. Ogden*, the *Charles River Bridge Case* marked an inflection point. In the first few decades of American development, charters and grants reassured investors with property rights to foster growth. But in the decades up to the Civil War, a new era of entrepreneurs operating under laissez-faire brought a wave of innovation, challenging incumbents with an intense period of (perhaps ultimately excessive) competition.[40]

The *Charles River Bridge* case explicitly balanced property rights against the right to compete, with implications far beyond bridges. The judges worried that the older bridge, turnpike, and canal monopolies might restrict the growth of railroads, which were starting to spread across the country. The case starred important legal minds, including Daniel Webster, who represented the original bridge owners (and had argued in both the *Dartmouth* and *Gibbons* cases), and Justice Joseph Story, a staunch advocate of preserving established rights. In the middle of the case, long-serving but ailing Chief Justice Marshall stepped down, replaced by President Jackson with Roger Taney, who shared Jackson's bias for open development.

In ruling against any compensation for the owners of the original bridge, the court supported the imperative of economic progress and signaled that a new era of expansion was underway. The older bridge, which had been among the most lucrative endeavors in North America, lost most of its customers and went out of business soon after.[41]

America's Dynamic Economic Elites

Jackson's attack on established power thus confirmed an environment where economic incumbency was difficult to maintain, and innovation and productivity were hard to hold back. Even as the economy established a solid foundation for investment and growth, it showed a notable churn rate among elites. Fortunes were won, lost, and won again, and successful entrepreneurs who wanted to maintain their position among the economic elite would have to stay sharp. Despite attempted cronyism at both the national and state level, political elites would not be sheltered. The fates of Robert Morris, the Livingstons, John Hancock's descendants, and others showed that no position was guaranteed, and though some descendants could remain successful, the economy would not stand still to protect a privileged few. Those that would be successful, such as the Browns or Vanderbilt, would need to continue to innovate or move into new ventures to keep ahead.

Schumpeter noted how "creative destruction" could undermine elites, with even some of the most successful families going from "shirtsleeves to shirtsleeves in three generations." While this may be an overstatement, America has witnessed new elites superseding the old almost continually, usually raising the bar overall. Established elites may still preserve their wealth, often by deploying it in new opportunities or investing it in secure but less dynamic areas, but new entrepreneurs propel themselves – and the economy – to new heights. While Elias Hasket Derby had become a millionaire by his death in 1799, John Jacob Astor was worth \$25 million when he died in 1848. Vanderbilt's wealth exceeded \$100 million when he died 30 years later.

This phenomenon can be seen today in the *Forbes 400* list of wealthiest Americans. The list was started in 1982, and in the nearly 40 years of its existence the fluidity of the list is notable. Few families on the list have remained on it continuously, and many have dropped off as their businesses faced challenges or were superseded by new players.[42]

Not only are the list members churning, but an increasing percentage are now first-generation entrepreneurs as opposed to scions of inherited wealth. When the first list came out in 1982, people with inherited wealth represented a large percentage. By 2007, only 74 people on the list (19%) came from inherited fortunes, while more than half were self-made, a metric that holds true in 2021. Not surprisingly, entrepreneurs with technology backgrounds and immigrants with engineering backgrounds continue to take more spots on the lists.

Moreover, the bar for reaching the *Forbes 400* list continues to rise impressively, suggesting that successful entrepreneurs have pushed the economy as a whole forward and themselves into the upper echelon by generating exceptional performance, or growth beyond that of the market generally.[43] The aggregate net worth of *Forbes 400* members increased by 423% from 1982 to 2002, while the S&P 500 increased by 353%. In 1982 three families (the Hunts, Rockefellers, and DuPonts) accounted for 53 members of the list (13% of the total); by 2002, only three members of those same families (all Rockefellers) still appeared at all.[44]

While it is unlikely that those who fell off the initial list were reduced to "shirtsleeves," the entrepreneurial dynamism of upstarts continues to raise the bar for inclusion. In 1982, the threshold for membership on the list was \$75 million. By 2021, that hurdle was just shy of \$3 billion.[45] Of course, an important and worrying aspect of this phenomenon is that the combined net worth represented by these individuals as a percentage of GDP has increased markedly, signaling dramatic levels of inequality between the very rich and everyone else.

By contrast, inherited wealth has traditionally dominated the lists abroad. This is beginning to change with the increase in entrepreneurship globally, but other countries continue to show less dynamism. In some places, such as the former Soviet Union, most dynamism is linked to cronyism. Some researchers have analyzed the persistent and concentrated power of a small number of families in many non-U.S. countries, and the results suggest hierarchies are far more static there. According to one study, ownership of company assets by the 15 richest families in the United States amounted to 3% of total assets in 1996, whereas in some Asian countries the range was an astounding 20% or higher.

We also see a link between economic power and political control in many nations with concentrated wealth: "where a few families control the state, they can use it to suppress economic competitors and secure monopoly profits."[46] Evidence also suggests a link between cronyism and concentrated banking and finance. This is consistent with the claim that a broad dispersion of economic and political power, and increased social mobility in countries, supports higher rates of growth, productivity, competitiveness, and innovation, while the opposite holds in less dynamic regimes.

The North-South Divide

For all of its entrepreneurial success, America was still an immature economy in the decades leading up to the Civil War. A frenzy of competition ensued from the 1830s, triggered by Jackson as well as the general movement to open corporation laws, the proliferation of banks, and continued westward expansion. Two major panics, in 1837 and 1857, added to the instability. To some it was the conquest of the self-made man and new entrepreneurs (generally small businesses) over the merchants and capitalists of the first decades after independence.[47] Yet the myriad railroad networks brought duplication and confusion, with over 20,000 miles of track built by 1850 yet little standardization in width of track.[48] Policymakers in some states lamented the competition that made transportation networks unprofitable. The fledgling New York Stock Exchange struggled to build up a regular market in railroad and government securities.

In effect, too much entrepreneurship had unsettled many industries. By the end of the 1850s, open competition had arguably gone too far, bringing inefficiencies across sectors of the economy and failed banks in many states. The legal system, so flexible and adaptive after 1790, began to ossify, as local elites secured their positions using protective legislation. Judges relied more on technical rules to limit action, a move now known as "formalism."[49]

The bigger problem was that this openness had not integrated North and South as it had tied together North and West. Together, the northeastern and midwestern states developed diverse mixes of agriculture, industry, and commerce. These regions accounted for almost all manufacturing, as well as over 90% of all patentees between 1790 and 1860.[50]

Meanwhile the South specialized in high-margin crops, especially cotton. The development of the cotton gin and cotton loom resulted in massive increase in demand, which Southerners not surprisingly rushed to supply. By 1860, more than half of the richest 7,500 people in the country lived in the South, and slave-trading Natchez, Mississippi, was among the wealthiest towns in the nation, despite the North's relative strength overall.[51]

This lucrative specialization led white Southerners to expand their horrific reliance on enslaved Black laborers. Slavery was the stain on the American economy as a whole, and both Northerners and Southerners benefitted – "lords of the lash" supplying the "lords of the loom." The South's emphasis on large-scale production of agricultural commodities meant that business in the South lost much of its capacity for dynamic development. Planter dominance within strong social hierarchies prevented the openness to upstarts that drove innovation in the North. The South certainly had elements of entrepreneurship, including advanced capital accounting and inventors such as Cyrus McCormick, who developed his mechanical reaper in Virginia before perfecting it in Illinois. But these innovations happened within the narrow band of slave-produced export crops.[52]

A hint of the dynamism and creativity the South lost from slavery comes in the life of Robert Gordon. He was born enslaved to a wealthy Virginian who spent much of his time with yachts. Gordon was put in charge of the master's coal yard and allowed to do what he liked with the waste coal dust. Gordon collected the dust, found ways to sell it, and eventually bought his freedom in 1846. He traveled north and settled in Cincinnati, where he set up a coal yard. Cincinnati was hardly free of racism, with a race riot as recently as 1841, and its white coal dealers banded together to lower their prices and squeeze Gordon out. But Gordon hired some light-skinned men to pass for white and buy a large volume of coal at the low price, which Gordon held for a while before reselling. His maneuver worked, and Gordon went on to expand and amass a large fortune.[53]

Falling behind in development, Southern planters clamored for new territories – the only way they could imagine sustaining their position. Northerners distrusted what they saw as an entrenched "Slave Power," and "Free Soil, Free Labor, Free Men" became the rallying cry of the emergent Republican Party in the 1850s. Northerners were determined to prevent the Southern upper class from claiming the new lands out west.[54]

Amidst these changes, signs of new opportunity were becoming apparent. Railroads were expanding the commercial frontier and bringing economic and demographic transformation along with it, and the discovery of gold sparked a new wave of migration. A new form of communication – the telegraph – also appeared and was aided by congressional appropriations that drove growth from 40 miles in 1846 to over 23,000 miles a mere six years later.[55] The need to rationalize the economy and the opportunity for nationwide expansion opened a path for a new generation of entrepreneurial upstarts.

Conclusion

The early American republic failed to eliminate slavery, and it culminated in a devastating civil war. Yet it accomplished something remarkable: a solid foundation for entrepreneurship that protected most property rights while encouraging sustained innovation and scale. Thanks to its favorable geography and democratic ambitions, as well as some farsighted leaders, the country continued to empower entrepreneurs who sought out and embraced opportunity. Because of its balanced legal and political framework, it largely contained the dangers of crony capitalism and populist disorder. Too many other developing countries, especially in the 20th century, have failed to maintain the entrepreneurial balance between property rights and the right to compete. They never break the hold of early elites, so they struggle to evolve over time.

By 1860, the first big development cycle – from investment to competition to consolidation to disruption – had reached completion. Derby, Livingston, and other early innovators had played their part, then new players such as Girard and Vanderbilt overshadowed them. They, too, soon faced competition as new market opportunities, technologies, and entrepreneurs upset the balance. Maintaining that momentum required new fields to be conquered, both geographical and industrial. A new breed of entrepreneurs, especially ones who could consolidate and rationalize, would soon find their chance. They would build not just new enterprises, but ones of unprecedented scale. The first unicorns were coming.

Endnotes

1. Brown actually wrote a long report to Hamilton, who had reached out to all the states asking for their experiences with manufacturing. It is unclear whether Hamilton received or read the report from Brown.

2. See Barbara Tucker, *Samuel Slater and the Origins of the American Textile Industry* (New York: Cornell University Press, 1984); Ron Chernow, *Hamilton* (New York: Penguin Press, 2004); and Doran S. Ben-Atar, *Trade Secrets: Intellectual Piracy and the Origins of American Industrial Power* (New Haven: Yale University Press, 2004). See also Michael Lind, *Land of Promise: An Economic History of the United States* (New York: HarperCollins, 2012), 1–8.

3. Jefferson was apparently inspired by the writings of Jean-Baptiste Say, a Frenchman with Dutch roots who was supposedly the first to coin the term "entrepreneur" and whose *Treatise on Political Economy* (1809) highlighted the special role that these adventurers played in creating new goods and services and anticipating new consumer needs and wants ("Say's Law" is the proposition that supply creates its own demand). The book was so disruptive that Napoleon had it banned for a time. Say also translated Adam Smith's *Wealth of Nations* and Benjamin Franklin's works for the French public. Jean-Baptiste Say, *A Treatise on Political Economy, or the Production, Distribution and Consumption of Wealth* (New York: A.M. Kelly, 1809), transl. by C.R. Prinsep (1841). See also Louis Uchitelle, "The Accidental Inventor of Today's Capitalism: Jean-Baptiste Say, No Longer a Villain," *New York Times*, February 21, 1998, and Evert Schoorl, *Jean-Baptists Say: Revolutionary, Entrepreneur, Economist* (Oxford, UK: Routledge, 2013).

4. See William Rosen, *The Most Powerful Idea in the World: A Story of Steam, Industry & Invention* (Chicago: University of Chicago Press, 2010), 276–288; and Craig Nard and Andrew Morriss, "Constitutionalizing Patents from Venice to Philadelphia," Case Western Reserve, *Review of Law and Economics*, January 2006.

5. See Bruce Mann, *Republic of Debtors: Bankruptcy in the Age of Independence* (Cambridge, MA: Harvard University Press, 2002).

6. Hamilton, "Defense of the Funding System," July 1795.

7. Hamilton, "Report on Manufactures," December 5, 1791. See also Chernow, *Hamilton*, 374.

8. For more on this struggle, see Stanley Elkins and Eric McKitrick, *The Age of Federalism: The Early American Republic, 1788–1800* (New York: Oxford University Press, 1993).

9. See Gordon S. Wood, *Empire of Liberty: A History of the Early Republic, 1789–1815* (New York: Oxford University Press, 2011), and Joyce Appleby, *Capitalism and a New Social Order: The Republican Vision of the 1790s* (New York: New York University Press, 1984).

10. See John E. Crowley, *The Privileges of Independence: Neomercantilism and the American Revolution* (Baltimore: John Hopkins University Press, 1993), 23–25, 127–131, 134–153; and Ned W. Downing, *The Revolutionary Beginning of the American Stock Market* (New York: Museum of American Finance, 2010), Appendix 1 and 2 (listing the various state charters). See also Alan Greenspan and Adrian Wooldridge, *Capitalism in America: An Economic History of the United States* (New York: Penguin Press, 2018), 135. (More than 350 corporate charters were granted between 1783 and 1801, with two-thirds of them for transportation projects such as turnpikes and bridges; the balance were for banks, insurance companies, and small manufacturing.)

11. Charles Sellers, *The Market Revolution: Jacksonian America, 1815–1846* (New York: Oxford University Press, 1991), 38–85. By 1850, over 3,700 miles of canals had been completed, with transportation costs much cheaper than the turnpikes and roads of the prior generation. Greenspan and Wooldridge, *Capitalism in America*, 50.

12. See, e.g., Eric Jay Dolin, *When America First Met China: An Exotic History of Tea, Drugs, and Money in the Age of Sail* (New York: Liveright Publishing Corporation, 2002); Eric Jay Dolin, *Fur, Fortune and Empire: The Epic History of the Fur Trade in America* (New York: Liveright Publishing Corporation, 2012); and Eric Jay Dolin, *Leviathan: The History of Whaling in America* (New York: Liveright Publishing Corporation, 2007). See also Richard Kluger, *Seizing Destiny: The Relentless Expansion of American Territory* (New York: Vintage Books, 2007).

13. The country's size increased from 864,746 square miles in 1800 to 2,940,042 by 1850, with new territories including the Louisiana Purchase (1803), Florida (1821), Texas (1805), and the Mexican-American War (1850). Greenspan and Wooldridge, *Capitalism in America*, 10.

14. Charles R. Morris, *The Dawn of Innovation: The First American Industrial Revolution* (New York: Public Affairs, 2012).

15. Greenspan and Wooldridge, *Capitalism in America*, 40–42.

16. *Salem: Maritime Salem in the Age of Sail*, 48 (National Park Service Handbook), 26.

17. There were 338 banks in 1810 and 27,864 banks by 1914. Greenspan and Wooldridge, *Capitalism in America*, 10.

18. Greenspan and Wooldridge, *Capitalism in America*, 46, 179.

19. Daren Acemoglu and James A. Robinson, *Why Nations Fail: The Origins of Power, Prosperity, and Poverty* (New York: Random House, Crown Business, 2012), 33.

20. See David A. Hounsell, *From the American System to Mass Production, 1800–1932* (Baltimore: John Hopkins University Press, 1984) and Morris, *The Dawn of Innovation*, 113–158.

21. Greenspan and Wooldridge, *Capitalism in America*, 50–54.

22. Robert F. Dalzell, Jr., *Enterprising Elite: The Boston Associates and the World They Made* (Cambridge, MA: Harvard University Press, 1987). Later, John Murray Forbes and others would continue this tradition, deploying his fortune from the China trade into a series of railroad investments. John Lauritz Larson, *Bonds of Enterprise: John Murray Forbes and Western Development in America's Railway Age* (Cambridge, MA: Harvard University Press, 1989).

23. Wood, *Empire of Liberty*, 2, 25, 101.

24. *Democracy in America*, John Canfield, trans., 322.

25. Ibid., 232.

26. Sellers, *The Market Revolution*, 376–377.

27. Stuart Bruchey, *Enterprise: The Dynamic Economy of a Free People* (Cambridge, MA: Harvard University Press, 1990), 113.

28. See Mike Wallace and Edwin G. Burrows, *Gotham: A History of New York City to 1898* (New York: Oxford University Press, 1998), 432–433. See also Jean Edward Smith, *John Marshall: Definer of a Nation* (New York: Henry Holt and Company, 1996), 477–481 and Daniel Walker Howe, *What Hath God Wrought: The Transformation of America, 1815–1848* (New York: Oxford University Press, 2007), 439–445.

29. Morton Horwitz, *The Transformation of American Law, 1780–1860* (Massachusetts: Harvard University Press, 1977). See also Herbert Hovenkamp, *Enterprise and American Law, 1836–1937* (Cambridge, MA: Harvard University Press, 2014).

30. James Willard Hurst, *Law and the Conditions of Freedom in the Nineteenth Century of United States* (Madison, WI: University of Wisconsin Press, 1956), 24.

31. Thomas Cochran, *Frontiers of Change: Early Industrialism in America* (New York: Oxford University Press, 1983), 121. Massachusetts passed general acts for manufacturing in 1809, New York in 1811; by the 1840s, most state had general acts and some began to prohibit the issue of special business charters. In New York, for example, there were 220 incorporations between 1800 and 1810 alone.

32. James Willard Hurst, *The Legitimacy of the Business Corporation in the Law of the United States, 1780–1970* (Charlottesville: University Press of Virginia, 1970), 13–57, Chapter 1, "From Special Privileges to General Utility, 1780–1890" ("After independence, the desire of businessman to use the corporation mounted rapidly; state legislatures chartered 317 business corporations from 1780 to 1801"), and 33–39 (noting the confusion between 1830 and 1870 between nature and status of a corporation and any special franchise right associated with it). See also Arthur S. Schlesinger, Jr., *The Age of Jackson* (New York: Penguin Group, 1949), 334–349 (Jacksonian Democracy and Industrialism).

33. T.J. Stiles, *The First Tycoon: The Epic Life of Cornelius Vanderbilt* (New York: First Vintage Books, 2010).

34. Sellers, *The Market Revolution*.

35. Greenspan and Wooldridge, *Capitalism in America*, 57.

36. See Schlesinger, *The Age of Jackson*; Bray Hammond, *Banks and Politics in America: From the Revolution to the Civil War* (Princeton, NJ: Princeton University Press, 1957), and Greenspan and Wooldridge, *Capitalism in America*, 69. On state banks' role in promoting local economic development, see Naomi Lamoreaux, *Insider Lending: Banks, Personal Connections, and Economic Development in Industrial New England* (Cambridge, UK: Cambridge University Press, 1996).

37. Carl Lane, "The Elimination of the National Debt in 1835 and the Meaning of Jacksonian Democracy," *Essays in Economics and Business History* 25, no. 1 (2007).

38. See Charles W. Calomiris and Stephen H. Haber, *Fragile by Design: The Political Origins of Banking Crises and Scarce Credit* (Princeton, NJ: Princeton University Press, 2014).

39. Luigi Zingales, *A Capitalism for the People: Recapturing the Lost Genius of American Prosperity* (New York, Basic Books, 2014), ch. 4; and Mark J. Roe, *Strong Managers, Weak Owners: The Political Roots of American Corporate Finance* (Princeton, NJ: Princeton University Press, 1994).

40. See Horwitz, *The Transformation of American Law*, 109–139 ("By the second quarter of the century, it was becoming clear in a number of areas of the law that a conception of property as monopolistic and exclusionary placed an unmanageable burden on continued economic growth.")

41. Stanley I. Kutler, *Privilege and Creative Destruction: The Charles River Bridge Case* (Baltimore: John Hopkins University Press, 1989).

42. Steve Kaplan and Joshua Rauh, "Family, Education and Sources of Wealth Among the Richest Americans, 1982–2012." *American Economic Review* 103, no. 3 (May 2013): 158–162. According to one study, 60 people have been on the list continuously, while 156 died but likely would have been on the list at the time of their death. But at least 191 fell off the list due to business conditions or other challenges.

43. Peter Bernstein and Annalyn Swan, *All the Money in the World* (New York: Vintage Books, 2008), 5 (from 1982 to 2006, the average net worth has gone from $230M to $3.1B and the minimum has gone from $75M to $1B), 65 (from 1982 to 2006, the number who have inherited their wealth has dropped from 47% to 30%), 71 (only 36 people from the original list on the list in 1982 were still in 2006; only 14 of those saw their wealth increase more than the S&P 500).

44. William P. Barrett, "The March of the 400: If You Get to $1B, Don't Rest on Your Laurels: Capitalism Has a Knack for Crushing Old Fortunes and Churning Up New Ones," *Forbes*, September 30, 2002. See also Kevin

Phillips, *Wealth and Democracy: A Political History of the American Rich* (New York: Broadway Books, 2002).

45. Kerry A. Dolan, *The 2021 Forbes 400 List of Richest Americans: Facts and Figures*, Forbes.com, October 5, 2021.

46. Robert D. Cooter and Hans-Bernard Schäfer, *Solomon's Knot: How Law Can End the Poverty of Nations* (Princeton, NJ: Princeton University Press, 2012), 56.

47. See Herbert Hovenkamp, *Enterprise and the Law*, 2, 13, 234 (1830s and 1840s were the democratization of opportunity). See also Hammond, *Banks and Politics in America*, 145, 322, 746, noting the difference between "mechanics banks" and "merchants banks" during this period.

48. Greenspan and Wooldridge, *Capitalism in America*, 53.

49. Morton Horowitz, *The Transformation of American Law*, Chapter 11. See also Herbert Hovenkamp, *Enterprise and the Law*, 6 (formalism occurs "when a dominant group achieves its political goals and then attempt to freeze them in place").

50. Greenspan and Wooldridge, *Capitalism in America*, 69, 80. Similarly, the North had 70% of the nation's wealth and 80% of its banking assets.

51. Greenspan and Wooldridge, *Capitalism in America*, 74–78 (Whitney's cotton gin helped make it possible to cultivate non–long staple cotton in upland areas, while new seed varieties also increased productivity).

52. Sven Beckert and Seth Rockman, eds., *Slavery's Capitalism: A New History of American Economic Development* (Philadelphia: University of Pennsylvania Press, 2016). Some historians have argued that entrepreneurial capitalism gradually undermined the cultural basis of slavery: Thomas Bender, ed., *The Antislavery Debate: Capitalism and Abolitionism as a Problem in Historical Interpretation* (Berkeley: University of California Press, 1991).

53. Carter Woodson, "The Negroes of Cincinnati Prior to the Civil War," *Journal of Negro History*, January 1916.

54. Eric Foner, *Free Soil, Free Labor, Free Men: The Ideology of the Republican Party before the Civil War* (New York: Oxford University Press, 1995). See also the "Beard-Hacker" thesis, which argues that the Civil War represented the success of Northern industrial capitalism over Southern agrarianism.

55. Howe, *What Hath God Wrought*, 690.

6

The Evolution from Small Business to Big

The stench was so bad it could be smelled throughout New Orleans. More important, the offal from butchered animals was contaminating the water supply and sickening residents. To remedy this chaotic situation, the Louisiana legislature in 1869 gave the newly chartered Crescent City Livestock Landing and Slaughterhouse Company an exclusive right to operate a single meat-packing plant. The facility was to be located just south of New Orleans, across the Mississippi and downstream from the main population area. It had the right to operate for a 25-year period and to charge butchers to use wharves and other facilities.

In response, a group of 400 long-standing independent butchers sued to stop the monopoly. Arguing that the legislation conferred an "odious and exclusive privilege" to the new company, the butchers claimed that it deprived them of their livelihood. Undercurrents of racism and scars from the Civil War were at play, as many of the (white) butchers felt that the new facility would help newly freed Blacks and northern carpetbaggers at their expense. With more than a bit of irony, the attorney for the butchers used the recently enacted 14th Amendment, intended to protect the freedmen, to claim that their rights were being violated.

In ruling against the butchers in the *Slaughterhouse Cases* (1873), the U.S. Supreme Court narrowly interpreted the 14th Amendment, specifically the "privileges and immunities" provision. The majority opinion concluded it did not protect the "right to ply one's trade" under that clause and that the local charters could move ahead. Yet this was a narrow 5–4 decision, with influential dissenting opinions.

In particular, Justice Stephen Field argued for an individual's right "to pursue happiness and trade," a strong endorsement of the right to compete and condemnation of state-sanctioned monopoly. He also supported an expansive view of the 14th Amendment for economic rights. Field dissented again several years later against the states' right to regulate grain storage rates. He sought to limit what states could claim as a public interest, in support of the "new entrepreneurialism."[1]

Field's view eventually won out. The Slaughterhouse cases, never overturned, neutered the privileges and immunities clause, but other provisions of the 14th Amendment – equal protection and due process – were ultimately deployed to support economic growth. Not just entrepreneurs but soon large corporations benefitted from fewer government constraints. However, as these corporations gained heft with capital-intensive industrialization, and as the entrepreneurs who built them morphed into oligopolists, the federal government eventually found ways to rein them in. By the early 20th century, reformers were challenging these new incumbents and recalibrating the government's role in managing competition.[2]

Upstarts in the New National Market

One outcome of the Civil War was that it validated the Northern economic model as the path for national development. Republican Abraham Lincoln, who had done legal work for railroads before becoming president, pushed to integrate the nation. Free from Southern objections, Congress passed the Homestead Act (1862), which gave free land to settlers and the railroads that connected them to markets, as well as the Morrill Land-Grant Acts (1862), which promoted technical education and land-grant universities. It also passed acts to subsidize a transcontinental railroad. The huge western part of the continent was now opening up to entrepreneurs for exploitation and development, from farming and herding to mining and processing.[3]

The speed and scope of the railroads' progress were remarkable. Total mileage in the United States grew from 30,000 in 1860 to 190,000 by 1900.[4] Regional combinations operated most of this track, which yielded operations of immense scale as they finally standardized track gauges. To run them efficiently and safely, the railroads innovated in administration and capital management, and in turn spawned equally capital-intensive industries from telegraphs to steel to sleeping cars. The cost of transporting goods fell dramatically. The telegraph, which had been growing as a means of communication prior to the war, was critical in speeding the flow of information and improving efficiency.

Success required not just daring and hard work, but also large sums of capital from faraway investors. To encourage this risky investment, the corporate legal form and capital markets expanded and evolved to favor investors.[5] And it was just in time. Antebellum investments in textile mills and eastern railroads were showing decreasing returns, as their high profits had attracted imitators. So investors shifted westward to capture the new possibilities. From a copper mine in Michigan to a stockyard in Kansas City, and with railroads from Texas to Montana, western areas took off due to eastern capital and advice.[6]

At the same time, in an echo of the antebellum situation, the excess competition in certain areas led to opportunities for those who could pick up the pieces and master the legal, financial, or technical mechanisms. State banks had sprouted up everywhere, and many proved reckless, leaving opportunities in their wake. Western expansion depended on unpredictable rates of settlement and exploitation, while expanding manufacturing and industrial firms had to compete in an open market with little protection; this led to waste but also opportunity. The railroads had already built costly networks of tracks, stations, engines, and cars, and these fixed costs led to aggressive price-cutting as competing lines vied for incremental revenue. The result was, in the words of railroad regulator Charles Francis Adams, "ruinous competition" and calls for government intervention, mostly to limit the frenzy and protect investor and other interests.[7] Ultimately, it would be a new class of smart entrepreneurs that succeeded in consolidating and rationalizing the networks.

Even industries that did not directly serve the railroads drew from entrepreneurs who got their start in that ecosystem, from merchandiser Richard Sears (a station master) to inventor Thomas Edison (a telegraph operator). Aggressive upstarts, who understood better than incumbents the possibilities for scale and efficiency, jumped in. As new businesses developed to leverage these technologies, end consumers often enjoyed broader selection, safer products, and lower prices.

Gustavus Swift developed refrigerated cars to ship frozen packaged meat over long distances, saving the trouble of sending live animals across the country. The big railroads, preferring to own all the freight cars, initially refused to transport Swift's cars, but they eventually capitulated as Swift found workarounds using smaller or Canadian roads. Swift also developed lucrative markets in the byproducts of animal slaughter, harvesting "everything but the squeal." Expanded scale in turn encouraged improvements in production, especially the automated "disassembly line" that later inspired Henry Ford.

Other entrepreneurs, from H.J. Heinz in food processing to James Duke in cigarettes, likewise triumphed with improved efficiencies and consolidation, often brought about by low transportation costs and other innovations. Retailing joined the trend with department store magnates and mail order giants – using fast railroad shipping to expand nationally. Isaac Merritt Singer mass-produced sewing machines using interchangeable parts, winning customers not just with low prices but also innovations such as installment purchasing and trade-ins.

Local Incumbents Left in the Dust

Of course, as these new enterprises grew they left behind a trail of incumbents from an earlier era. Most of those were small local or regional businesses that had emerged in the years prior to the Civil War, amid the first surges of westward expansion. Initially the new consolidating enterprises coexisted with many established entities, as these provided access to markets and encouraged settlement and development. But over time the consolidators squeezed out the smaller firms with increasingly efficient operations. The pressure for scale eventually convinced many smaller incumbents to give up their independence, as they found themselves with overcapacity and little ability to differentiate their product.

John D. Rockefeller was more conscious than most upstarts of economies of scale and network power. As he built his empire in oil refining, he understood the railroad shippers' need for volume and convinced them to give him favorable rates, which in turn provided unique competitive advantage that enabled him to buy out rivals. Those who declined to join forces found themselves crushed by Standard Oil's low prices. The greater the volume of throughput, the lower the cost, and not just in shipping. Rockefeller eventually controlled nearly 90% of U.S. oil refining, while expanding vertically into oil drilling and distribution. But consumers benefitted with lower-cost fuel. "We are refining oil for the poor man," Rockefeller said.[8]

Those incumbents sought to create barriers through state courts and legislatures, often winning temporary protections. But the national entrepreneurs, seeking the right to compete, challenged state limitations. A series of cases, combining the dormant commerce clause and Field's argument for economic rights, swept many of those roadblocks aside.

While entrepreneurs played the leading role in national development, the federal and even certain state governments helped with crucial infrastructure. Initially passed to support the war effort, the National Banking Acts of 1863–1866 created a more stable, nationwide banking system that supported the flow of investment west. The newly chartered national banks, despite limits on branches, also expanded lending by disrupting local bank monopolies. The legislation bolstered investors' confidence in the soundness of money, making them more willing to invest in long-term western development.[9] At the same time, even as large national banks developed in New York, Congress refused to create a strong central banking system similar to what European countries established. It was the old Jacksonian concern with entrenching incumbents through centralized finance.

The New York Stock Exchange and other emerging securities markets channeled ever more capital to large-scale enterprises. Like national banks, these markets had gotten their initial push during the Civil War, as the federal government looked to Jay Cooke and other brokers to sell war bonds. From there the exchanges readily took on railroad and other corporate securities, much of which were bought by European investors. Over time, the railroad consolidators used the exchanges to gain control of adjacent or competing lines, often rationalizing the duplication and fragmentation in the system and creating efficiency through acquisitions and other tactics. In addition, Massachusetts and some other states encouraged private investment in new ventures by relaxing the "prudent man" standard for fiduciaries, enabling them to invest in equities along with the safer bonds. This growth in national financial markets made up for the weakness of the still-fragmented commercial banking system.

With these opportunities for growth and the benefits of efficiency, corporate law and the general perpetual corporation evolved into something bigger and broader. First it was used to facilitate loose "pools" of allied firms, then it supported the development of combined trusts. When the Sherman Act limited trusts in 1890, Rockefeller chartered his Standard Oil Corporation as a holding company under New Jersey legislation allowing corporate entities to own stock in other firms. Clever bankers, notably J.P. Morgan toward the end of the century, pushed further to consolidate entire industries, rationalizing costs, operations, and pricing along the way. Local incumbents didn't stand a chance.[10]

New Rights for Big Business

These countrywide developments eventually forced the federal government to take up a new question: Could entrepreneurs succeed so well that they became entrenched incumbents that stifle competition? Courts had long worked to remove privileges and promote open competition and freedom of contract. But what about firms whose competitive advantage came largely from scale economies rather than chartered monopoly?

The doctrine of "natural monopoly," and the evident chaos of "ruinous competition," had initially led justices to allow consolidation. Despite periodic panics and failures from overcapacity, the economy was growing, productivity increasing, and efficiencies proving themselves out. The courts often relied on the commerce clause of the Constitution to push back against state protectionism, such as a law subjecting Singer sales branches to licensing fees. Similarly, the Court forbade state regulators from requiring local meat inspectors for the national Armour meat-packing company. The Court also limited state rate regulation of interstate railroads, a rebuke that set the stage for federal regulation under the Interstate Commerce Commission.[11]

Most significant was the Supreme Court's extending "personhood" under the 14th Amendment to corporations, the ultimate triumph of Field's argument. In *Santa Clara v. Southern Pacific* (1886), the Court gave these businesses the same rights of equal protection as natural persons, thereby safeguarding them against arbitrary state action. "Arbitrary" came to mean any rule without a strong consumer rationale – protecting incumbents (or local workers) would not be enough.[12]

With personhood, corporations could avail themselves of the 5th and 14th Amendment protections against being deprived of "life, liberty, or property, without due process of law" at both the state and federal level, rights that became known as "substantive due process." These rights expanded over the next century and beyond, continuing to the present with controversial cases such as corporate political donations.

While the states were stymied, early federal efforts at regulation were only partially effective – and often helped these new incumbents. The Interstate Commerce Commission (ICC), formed in 1887, established federal regulatory control over large enterprises such as railroads, but did little at first. Most of its efforts centered on rationalizing rates and competition for the benefit of established corporations. Only later did the ICC discourage the sort of discriminatory freight rates that Rockefeller had used to squelch his opponents. Likewise, the Sherman Antitrust Act of 1890 promoted open, fair competition, but set no enforceable policy.[13]

Moreover, a conservative Supreme Court seemed to lag the sentiment of Congress by at least a decade.[14] In one well-known case, the Court decided that the Sherman Act would not even apply to manufacturing.[15] In another, the Court said the federal government could prohibit egregious restraints on trade, but monopolies per se were not illegal and were perhaps a fact of economic life.[16] Ironically, in supporting these new enterprises the Court sometimes took a limited view of the definition of interstate commerce (they had often used a broad interpretation to curb state actions) or deferred to the states' chartering authority over corporations as a justification for limiting the intervention of the federal government. As was often be the case in American history, the separation of powers made it difficult for governments to work in lockstep.[17]

Carnegie as an Entrepreneur of Scale

Andrew Carnegie was driven. He'd arrived in America in 1848 at the age of 13, the son of a Scottish weaver impoverished by the new mechanized looms. Carnegie's relentless energy and innate intelligence, along with supportive bosses at the Pennsylvania Railroad, eventually landed him shares of stock in that company. In 1865 he quit the railroad and worked full-time on investments, eventually putting all of his eggs into the single basket of steel manufacturing. Carnegie focused on the innovative new Bessemer process, developed in Britain, and began building these new mills in 1872.

Carnegie improved substantially on the invention by applying rigorous cost-accounting, vertical integration, and other aggressive managerial techniques. He instinctively understood economies of scale, and he had the discipline to live frugally and plow earnings back into the business – rather than rely on outside investors who might slow his pace.

Those efforts captured the enormous potential savings from the Bessemer process, but unlike the textile mills that took off before the Civil War, steel plants required a great deal of up-front capital to achieve full efficiency. They also needed to run this expensive equipment as much as possible to cover the cost of capital – which meant a steady, high flow of materials into production. During a period of rapid growth, with mines and transportation links still developing, such a throughput required backward integration either by direct ownership or tight contracts with suppliers. Carnegie took his early profits as a Bessemer pioneer and plowed them back into the enterprise by acquiring his main suppliers, similar to what Rockefeller had done in buying oil leases. Once he had control, he could orchestrate steel production at amazingly low costs. With low prices he gained ever more contracts for steel delivery, and with greater scale came still lower costs.

He summed up the entrepreneurial achievement as follows:

"Two pounds of iron stone mined upon Lake Superior and transported 900 miles to Pittsburgh; one and a half pound of Pennsylvania coal mined and manufactured into coke and transported to Pittsburgh; a small amount of manganese ore mined in Virginia and brought to Pittsburgh – and these four pounds of materials made into one pound of steel, for which the consumer pays one cent."

With that achievement Carnegie disrupted the incumbent providers of both iron and steel rails. Before the 1870s, iron and steel was a largely regional industry, but Carnegie helped to make it a national one. While the booming economy of the late 19th century supported a number of steel firms, in the troughs of the business cycle only Carnegie's firm kept operating near capacity.

In 1900, Carnegie Steel was not just the most efficient but by far the largest steel company in the world. Its products went into rails, bridges, and the new skyscrapers rising over cities. He also marketed aggressively, sending his products worldwide. And he wasn't finished. At age 65, he was planning to integrate forward into finished steel for the emerging industries of cars and appliances.

Complaining of ruinous competition, Carnegie's rivals enlisted the help of J.P. Morgan & Company, which had just come from rescuing the railroads. He offered Carnegie $480 million to sell out to his massive combination. Unable to resist the chance to finally realize his long-held ambitions for philanthropy, Carnegie accepted.[18]

The result was the United States Steel Company, capitalized in 1901 at $1.4 billion (equal to $41 billion now). The consolidation handled two-thirds of domestic steel production and formed by far the largest corporation yet. That market share reached 80–90%, varying by category, in 1907, when U.S. Steel acquired its largest remaining rival, the Tennessee Coal and Iron Company. President Theodore Roosevelt made a "gentlemen's agreement" with J.P. Morgan that federal government would not challenge the deal. Carnegie Steel had gone from industry disruptor to the biggest incumbent of the land.

Combining Incumbents

Already by 1900, widespread consolidation in the economy was bringing calls for action. Even as innovations such as the telephone and electricity spread, with rising productivity and falling costs, large firms were using their scale advantages and accumulated assets to both crush smaller rivals and prevent new upstarts from challenging their position. Small producers, farmers, and others continued to raise their voices. Back in 1867, Mark Twain had ridiculed the "upstart princes of shoddy," whose shallow glitz prompted him to coin the term the "Gilded Age." But now most people thought they needed reining in.[19] Even the Horatio Alger stories so popular in the era, touting rags to respectability, suggested that luck and pluck rather than pure opportunity might be needed for success.

While elite opinion continued to preach the advantages of scale and efficiency, critics pointed to large companies growing complacent and failing to innovate. For instance, back in the 1870s, Western Union controlled nearly all national communication through its dominance in telegraphs. When Alexander Graham Bell patented telephone communications in 1876, he offered to sell the rights to the telegraph giant. But Western Union, skeptical of the technology, refused him. Bell set up his own company to commercialize the innovation, and it eventually became so strong that it acquired Western Union in 1909.

Developments in economic theory also supported arguments for government intervention, even as most economists maintained a strong belief in the virtues of economies of scale. The doctrine of "marginalism," describing how firms set prices and created value, suggested that large firms were capturing more of this value at the expense of workers and others. Related concepts such as "utilitarianism" argued that overall social welfare would rise if more of the incremental production went to those who needed it rather than to wealthy people who already had plenty. Some legal critics argued for less formalism and more awareness of social implications, culminating in the "legal realism" of the 1920s and '30s. These and related concepts supported calls for greater government control and a move away from the basic balance established by the end of the 19th century.[20]

The new entrepreneurs proved clever in staying ahead, and many copied innovations such as Standard Oil's use of the New Jersey holding company statute to circumvent the regulation of trusts.[21] When the panic of 1893 led to concerns about overcapacity and price competition, the "great merger movement" in American business began. From 1895 to 1904, more than 1,800 firms consolidated into a much smaller number of companies, with 72 entities (including U.S. Steel) controlling over 40% of their industries and some controlling over 70%.[22]

Alongside the growth of these entities – and a significant driver of it – was the development of broad managerial systems. The second half of the 19th century saw the creation of a new type of employee – the professional manager – and an organizational framework for controlling large-scale enterprise. In the early 20th century, universities helped develop both a capable workforce and techniques of systematic management.[23] Patents were increasingly held by corporate entities, though individual inventors (especially Thomas Edison) continued to operate.[24] The economy was transitioning from one based on the self-employed small producer or farmer, to one with large corporate employers and their labor force at the center.[25]

Many of the consolidations eventually lost out to new upstarts. Only those that vertically integrated or otherwise used their size to create sustained advantage maintained strong market positions well into the 20th century.[26] Nevertheless, what had been a fragmented economic landscape of small- and mid-scale producers supplying local markets became a stark terrain of massive enterprises with national spheres of operation. Local shopkeepers and small producers that did survive found themselves doing business on substantially altered terms.

The Progressive Response

One of the most prominent critics of these large and dominant firms was Louis Brandeis. A native of Kentucky and the son of a small businessman, Brandeis came out of the Southern anti-monopoly tradition of Jefferson and Jackson and was naturally suspect of the increasing concentration of power by the large corporations. Although the large enterprises created by the trusts were demonstrating managerial efficiency and lower prices, Brandeis believed that these companies were becoming less innovative and less efficient over time. He called them "clumsy dinosaurs" and believed that once these entities controlled a market, they would increase prices, block out new competitors, and deter innovation.[27]

Brandeis also railed against the concentration of the financial system in the "money trust." He wrote *Other People's Money and How the Bankers Use It* (1914) to publicize Congress's Pujo Committee investigation into the power of J.P. Morgan and other bankers. The committee found that they influenced large swaths of the economy through interlocking directorates and financing.

Brandeis's arguments brought with them a decidedly moral tone that ran against corporate property rights. While much of American law up to that point had supported efficiency, he and other Progressives argued for "distributive justice" and "industrial democracy" and a rebalancing of interests toward small businesses and the growing working class. Consumer prices were secondary. While Brandeis thought a small-business economy would in practice lead to innovation, efficiency, and choice, he proved willing to protect small firms even if that meant consumers paid higher prices.[28]

He therefore had little interest in disruptive competition by new market entrants. For him and others who championed small businessmen, the rise of the new entrepreneurs into large incumbents had shown the pitfalls of market access and scale, as vertical integration and professional management made it harder for small business incumbents to compete.

While he spoke for many Progressives, others aimed simply to rein in and manage the large corporate entities – not necessarily to foster challengers or even support small producers, but simply to limit their growing power. They believed that government would better rationalize ruinous competition than the bankers had. In conjunction with the rise of "scientific management," they argued that thoughtful collective government regulation would better manage competition among the various players than the marketplace itself. Both of these strands affected politics, though in practice government regulation (favored by both wings) often ensconced incumbents and deterred new entrants.

Official government policies changed decisively at the turn of century, after the assassination of President McKinley. McKinley had defeated populist William Jennings Bryan in two straight elections, confirmed the country's commitment to the gold standard, and overcame the economic recession in the late 1890s. But the merger movement had put the "trust question" front and center in politics. The three presidents who followed – Theodore Roosevelt, William Howard Taft, and Woodrow Wilson – shared some assumptions about the importance of the private sector in generating wealth and prosperity, but differed on whether, how, and to what extent the government should intervene.

Though a Republican like his predecessor, Roosevelt surprised many observers with his activist approach to regulating large corporations. He was eager to rein in corporate abuse, but he believed that bigness itself was not a corporate crime or sin; in fact, he saw large corporate entities generating wealth domestically and projecting power abroad. Rather than go back to an early era of small-producer competition, Roosevelt distinguished between "good" and "bad" trusts. The good trusts competed fairly and achieved competitive advantage through scale-based efficiencies. The bad ones used their monopoly power to squelch competition with unfair tactics.

Roosevelt advocated for a strong federal role and what might be called a "statist" approach to the managing the economy. To sort one from the other and punish accordingly, he persuaded Congress in 1903 to establish a Bureau of Corporations.[29] But Congress gave the bureau only an investigatory role, without licensing power, as even some of Roosevelt's supporters saw that as a risk of overreach.[30]

He also went on the offensive with antitrust prosecution. Bolstered by court decisions giving the federal government more power to intervene, he initiated actions against Rockefeller's Standard Oil, James Duke's American Tobacco, and other giants.[31]

Roosevelt decided against seeking a second full term in 1908 and instead supported William Howard Taft, a traditional conservative. Taft defeated William Jennings Bryan in the general election and then continued T.R.'s action against the big firms, bringing 70 cases under the Sherman Act (more than Roosevelt himself). Taft was in office when the Supreme Court broke up both Standard Oil and American Tobacco. The court established the "Rule of Reason," which followed Roosevelt's formula in assessing whether a company was a good or a bad trust, but kept decision power in the courts.[32] Taft went on to challenge U.S. Steel as well, with an implicit rebuke of Roosevelt for his "gentleman's agreement" on the Tennessee Coal deal. Angered, Roosevelt ran against Taft in 1912, splitting Republican votes and enabling Democrat Woodrow Wilson to become president.

Wilson was more of a Brandeisian Progressive, ready for government to intervene in the economy and skeptical of big business as the answer. Rather than influencing large corporations through government coercion, Wilson preferred to break them up and decentralize them. The Pujo Committee findings helped to motivate him to these reforms.

With his two terms, Wilson had a lasting impact on America's entrepreneurial ecosystem. First, he helped bring about a federal income tax with the 16th Amendment, which increased federal power over wealthy incumbents. Second, he helped create the Federal Reserve System, to prevent a repeat of the Panic of 1907 where the economy depended on a rescue from Morgan and other private bankers – but which still had a regional structure to decentralize decision making. Finally, with the Clayton Antitrust Act, he brought about the Federal Trade Commission, empowered to check price discrimination, dismantle interlocking corporate directorates, and prohibit exclusive dealings or tied purchase arrangements. It also strengthened federal antitrust oversight, though it led to no new corporate breakups. Here again, Congress stopped short of giving the agency licensing or similar positive authority; it could intervene only after finding a problem.[33,34]

America's Tradition of Corporate Autonomy

The difference between Roosevelt, Taft, and Wilson is essential to understand. Roosevelt's "New Nationalism" sought to control – and favor – large firms and to use them to help develop the economy. His was a "progressive version of America's tradition of Hamiltonian developmental capitalism." Taft had more of a hands-off approach, allowing concentration with the understanding that the courts would use their judgment to avoid unfair competition. Wilson's "New Freedom" opposed large, centralized firms as a matter of principle, favoring small businesses even as it recognized that a return to individual competition and the Jeffersonian ideal was unrealistic.[35]

From these differences the federal government developed a consensus of sorts: tolerate big business but keep it from actively undercutting the right of small firms to compete. Government would have an active but still secondary role in the economy. This "corporate reconstruction of American capitalism" was a reasonable compromise that largely preserved the entrepreneurial balancing act, though in practice tilted to incumbents. The country would benefit from scale economies, while preserving space for upstarts to challenge the giants as these grew complacent.[36]

Federal oversight still mattered, even where it left giant companies intact. For instance, the leaders of U.S. Steel made a point of not crushing rivals when these went into new areas, a policy of "live and let live." When Bethlehem Steel, led by an aggressive former Carnegie executive, invested heavily in structural steel for skyscrapers, U.S. Steel largely ceded that market rather than risk antitrust attention.[37]

As for the farmers and small businesses resentful of national domination, they experienced these changes in the economy both directly and generationally. Many sons of middle-class shopkeepers and local entrepreneurs joined big business, but as quasi-professional managers with a degree of autonomy. As for wage workers, large corporations sought to assuage them and preempt unionization with the variety of benefits known as "welfare capitalism."[38] The country moved toward a "corporate-administered" marketplace, with an active government but one that deferred to private ordering.[39]

That last point was essential to maintaining the entrepreneurial balancing act. Over the course of the 19th century and despite government intervention in the Progressive era, American corporations had developed a degree of independence unmatched elsewhere. Both large and small firms operated mostly unconstrained by government in terms of access, scope, and freedom, bolstered by constitutionally protected rights. With a plethora of state and local banks, as well as a robust stock market, aspiring entrepreneurs could choose from a range of capital sources far beyond the experiences of their counterparts in other countries – freeing them from domination by big banks or investors. Even J.P. Morgan & Co. gradually pulled back from the mergers it had organized, and trading on public exchanges soon gave these behemoths broad and dispersed shareholding. As a result, American corporations came into the 20th century more independent, less influenced by third-party constituencies, arguably more willing to take risks, and, at the same time, more vulnerable and less protected than corporate entities elsewhere in the world. For all of their rhetoric against big business, Progressive reforms from 1901 to 1920 did not fundamentally change this dynamic.

That independence still largely holds true today, and it sets America apart from other countries. Corporate independence has some drawbacks, especially to those who believe companies have gone too far in areas such as free speech, both commercial and political, or that they have acted without regard to non-shareholder constituencies.[40] But it also gives companies a freer hand to pursue new strategies and innovations, and fewer means of protection when upstarts challenge them. The independence also means that firms in need of assistance generally find little recourse to the government, which allows firms to fail and forces them to find other private firms or capital to rescue them rather than stepping in.

By comparison, Germany and France developed strong state administrative roles in corporate governance, often leading to political interference or pressure such as the mandate of worker councils. In many cases, trade-offs or issues that many American firms might deem beyond the scope of companies are addressed within the corporate organization itself. Political factors can spill into the boardroom, especially in Continental Europe. The Anglo-Saxon model, prevalent in the UK and America, involves a single governing board representing shareholders. By comparison the two-tiered European-Asian model features two boards, one for management and the other a supervisory board often influenced by governments and stakeholders.

Corporations elsewhere must also deal with more direct financial oversight by banks. In many countries large banks are the main sources of finance for corporations, and they often have interlocking directorates. In both Germany and Japan, for instance, a handful of large banks have a strong hand in corporate governance, including (in Germany) the ability to vote shares they hold on behalf of others.[41] Moreover, most of the large banks are themselves heavily controlled by the government, a further source of political pressure that can limit innovation that might hurt non-shareholder constituencies. Bank-controlled corporations, compared those oriented to investors, are more likely to seek stability (and the return of loans) over risk-taking. By contrast, even the largest money center banks have little control over corporate America, and the capital markets play a larger role in company financing, so large corporations have more freedom to operate. Coupled with the country's tradition of decentralized finance, it also means that entrepreneurs looking to disrupt established industries are less likely to be boxed out from getting access to capital than in bank-dominated countries.

Shareholdings in the United States are also more dispersed than elsewhere. One study, for instance, compared the shareholders of Daimler-Benz, Toyota, and General Motors in 1990s and found that the top five owners constituted 74% of the equity in the case of Daimler and 21% of Toyota. With GM, the top five owners accounted for less than 5%.[42] While U.S. institutional investors control a large percentage of the shares in American public companies, these funds do not exert control as do concentrated shareholders in other countries.

Similarly, governments hold very little corporate equity in the United States (less than 3%), with most shares held by relatively passive institutional investors such as mutual funds and pensions (72%). In Japan, major shareholding is split between public and institutional investors (23% each) with a large component of interlocking private ownership among the major "zaibutsu" business groups. In China, public-sector investment represents an extraordinary 38%, while institutional investors are at only 9%. In general, European companies have greater ownership by institutional investors (38%) and private corporations (13%) rather than government. In many other parts of the world, either governments or wealthy families own much of the corporate equity and control those firms.[43] (See figures 6.1 and 6.2)

This independence from concentrated ownership has given corporate executives enormous autonomy and power historically. In the early 1930s, future New Dealers Adolph Berle and Gardner Means were using this managerialist power as a justification for increased regulation. In the 1970s, Michael Jensen similarly developed "agency theory," but to support shareholder activism rather than government intervention. The primacy of shareholders and their ability to challenge boards and management teams continues to the present, ranging from those who

The table shows the distribution of total holdings by investor category in each country/ region for the 10,000 largest listed companies. The ownership by category of investor is aggregated at market value in USD terms as of end 2017 and expressed as share of the total market capitalisation in each market. The data covers ownership by both domestic and foreign origin. For example, in European listed companies strategic individuals and families own 8% of the total market capitalisation; the public sector owns 9%; private corporations own 13%; institutional investors own 38% and the remaining ownership share corresponds to other free-float including retail investors.

	Private corporations	Public sector	Strategic individuals	Institutional investors	Other free-float
United States	2%	3%	4%	72%	19%
Advanced Asia	17%	23%	7%	23%	30%
Europe	13%	9%	8%	38%	32%
China	11%	38%	13%	9%	28%
Emerging Asia excl. China	34%	19%	10%	16%	21%
Other Advanced	7%	4%	4%	39%	47%
Latin America	34%	7%	17%	20%	21%
Other Emerging	15%	28%	6%	20%	31%
Global average	**11%**	**14%**	**7%**	**41%**	**27%**

Figure 6.1 Regional ownership distribution by investor category.

Source: A. De La Cruz, A. Medina, and Y. Tang (2019), "Owners of the World's Listed Companies," OECD Capital Market Series, Paris, www.oecd.org/corporate/Owners-of-the-Worlds-Listed-Companies.htm. OECD Capital Market Series dataset, FactSet, Thomson Reuters, Bloomberg.

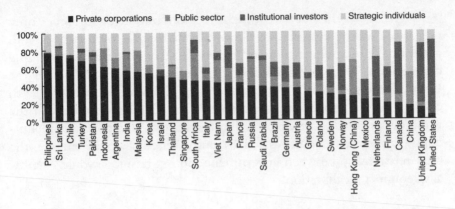

Figure 6.2 Category of the largest investors at the company level.

Source: A. De La Cruz, A. Medina, and Y. Tang (2019), "Owners of the World's Listed Companies," OECD Capital Market Series, Paris, www.oecd.org/corporate/Owners-of-the-Worlds-Listed-Companies.htm.

seek higher stock prices or a sale of the company to those pursuing goals around environmental, social, and governance issues.[44]

American corporate independence may have also come about simply as a result of the historical evolution of the federal government. In Germany and Japan, industrial policy and the administrative state took an active role beginning in the late 19th century. Both of those countries largely came into being as modern states in the 1860s and 1870s, and the governments quickly came around to developing large national enterprises as a matter of industrial policy. The objective was in part to create "national champions" to compete globally while managing other constituencies such as workers, farmers, and small businesses. As such, political and administrative factors influenced corporate development more directly in these countries than it did in the less centralized and cohesive United States, where the national government began small and most economic development commenced at the state level.[45]

The years between the Civil War and World War I transformed the American economy, with the country becoming fully connected and large independent corporations emerging to take advantage of scale and efficiency. The political, legal, and institutional response wrestled with how far to go in allowing these new firms to compete and what administrative agencies and antitrust legislation would be needed to keep them in check. The process of working through these issues helped America's entrepreneurial balancing act survive both the merger movement and the Progressive era, even if the result was a stronger hand for big business and big government.

Fighting World War I required the mobilization of resources on a previously unknown scale. The largest firms rose to the occasion, with government temporarily intervening in the economy and discouraging competition. This new approach returned on a larger scale with the Great Depression, World War II, and the Cold War. Most of the 20th century saw continued intervention by the federal government in the economy, greatly influencing the dynamics between upstarts and incumbents. While new industries led by entrepreneurs would emerge, the cozy relationship between government and big business would eventually require a recalibration.

Endnotes

1. Munn v. Illinois (1877) (allowing state regulation in areas related to a public purpose; the case was initiated in large measure by the Granger Movement, whose "Farmer's Declaration of Rights" railed against emerging railroad monopolies). See also Rudolph J. R. Peritz, *Competition Law in America: History, Law, Rhetoric* (New York: Oxford University Press, 2001), 70 ("state monopoly laws encroach on the right to pursue happiness and trade" – Field).

2. Adam Winkler, *We the Corporations: How American Businesses Won Their Civil Rights* (New York: Liveright, 2018), 125–128.

3. Michael Lind, *Land of Promise: An Economic History of the United States* (New York: HarperCollins, 2012), 143. See also Hurd vs. Rock Island Bridge Company (1857) (Lincoln's famous railroad case, supporting the railroad's right to cross rivers).

4. John Steele Gordon, *An Empire of Wealth: The Epic Story of American Economic Power* (New York: HarperCollins, 2004), 235.

5. Gerard Berk, *Alternative Tracks: The Constitution of American Industrial Order, 1865–1917* (Johns Hopkins University Press, 1997).

6. Noam Maggor, *Brahmin Capitalism: Frontiers of Wealth and Populism in America's First Gilded Age* (Cambridge, MA: Harvard University Press, 2017).

7. Thomas K. McCraw, *Prophets of Regulation* (Cambridge, MA: Harvard University Press, 1984).

8. Ron Chernow, *Titan: John D. Rockefeller, Sr.* (New York: Random House, 1998), 133.

9. Berk, *Alternative Tracks,* especially Chapter 2, on the legal and financial foundations of big business.

10. See Morton J. Horwitz, *The Transformation of American Law, 1870–1960* (Cambridge, MA: Harvard University Press, 1977), 83; Herbert Hovenkamp, *Enterprise and American Law, 1837–1937* (Cambridge MA: Harvard University Press, 1991); Maggor, *Brahmin Capitalism,* Chapter 5. See also Alan Greenspan and Adrian Wooldridge, *Capitalism in America: An Economic*

History of the United States (New York: Penguin Press, 2018), 129 ("For Rockefeller, business combinations were the organizational equivalent of the steam engine").

11. See, Welton v. Missouri (1876) (Singer case), Minnesota v. Barber (1890) (Armour case), Wabash, St. Louis and Pacific Railway Co. v. Illinois (1886) (compare with the Munn case in note 1). See also Stuart Bruchey, *Enterprise: The Dynamic Economy of a Free People* (Cambridge, MA: Harvard University Press, 1990), 390–310, 336.

12. See Winkler, *We the Corporations*.

13. "If we will not endure a king as a political power, we should not endure a king over the production, transportation, or sale of any of the necessities of life" – John Sherman. Nonetheless, some have argued that the Sherman Act was undercut from inception by the New Jersey holding company act, which supplanted traditional trusts that would otherwise be covered by the act.

14. Arnold M. Paul, *Conservative Crisis and the Rule of Law: Attitudes of Bar and Bench, 1887–1895* (Gloucester, MA: Peter Smith, 1976).

15. United States v. E.C. Knight (1895) (Sherman Act does not apply to manufacturing and sugar refining is intrastate commerce).

16. Addyston Pipe and Steel Company v. United States (1899), (bid rigging is clearly illegal but some restraints of trade could be permissible under the Sherman Act).

17. Hovenkamp, *Enterprise and American Law*, 176 (noting that at the turn of the century, there was a gap between the judiciary, which clung to laissez-faire, and the legislature, which wanted reform).

18. Gordon, *An Empire of Wealth*, 260. As noted in the previous chapter, the net worth for the richest men in the country continued to rise, demonstrating how entrepreneurs continued to raise the bar. At his death in 1848, John Jacob Astor was reportedly worth $25M; Cornelius Vanderbilt was in turn worth $105M upon his death in 1878; and John D. Rockefeller was worth $2B in 1916 (he died in 1937). Carnegie was worth $900M when he died in 1919.

19. Twain wrote in 1867 that the old Knickerbocker families were supplanted by "upstart princes of shoddy, vulgar and with unknown grandfathers." Quoted in Gordon, *Empire of Wealth*, 260.

20. See Hovenkamp, *Enterprise and American Law*, 190–192 (marginalism in support of the argument for wealth transfer), and 218–219 (economies of scale). See also John Stuart Mill, *Utilitarianism* (1863), and Oliver Wendell Holmes, "The Path of the Law" (forerunner to legal realism).

21. By 1901 roughly two-thirds of all firms with assets over $10M were in New Jersey. Greenspan and Wooldridge, *Capitalism in America*, 143. Hovenkamp, *Enterprise and American Law*, 77 (by 1890, three-quarters of all wealth was held by corporations).

22. Naomi Lamoreaux, *The Great Merger Movement in American Business, 1895–1904* (Cambridge, UK: Cambridge University Press, 1988), 153 ("In most cases, there was no dominant firm with competitive advantage, so it was less likely there would be real barriers to entry" unless there was vertical integration); and 189 (which describes new companies with up-to-date technology entering the markets).

23. Alfred D. Chandler, Jr. *The Visible Hand: The Managerial Revolution in American Business* (Cambridge, MA: Belknap Press, 1977).

24. Greenspan and Wooldridge, *Capitalism in America,* 143 (Individual patentees would drop from 95% to 42% by the end of the century).

25. Martin J. Sklar, *The Corporate Reconstruction of American Capitalism, 1890–1916: The Market, The Law, and Politics* (Cambridge, UK: Cambridge University Press, 1988), 4.

26. Greenspan and Wooldridge, *Capitalism in America*, 91 (in 2000, 53 of the Fortune 500 were founded in the 1880s, 39 in the 1890s, and 52 in the 1900s).

27. See Louis D. Brandeis, "The Regulation of Competition Versus the Regulation of Monopoly" – Speech to the Economic Club of New York – 1912. See also Adam Smith, *An Inquiry Into the Nature and Causes of the Wealth of Nations* (1776), Book 1, Chapter 10 ("People of the same trade seldom meet together, even for merriment and diversion, but the conversation ends in a conspiracy against the public, or some contrivance to raise prices").

28. See, e.g., Dr. Miles v. Park & Sons, Inc. (1911)(the Court found minimum retail price agreements per se illegal under the Sherman Act; Brandeis as an advocate sought price uniformity so that large department stores would not have undue price advantages over smaller retailers).

29. Sklar, *The Corporate Reconstruction of American Capitalism*, 185. There was significant debate about the range of authority for the Bureau of Corporations, including its ability to oversee licensing and to review contracts. The bureau eventually became part of the Federal Trade Commission when the latter was formed.

30. "Shall we confer power upon the mere head of a bureau that the Parliament of England were unwilling to accord to the king, and which they regarded as a menace to their liberties." Quoted in Lamoreaux, *The Great Merger Movement*, 173. See also Sklar, *The Corporate Reconstruction of American Capitalism*, 232 (Roosevelt's efforts to include registration and licensing powers in the Hepburn bill were rebuked as being too statist).

31. See Northern Securities v. United States (1904) (disbanding railroad holding company) and Swift & Co. v. United States (1905) (meatpacking is in the stream of commerce and subject to regulation even if the work itself is intrastate).

32. In fact, Taft had initially developed the formulation as a circuit court judge in the *Addyston Pipe* case. See Lamoreaux, *The Great Merger Movement*, 174;

Peritz *Competition Law in America*, 36, 59–63; Hovenkamp, *Enterprise and American Law*, 332. See also Sklar, *The Corporate Reconstruction of American Capitalism*, 175 (the Rule of Reason "rejected a statist for a liberal form" as it took power away from the executive and legislature and gave it to the courts).

33. Sklar, 325 (Wilson's trade commission with no licensing power was aligned with the judicial process and reflected a non-statist approach compared with simply a judicial process [Taft] or a trade commission that included a licensing system [TR]).

34. McCraw, *Prophets of Regulation*.

35 Lind, *Land of Promise*, 226–230.

36. Martin Sklar, *The Corporate Reconstruction of American Capitalism, 1890–1916* (Cambridge, UK: Cambridge University Press) (characterizing three types of corporate oversight: statist-tending [Roosevelt] minimalist-regulatory [Taft], and regulatory-corporate [Wilson]).

37. Robert Hessen, *Steel Titan: The Life of Charles M. Schwab* (New York: Oxford University Press), 1975.

38. John Landry, "Corporate Incentives for Managers in American Industry 1900–1940," PhD dissertation, Brown University, 1995; and Stuart Brandes, *American Welfare Capitalism, 1880–1940* (Chicago: University of Chicago Press, 1976).

39. Sklar, *The Corporate Reconstruction of American Capitalism*, 431 ("republican principles shifted from their old roots in the self-employed producer to new roots in principles of citizenship, individuality, opportunity and the general welfare").

40. See, e.g., Virginia State Pharmacy Board v. Virginia Citizens Consumer Council (1976) (allowing pharmacists to advertise prescription drug prices); Citizens United v. FEC (2010; permitting independent expenditures for political campaigns by corporations). See also Adam Winkler, *We the Corporations: How American Businesses Won Their Civil Rights* (New York: W.W. Norton & Company, 2018).

41. Thomas K. McCraw, ed., *Creating Modern Capitalism: How Entrepreneurs, Companies and Countries Triumphed in Three Industrial Revolutions* (Cambridge MA: Harvard University Press, 1997), 143.

42. See, e.g., Mark J. Roe, *Strong Managers, Weak Owners: The Political Roots of American Corporate Finance* (Princeton, NJ: Princeton University Press, 1994), 171. See also Mark Roe, *The Political Determinants of Corporate Governance* (New York: Oxford University Press, 2006) (suggesting that limited political pressure on public companies in the United States has allowed dispersed ownership and enabled managerial control).

43. OECD Capital Market Series, "Owners of the World's Listed Companies," October 17, 2019. See also Robert D. Cooter and Hans-Bernd Schafer, *Solomon's Knot: How Law Can End the Poverty of Nations* (Princeton, NJ: Princeton University Press, 2011).

44. Berle and Means, *The Modern Corporation and Private Power* (New York: Harcourt, 1932); and Michael Jensen and William Meckling, "Theory of the Firm: Managerial Behavior, Agency Costs and Ownership Structure," *Journal of Financial Economics* 3, no. 4 (October 1976): 305–360.

45. Just as corporate law experts have compared governance across regions, business historians have studied "modes of capitalism" and noted the difference across regions and even within them. For instance, some characterize the differences to include the clubby nature of investment in the United Kingdom ("personal capitalism"), the heavy-industry, oligopolistic nature of German activity ("cooperative managerial capitalism"), and the Japanese tradition of family-based *zaibatsu* and enterprise-based *kigyou shudan* ("communitarian capitalism"). See, e.g., Thomas McCraw, *Creating Modern Capitalism*; Alfred D. Chandler, Jr., *Scale and Scape: The Dynamics of Industrial Capitalism* (Cambridge, MA: Harvard University Press, 1990); Alfred Chandler, Franco Amatori, and Takashi Hikino, *Big Business and the Wealth of Nations* (Cambridge, UK: Cambridge University Press, 2000); and Ulrich Wengenroth, *Germany: Competition Abroad – Cooperation at Home, 1870–1990* (Cambridge, UK: Cambridge University Press, 1997).

7

The Age and Aging of Incumbents

In the land of the giants, three companies stood the highest. Among the largest enterprises the world had ever known, their combined value dwarfed much of the rest of the economy. By 1907, Standard Oil, American Telephone and Telegraph (AT&T), and U.S. Steel were so big that they each controlled well over two-thirds of the market share of their respective industries. While the federal government took action against all three companies, the results varied enormously.

Standard Oil was the only one to be broken up, yet the resulting entities went on to dominate the energy sector. AT&T avoided breakup by proactively entering into a compromise with the government, one that secured its natural monopoly in long-distance telephone. It dominated its industry until deregulation finally restored the right to compete to new entrants toward the end of the century. U.S. Steel won its battle with the government and remained the largest corporation in the world for decades, only to be undone by its internal bureaucracy, challenges with the workers union, and new technologies commercialized by up-starts who never lost the right to compete.

Their continuing market dominance stemmed partly from the broad global backdrop. Government-business relations in the 20th century took place in the context of two world wars, the Great Depression, and a high-stakes Cold War. In rising to these challenges, the government intervened more aggressively to bolster these large firms than at any point prior – to some extent clipping smaller firms' right to compete with them. Yet the balancing act ultimately continued as the country avoided the state-controlled approaches of other countries. When the need to liberalize arose at the end of the century, American society pivoted back to competition and positioned the economy for success.

As described in the previous chapter, Standard Oil substantially reduced prices for users, but its aggressive deals with railroads and creative corporate organization had forced out many small rivals. The Supreme Court's decision in 1911 broke the giant into 34 smaller companies, including the future ExxonMobil, Chevron, and Amoco.

While the government won its case, founder John D. Rockefeller was in many respects the ultimate beneficiary. Standard Oil had already begun to see competition from new entrants such as Texaco, Gulf, Citco, Unocal, and Shell, and its market share had dropped to 65% in 1905. Its progeny, smaller and more agile than the behemoth, had higher profits after the breakup, and Rockefeller's interest in them made him the richest person in the world up to that point.[1]

AT&T's now-infamous 1913 "Kingsbury Commitment" with the federal government required only that it divest itself of its Western Union telegraph subsidiary. The giant also had to give local telephone service operators access to its long-distance network, but the agreement allowed the company to acquire those operators in certain markets. It made over 500 acquisitions over the next two decades.

AT&T's government-sanctioned monopoly enabled it to become one of the strongest and most powerful companies in America throughout the 20th century, and a mainstay in the economy with over one million American shareholders at its peak.[2] But even with this government support and a seemingly "natural monopoly," the company's protected position could not last. Upstarts kept seeking market entry using new technologies, while a 1956 consent decree with the government forced the company to license its patents royalty-free. In 1950, the company failed to prevent an inventor from marketing a mechanical device that could be connected to an AT&T telephone.[3] In 1968, another upstart won the ability to connect any lawful device, such as answering machines, fax machines, and modems, to the network.[4] That decision helped spawn MCI, the first real challenge to AT&T's monopoly on long-distance phone service itself.

The dam broke in the 1970s, when both MCI and the DOJ sued AT&T on antitrust grounds. MCI won a financial settlement and then raised over $1 billion in high-yield ("junk") bonds to enter the market. Separately, AT&T agreed to spin off its seven regional operating companies (the Baby Bells), as well as its Western Electric hardware division. AT&T continued as only the traditional long-distance firm, now vulnerable to

MCI and other upstarts, while gaining the freedom to move beyond long-distance telephony, including a late-in-the-game effort in computers.[5]

U.S. Steel was allowed to continue, but with no protection. For many years it was so dominant that it was known simply as "The Corporation." The government did in fact attempt to limit its power and brought suit in 1911. However, in deciding the case on the heels of World War I, the Supreme Court concluded that "the law does not make mere size an offense."[6] Like many other seemingly dominant incumbents from the great merger movement, the behemoth eventually lost its hard-charging edge as professional managers took over. Under continuing government scrutiny, stability, not Carnegie's relentless competitiveness, was the order of the day.

Charles Schwab, a Carnegie executive and the first CEO of the company in 1901, soon left in frustration to take over a moribund producer of steel plating, Bethlehem Steel. Rather than compete head-on, U.S. Steel allowed the new company as well as some other small producers to gradually take market share while preserving its dominance. Schwab and others learned they could operate a profitable business, including exploiting new markets such as structural steel for skyscrapers, as long as they didn't compete aggressively. The incumbent disciplined the upstarts into cooperating in a stable, comfortable oligopoly, aided by high industrial tariffs.[7] By the time of the antitrust suit, U.S. Steel's market share had fallen to only 50%.

Though the company remained large and profitable as the industrial economy grew throughout the 20th century, it suffered from the failings of size and embedded technology. It fought battle after battle with the steel workers union, and its reliance on blast furnace technology was disrupted by cost-effective and flexible electric arc mini-mills. New entrants could leverage that technology with a clean slate. Moreover, the company proved vulnerable during the Oil Crisis in the 1970s and the emergence of foreign competition in the 1980s. What the government would not or could not do in 1911, the marketplace ultimately accomplished. In 1991 U.S. Steel left the Dow Jones index after a 90-year run, and it left the S&P 500 index in 2014. Today, it barely makes the list of the world's 40 largest steel producers.

The Push for Bigness

The era of bigness began tentatively with World War I, which showed Americans the payoff from the federal government directing the economy through large enterprises. The war created an abrupt, sharp demand for industrial conversion, and the giants devoted their massive production capacity to the war effort. DuPont, for example, grew its military business by a factor of 236 and the stock prices of many companies increased substantially.[8] To coordinate activities, the federal War Industries Board asserted broad temporary powers over business. Business leaders lent management expertise as "Dollar-a-Year Men" to answer the exigency. The rapid rise in output convinced many observers that governments could improve on markets, even as the importance of business was evident.

Americans were coming to terms, albeit ambivalently, with a transformed economic landscape.[9] "The chief business of the American people is business," President Calvin Coolidge reminded his constituents in 1925. As trenchant as the Progressive critique of the new industrial behemoths had been, large corporations found themselves at the center of the economy. Instead of dismantling the firms and their enormous productive capacity, American policymakers and judges focused on curbing anti-competitive abuses, implicitly accepting big business as a reality to work with rather than against.

Upstarts didn't go away, but they focused on new industries not yet caught up in bigness, or they pushed big companies in new directions. Thomas Edison became the iconic inventor-entrepreneur, while Henry Ford transformed the automobile industry – the cost of vehicles went down significantly and the number of cars on the road skyrocketed. Similarly, electricity altered both consumer and industrial markets. Many of their developments affected consumers directly, in an era characterized as the "democratization and dissemination of the great innovations of laissez-faire."[10] Several new fields, such as the nascent airline industry, benefitted from government support (in this case mail delivery contracts). But in this era of scale, even those start-ups aimed at rapid incumbency through size. Over time, these new technologies became platforms for innovation that challenged established industries and incumbent firms, creating opportunities for entrepreneurs much as the railroads did decades earlier.

The consensus for bigness was tested in the 1930s with a new emergency, the Great Depression. While some people blamed large firms for the downturn, most accepted the notion that modern technology and markets required large organizations. Instead of relying on the free market to rationalize through competition, they wanted the government to take an active role, either by closely supervising or perhaps nationalizing key areas. Many urged Washington to follow the European example of acquiring some industries outright and enforcing cartels in others.[11]

Impressed with business–government planning in World War I, President Franklin Roosevelt (FDR) initially opted for government-sponsored cartels. He hoped to build on the lobbying and information-sharing associations that had spread to much of the economy in the 1920s. He suspected that excessive competition had triggered the downturn, and believed that government intervention would restore confidence and rationalize big business.

With the National Industrial Recovery Act (1933), FDR embarked on an experimental, emergency-basis program allowing businesses to stabilize prices and thus restore prosperity. The act established the National Recovery Administration (NRA) to oversee industries as they set prices and production levels, improved wages and working conditions, and avoided wasteful competition. Many of the regulations and price controls were drafted with the collective help of industry-leading incumbents.[12] This was not a time for disruptive upstarts to make their mark.

The NRA proved controversial, with opponents ranging from consumer and labor groups to small businesses.[13] The Supreme Court's decision in *A.L.A. Schechter Poultry Corp. v. United States* (1935) concluded that the federal government had gone too far in regulating business, in this case setting rules for the sale of whole chickens. The decision was unanimous, as the legislation had delegated to the executive branch power over everything from work hours to local trade codes. Both conservatives, who naturally distrusted government oversight, and even some Progressives felt that big government was going too far. Justice Brandeis voiced concern about the risk of increased centralization, statism, and big government control.[14]

The NRA soon collapsed, ending intensive oversight of companies, but the federal government nevertheless assumed greater regulatory and administrative authority over markets. The Communications Act of 1934 set up the Federal Communications Commission (FCC) to oversee the airwaves. The Robinson–Patman Act of 1936 extended the FTC's purview to protecting smaller businesses from "unfair" competition – such as A&P's pricing arrangements (see Chapter 2).[15] The Civil Aeronautics Act of 1938 launched the predecessor to the Federal Aviation Administration, while the Agricultural Adjustment Act stabilized prices for the benefit of both large corporations as well as family farms. Despite the *Schechter Poultry* decision, the executive branch now wielded strong powers overall to regulate corporations.[16]

That oversight extended to corporate finance. Bolstered by policy-makers such as Adolph Berle, the new Securities and Exchange Commission worked to protect dispersed shareholders, a linchpin of what would develop into American shareholder capitalism decades later. Congress also passed the Glass–Steagall Act in 1933, which furthered the American tradition of decentralized finance by separating banking from investing.

If business leaders reluctantly accepted government management during the Great Depression, the benefits of public-private partnership grew more positive with America's entry into World War II – at least for big companies. Enlisted by the president to turn the nation into an "Arsenal of Democracy," incumbents converted factories to support the war effort and reaped most of the massive federal spending that resulted.[17] Half of all government spending went to 33 companies.[18] America's war production effort proved more effective than those of Germany, Japan, and Italy, as well as the allies. The successful Manhattan Project inspired a great many subsequent corporate and government development efforts, particularly in the area of science.

Big Science and Corporate Conglomerates

The post–World War II period initially seemed to confirm the new big business consensus. Large firms converted back to civilian production so quickly that the postwar dip was brief and mild. John Kenneth Galbraith, the prominent economist and a wartime price control administrator, published *American Capitalism* in 1952, arguing in support of large firms but also for "countervailing powers" such as big labor and big government to keep them in check. Big companies were henceforth to be disciplined not so much by upstarts as by equally powerful governments, labor unions, and other institutions.[19] Fueled by pent-up demand, European reconstruction, and the war's technological advances, the American economy began a long boom.[20] The government entered the R&D business, setting national priorities that suited its purposes but that also resulted in numerous commercial spin-offs. Scientific advances turned into practical goods. Federal and state governments helped to staff those labs with the GI Bill and heavily subsidized universities.[21]

While a few of the biggest companies engaged in fundamental research, most of them relied on public-private partnerships. The federal Office of Scientific Research and Development supported a host of technology initiatives. Vannevar Bush, its storied director, exemplified the close ties and the government's handmaiden role with innovation. A cofounder of Raytheon as well as a professor at MIT, he believed that central direction and investment were necessary to speed up the exciting technological development then unfolding. Frederick Terman at Stanford University adopted a similar alliance on the West Coast, helping to create what is now known as Silicon Valley.

The cozy business–government relationship and the imperative of scale often made it hard for disruptive companies to enter markets. Oligarchies dominated wide sectors of the economy, including steel, automobile manufacturing, aviation, radio and television broadcasting, and many consumer goods. From 1947 to 1968, the "Age of Oligopoly," the share of manufacturing handled by the 200 largest industrials rose from 30% to 41%, and their share of total incorporated production assets rose from 47% to 61%. A tighter group of 126 firms conducted three-quarters of all corporate research and development.[22]

Resisting the Lure of Central Planning

While the federal government played an important role in coordinating the economy, it nevertheless avoided the central planning or tight oversight of industry adopted by other countries after the war. Germany and Japan, bolstered by the Marshall Plan and other U.S. support, relied on overt industrial policy to rebuild their economies. In Japan, for instance, the Ministry of International Trade and Industry (MITI) helped to lead consortiums to resurrect and resuscitate new firms and industries. Several European countries, including Britain, France, and Italy, accommodated labor parties and moved to "socialist lite" models by nationalizing infrastructure-oriented industries such as banking and railroads.[23]

More menacingly, the communist states of China and the Soviet Union embarked on central state control. But while the Soviets made notable progress in areas such as science, particularly space exploration, its domestic production languished and consumers struggled. In China, Mao's central planning left the economy in shambles, with mass starvation. By 1968, the need for markets was apparent to virtually everyone within and outside those systems.[24]

While the U.S. government relied on intervention and oversight rather than outright control, it still took an active role in economic affairs. For instance, rather than force companies to provide health care or put workers on their boards, the government relied on private negotiations between companies and labor to recalibrate relations and secure benefits.[25] Congress also passed the Celler–Kefauver Act (1950) in order to close loopholes in the Clayton Act and discourage firms from acquiring direct rivals, suppliers, or distributors. The act limited vertical integration, which had allowed large corporations to erect barriers to entry in many markets.

The DOJ and FTC also became more aggressive in enforcement, with more than 2,000 antitrust suits brought in the 1950s. In some industries, the government worked to foster multiple suppliers, which created new enterprises of scale. Policymakers took pains to preserve the possibilities of entrepreneurship, or at least competition, forcing companies with large patent pools to license them and encouraging multiple competitors in key industries such as defense.[26] Similarly, the federal government challenged DuPont's acquisition of a 23% interest in General Motors in the late 1950s in order to limit the ability of the former to control the automaker. Officials may have gone too far in limiting some vertical mergers, such as when the Supreme Court backed the DOJ in the *Brown Shoe Company v. United States* case (1962) – prohibiting a relatively modest acquisition because it might lessen competition.

Checked from buttressing their incumbencies through horizontal or vertical acquisitions, many of the "entrepreneurs" of this era were ambitious corporate leaders who pursued new ways to deploy capital made inexpensive from postwar savings. Sensing the financial advantages of holding a diverse portfolio of industries, they assembled conglomerates of unrelated businesses. Gulf & Western (originally an automobile parts supplier) and International Telephone and Telegraph were particularly prominent. By 1970 more than three-quarters of the Fortune 500 had diversified.[27]

Management consultants supported this move, with the "growth share matrix" and "experience curve" explaining the benefits of portfolio management.[28] At the same time, some like Peter Drucker were seeing the risks of bloated companies.[29] Financial companies helped by gradually enticing investors back into stocks after the devastating losses of the 1930s, keeping capital costs low. The commercial paper market advanced, giving companies more options for short-term borrowing. But with stable revenue, big companies were increasingly comfortable reinvesting their earnings for growth.[30]

Even in this era of bigness, entrepreneurial activity continued in new areas, often related to infrastructure, demographic changes, or emerging technology. The postwar car boom, literally paved by the federal government with the interstate highway system, opened cities to suburbs and freed travelers from the constraints of train routes and timetables. The trucking industry grew significantly. Besides dethroning the original big business, railroads, these changes accelerated growth in the broad consumer market and fueled upstarts in industries from hotels (Howard Johnson's) and restaurants (McDonalds) to retailing (Walmart). Increased air travel, new appliances, suburban housing, and television opened other opportunities. Franchising helped some entrepreneurs rapidly scale up national brands with local flavor.

Some opportunities were so vast that they attracted both incumbents and upstarts, often in a kind of symbiosis. Military contracts spawned the computer industry, instilling in the early firms a culture of hierarchical, secretive research and development. While incumbents such as IBM and Raytheon prospered, so too did Route 128 upstarts Digital Equipment Corporation and Data General.[31] Innovation proceeded apace, in hardware and software, with help from the emergent venture capital industry.[32]

An Entrepreneur for the Age of Bigness

Only in the new era of big business could someone like David Sarnoff be an upstart. He was nine years old when his family immigrated to New York from Russia in 1900, and by age 15 he was working full-time to support them. He was fortunate enough to get a job as office boy at the Marconi Wireless Telegraph Company, the high-tech leader of its day.

Then in 1919, after World War I, in the interests of national security, the federal government wanted to use size to speed up the development of radio. Troubled that the key patents were owned by multiple companies – General Electric, Westinghouse, and AT&T as well as Marconi – it forced these companies to set up a patent pool. GE soon bought Marconi outright, then collected the patents in a subsidiary co-owned by the other patentees. GE called its new subsidiary the Radio Corporation of America, and the hard-driving Sarnoff was by then its commercial manager.

Sarnoff was a visionary who the saw the possibilities for broadcasting to masses of people. His bosses ignored his memos – until he arranged radio coverage of a major boxing match in 1921 that proved a success. Sales of home radio receivers took off, and in 1925 RCA launched the National Broadcasting Company to send programs to radio stations. Sarnoff led the push to standardize radio broadcasting around RCA's preferred format, and he signed recording contracts to ensure plenty of content while controlling the distribution of radio spectrum. Soon every household wanted a radio set.

By the late 1920s, as NBC was expanding its fledgling network, rival networks emerged and the federal government in 1932 forced GE to spin off RCA as an independent company so others could use its technology. Sarnoff, by then RCA's president, promptly pushed research in the next big thing, television, first broadcast in 1939. He again ensured that RCA's format would become the standard, and the company prospered in both the hardware of home receivers and the content of broadcasting through advertising. He won the next battle too, a tough fight with CBS over standards in color TV. And he did all of this despite knowing that television would likely cannibalize revenue from radio, which gradually declined.

Sarnoff thus benefitted from the federal government's de facto industrial policy: select a leading company and give it special privileges (mostly antitrust exemptions) to hasten development in a strategic area. In the post–Progressive period of 1920 to 1980, officials believed that managers of large organizations in capital-intensive industries would better carry out entrepreneurship than upstarts in small firms. But even as the federal government "picked winners," it limited those protections to foster competition over time.

Even with this support, like most incumbents, RCA eventually lost its way. In the 1970s, rather than compete with lower-cost foreign manufacturers, it diversified beyond consumer electronics. Efforts to enter the computer industry failed. In 1986, ironically, GE reacquired the company while selling off most of its assets.

The Great Dismantling

For all its apparent success, the bias for bigness came to halt in the 1970s. The end of the postwar economic boom broke the spell cast in World War II. Executives suddenly had to worry about factors they hadn't faced in a generation. Oil supply shocks and rising foreign competition took their toll, both economically and culturally. Slowing growth and stagflation undermined the prestige of large corporations. The 1970 bankruptcy of the Penn Central railroad, one of the 10 largest companies in the country, broadcast the pitfalls of bloated bureaucracy, overdiversification, and government regulation.

Large incumbents found themselves on the defensive. For conservatives, the Cold War fight against Soviet central planning favored markets over oligopoly and industrial policy, while libertarian thinkers centered at the University of Chicago blamed cozy business-government relationships and "regulatory capture" for the lost international competitiveness. Economists argued that consumers would benefit from greater competition even if that reduced the efficiency of large firms. Legal theorists questioned the effectiveness of antitrust as a policy tool. Business scholars claimed that large corporate bureaucracies were now less about efficient coordination and more about managerial fiefdoms.

Liberals distrusted big institutions of any type, while postwar affluence was creating a new generation concerned more with individual expression than organizing around a common goal. The disastrous Vietnam War, followed soon after by Watergate, cast doubt on experts leading any large organization, public or private. The consumer protection movement, led by Ralph Nader, challenged not just big manufacturers but the FTC as well. Meanwhile the Supreme Court gave corporations more freedom from regulation, recognizing commercial speech in overturning local restrictions on advertising.[33]

The malaise made itself felt among incumbents throughout the industrial economy, but perhaps most acutely in the centerpiece of the American economy: automobiles. Their nemesis was not so much Nader as it was the Japanese car industry, built up in the 1950s and now eager to sell overseas. Suffering from an initial reputation for shoddy cars, they made a virtue out of necessity and built low-cost, small, and fuel-efficient vehicles – a low-margin segment that Detroit automakers largely ignored. When the oil shocks of the 1970s encouraged Americans to try out the vehicles, they were impressed with their quality and dependability.[34] As Toyota, Nissan, and Honda gained brand acceptance and expanded their U.S. operations, they moved into the more attractive and lucrative luxury segment – leaving an opening for Korean upstarts Kia and Hyundai in the 1990s.

Though some saw the success of Japan and Germany as justification for an aggressive national industrial agenda, most policymakers began to withdraw from the big business–big government consensus that had prevailed in the prior decades. Entrepreneurs benefitted in many fields, including government-sponsored research. In the Bayh-Dole Act of 1980, for instance, Congress aimed to distribute the ownership rights of federally funded research. Many universities encouraged professors to commercialize their findings, fueling a wave of start-ups. And in response to concerns about overpricing at big pharmaceutical companies, the Hatch-Waxman Act of 1984 permitted the manufacture of generic alternatives to branded drugs.

Even the regulatory regime, which managed bigness but ultimately protected it, needed overhaul. A wave of deregulation began in the Carter administration in the late 1970s. The transportation (railroads, trucks, and airlines), finance (retail brokerage commissions), and tele-communications industries were all freed to pursue opportunities, including competing headlong against rivals.[35]

The Reagan administration intensified those efforts after 1980 with a larger and deeper critique of big government (if not big business), and it unleashed a wave of activity. Books such as Robert Bork's *The Antitrust Paradox*, George Stigler's work on "regulatory capture," and other "Chicago School" law and economics faculty led to officials emphasizing limited government and a focus on consumer interests more than competition between companies.

Antitrust enforcement diminished under Reagan, who had once been a spokesman for GE. Cases against AT&T and IBM, both commenced in the 1970s, had proved costly and largely unsuccessful. Reagan settled the AT&T dispute and dropped the IBM case on the same day in 1982. Policymakers, seeing how free markets generated efficiency, believed they could foster competition with less regulation, not more. Underlying this approach was the presumption that most markets were "contestable" – that new entrants would challenge incumbents and keep them in check, supplanting the need for most government action.[36] This may have seemed like a specious rationale at the time, but the next several decades of entrepreneurship bore it out.

The new openness hurt conglomerates and sleepy incumbents the most. Companies that could not unlock their embedded value were pried open. Financial deregulation, which had actually begun back in the late 1960s, was showing results. By the 1980s, a field that had long been the comfortable preserve of a handful of venerable investing firms, most named for long-dead founders, had opened to new challenges and challengers. Michael Milken's research showed that cautious investors had overstated the risk of default from low-grade corporate debt, and by the mid-1980s he had created a market for new securities. Insurers and savings banks put money into riskier high-yield "junk" bonds that funded upstarts in industries such as telecommunications. Changes to the tax code favored capital gains, and investors raised their appetites for initial public offerings. In the area of corporate governance, economist Milton Friedman's argument that the role of the corporation was to make money for shareholders, academic research such as by Michael Jensen on the agency costs of the firm, and legal decisions such as the Revlon Rule in Delaware (requiring boards to maximize shareholder value), ushered in an era of hostile takeovers and shareholder activism.[37]

Beatrice Foods, for example, had faced declining profitability by the late 1970s, yet continued to diversity by adding rental cars, motor oil, and pantyhose into its already broad portfolio. By 1986, a new kind of upstart forced the company's hand. Kohlberg, Kravis & Roberts, one of the largest of the new corporate takeover artists, bought Beatrice in a leveraged buyout for $8.7 billion, the largest ever at the time. Over the next four years they sold off nearly all of its divisions, with the once-central dairy business going to erstwhile rival ConAgra Foods.[38] The new era of corporate raiders and management buyouts had begun.

Financial liberalization also expanded venture capital. While several venture firms had cropped up beginning in the 1950s, most of those firms were funded by wealthy families and had only a modest amount of money. That changed with modifications to the pension guidelines in the early 1970s, which enabled pension funds to invest in venture capital and riskier asset classes.[39] The changes spurred the creation of investment firms dedicated to innovation – a major catalyst for the high technology industries that emerged in the 1990s.

The Cultural Shift

The movement away from large incumbents took on a decidedly cultural tone in the field of computers. The industry's anti-authoritarian streak began on the West Coast in the mid-1950s, when the "Traitorous Eight" left Shockley Semiconductor to found Fairchild Semiconductor, which in turn spawned numerous "Fairchildren," including Intel. This legendary "mutiny" created Silicon Valley lore that only increased with the Beat Generation in the 1960s. Personal computing became a huge growth area, spawning not just innovative hardware and software but ultimately the blossoming of electronic commerce. It was also a crucial factor in enabling the locus of entrepreneurship to shift back from big corporate groups to small teams. With so many resources now available to individuals – no more waiting to share time on a costly mainframe – anyone with a good idea and some software or engineering chops could start a company

Large, hierarchical East Coast companies gave way to nimble West Coast upstarts.[40] IBM, the very definition of an incumbent, had developed a personal computer in the late 1970s, but thought so little of it (or perhaps worried about antitrust threats) that it allowed a small Seattle software firm, Microsoft, to control the core intellectual property. Most of the East Coast firms, including one-time upstarts that had quickly become incumbents, failed to adapt and went under. They had done much to foster new technologies, but their inability to focus on new opportunities, or their fear of disrupting their existing businesses, prevented them from following through.

Xerox had developed much of the key personal computing technology at its legendary Palo Alto Research Center (PARC), while Bell Labs created much of the internet's foundations. Yet these companies lacked the appetite for creative destruction and proved unable to commercialize these advances. While the success of the Manhattan Project was the shining light for corporate America in the 1950s, PARC's willingness to allow Steve Jobs to imitate the "mouse," and IBM's ceding of its operating system to Bill Gates, became the next generation's proof text for the dangers of incumbency.[41]

America's Unique Corporate Dynamism

The speed and smoothness of this shift from bigness was truly remarkable. While most people celebrate entrepreneurs as the drivers of change, perhaps the more significant accomplishment was the overall social and political tolerance for failure. America's willingness to let large companies fail has been an essential part of its record of creative destruction.

Nowhere is the evidence of this dynamism stronger than in the indices of the country's largest companies. The Fortune 500 list, ranking the largest American companies by revenue, started in 1955, and roughly 2,100 companies appeared on the list in the first 60 years. But only 53 of the original 500 companies appeared continuously during that period and more than a third (769) showed up for just five or fewer years.[42] Incumbency, even at the highest levels of the economy, has been hard to maintain.[43]

This dynamism became acute in the 1970s, and the narrower Fortune 100 list actually declined from 1955 to 1988 as a percentage of both GDP and overall market capitalization.[44] Entrepreneurs played a major role in shifting the economy away from heavy industry. While many leading firms continued to dominate established markets, the manufacturing sector as a whole garnered a smaller share of the index.[45] By the mid-1970s, technology and other service sector firms were becoming a large part of the economy.[46]

The churn rate has increased even more in recent decades. One assessment showed that the average tenure of a member of the Standard and Poor's 500 index shrank from 61 years in 1958 to 18 years by 2012. This study noted the relatively modest performance of those firms that did survive and the difficulty of merely incremental approaches to sustaining companies amid disruption.[47] More recent studies have shown that the average tenure of top public company is now at an all-time low, with the corporate lifespan on the index projected to decline to 12 years by 2027.[48] (See Figure 7.1)

This turbulence is happening even as the largest companies have greater market capitalizations than ever. In 2000, General Electric was the largest firm on the S&P 500 index at $474 billion, and ExxonMobil was second at $302 billion. By 2018, Apple was in the top spot at $896 billion, and both GE and ExxonMobil had fallen off the top 10. While more than half of the companies on the 1995 list were no longer on it 20 years later, the list's overall share of U.S. GDP had actually doubled over its 60 years.[49] Today, with several companies sporting market values in excess of $1 trillion, this trend continues.

Comparing the United States to other countries suggests that America has an edge when it comes to creative destruction, even if it brings with it increased social costs.[50] While specific churn rates of comparable indices are difficult to find, most evidence suggests that

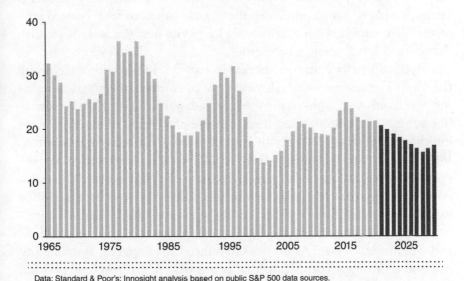

Data: Standard & Poor's: Innosight analysis based on public S&P 500 data sources.

Figure 7.1 Average company lifespan on the S&P Index.

Source: Innosight 2021 Corporate Longevity Forecast, Chart 1.

industries in countries such as Japan, Germany, and Britain are much more static compared with the U.S.[51] A large part of this can be explained both by culture and the protection of incumbent industries – either explicitly through regulation and industrial policy that favors certain "national champions" or implicitly through laws that protect the status quo or investors that are adverse to risk and innovation.

In some countries, a pecking order of large firms and their networks of suppliers and distributors encourages loyalty and stability but results in few young firms reaching the upper echelons. Germany, for instance, is known for its stable hierarchy of businesses, including the *Mittelstand* medium-sized companies that have been in place for long periods.[52]

One study of the FTSE 100, the London Stock Exchange index, found that an average of 10% of the companies listed on the index change every year. Of the 100 companies on the original list from 1984, only 24 remained in 2012. However, the study also noted that the typical age of the companies on the list is quite high, averaging over 90 years both 1984 and 2012.[53] This is far older than the average age of major firms appearing on the comparable index in the United States, which is now less than 20 years.[54]

There are several countries with long lists of firms in existence for more than a century.[55] The most striking example is Japan, where over 33,000 businesses are over a hundred years old. Shame associated with failure is one of the main reasons, and some argue that most managers are motivated to keep companies afloat, rather than to rejuvenate themselves.[56] To many, excessive corporate longevity and the lack of creative destruction is becoming a problem.

Dazzled by the country's success in two world wars, in overcoming the Great Depression, in developing new consumer goods, and in fighting the Cold War, 20th-century Americans put much of their trust in big business. In helping them rise to these challenges, the government intervened more aggressively in large firms than at any point prior, to some extent clipping smaller firms' ability to stay competitive. Yet the country never entrenched the giant companies and it avoided the state-controlled approaches of other countries. Similarly, it never abandoned its inherent belief in the right to compete. As a result, the major incumbents of midcentury failed to solidify their dominance through political and economic lock-in. As they ossified into bureaucracies and failed to respond to foreign competition or economic stagnation, the political economy refused to come to their rescue. That left an opening for nimble upstarts with a fresh approach. The upstart-incumbent balancing act thus proved more resilient than many experts would have expected.

And when the need to liberalize arose toward the end of the century, American society pivoted back to competition and new upstarts positioned the economy for success.

By the end of the 1980s, the tide had clearly turned. At the time of the fall of the Berlin Wall, the rise of the personal computer revolution, deregulation of major industries, and the growing venture capital and high technologies were all underway. Moreover, a new generation – the Baby Boomers – were becoming prominent and powerful, and with them the next new breed of entrepreneurs. Large companies, or at least those that remained static, had their day, and the corporate life cycle could not be postponed forever – especially in the American system that never wholeheartedly embraced bigness, and that maintained openings for new rivals. A great age of upstarts was emerging.

Endnotes

1. Daniel Yergin, *The Prize: The Epic Quest for Oil, Money & Power* (New York: Free Press, 1991).
2. Joyce Appleby, *The Relentless Revolution: A History of Capitalism* (New York: W.W. Norton, 2010), 324 (one million shareholders out of 6.5M shareholders in total; 76% of them earned less than $10,000/year).
3. Hush-A-Phone Corp v. United States (1956).
4. Federal Communications Commissions, Carterfone decision (13 F.C.C. 2d 420).
5. See Steve Coll, *The Deal of the Century: The Breakup of AT&T* (New York: Atheneum, 1986), and Tim Wu, *The Master Switch: The Rise and Fall of Information Empires* (New York: Atlantic Books, 2010).
6. United States v. United States Steel Corp. (1920).
7. John Landry, "Corporate Incentives for American Industry, 1900–1940," PhD dissertation, Brown University, 1995.
8. John Steele Gordon, *An Empire of Wealth: The Epic History of American Economic Power* (New York: HarperCollins, 2005), 289.
9. Unfortunately, the war did not change some long-standing racial animosities and barriers to entrepreneurship. In 1921, a mob of whites attacked a section of Tulsa with numerous thriving Black-owned businesses. They burnt most of the structures to the ground and killed dozens if not hundreds of residents. But abetted by the local corrupt police force, none of the perpetrators were ever convicted. James Hirsch, *Riot and Remembrance: The Tulsa Race Massacre and Its Legacy* (New York: Houghton Mifflin, 2002).
10. Alan Greenspan and Adrian Wooldridge, *Capitalism in America: An Economic History of the United States* (New York: Penguin Press, 2018), 107–203 (automobiles went from 468,000 to 9M between 1910 and 1920; stock market capitalization grew from $15B to $30B; electricity, trucking, buses, factories

all changed the landscape; the number of shareholder investors grew from 1M in 1900 to 7M in 1928).

11. Ellis W. Hawley, *The New Deal and the Problem of Monopoly: A Study in Economic Ambivalence* (Princeton, NJ: Princeton University Press, 1966).

12. Many of the production codes, in fact, were established by industry incumbents. For instance, tire production levels were established by Goodyear, Goodrich, and Firestone. Greenspan and Wooldridge, *Capitalism in America,* 252.

13. See Matt Stoller, *Goliath: The 100-Year War Between Monopoly Power and Democracy* (New York: Simon & Schuster, 2019), 209 (citing Richard Hofstadter, "American culture believes in entrepreneurial capitalism").

14. See Stoller, *Goliath,* 125 ("tell FDR we are not going to let the government centralize everything"), and 123 (Brandeis's concern about link between corporatism and state power).

15. See Barry Lynn, *Cornered: The New Monopoly Capitalism and the Economics of Destruction* (Hoboken, NJ: John Wiley & Sons, 2010), 50 (in favor of Robinson-Patman and the Miller-Tydings Act, which effectively overruled the Dr. Miles case). These price protections for small retailers are controversial as they limited discounting and cost consumers more. These acts were effectively repealed in the 1970s by the Consumer Goods Pricing Act, which gave large retailers more power to negotiate and set price, encouraging the success of big-box retailers and lowering consumer prices. See also Stoller, *Goliath,* 63–87 (Wright Patman and "egalitarian system of free enterprise" vs. argument that consumer prices were much higher as a result), 204 (two-thirds of Americans supported A&P over the government).

16. See Michael Lind, *The Land of Promise: An Economic History of the United States* (New York: HarperCollins, 2012), 250 ("Schechter was the last gasp of laissez-faire"). See, e.g., NLRB v. Jones & Laughlin Steel Corp. (1937) and U.S. v. Darby Lumber Co. (1941) (upholding federal labor laws). States would also reestablish more power vis-à-vis corporations during the mid-1930s. See, e.g., West Coast Hotel Co. v. Parrish (1937) (upholding state minimum wage laws and, in effect, reversing Lochner v. New York (1905) which had limited state regulations regarding bakers' hours) and U.S. v. Carolene Products Co. (1938)(in footnote 4, the Court suggested a "rational basis test" and minimal scrutiny of economic regulations by the states or Congress, compared with strict scrutiny for cases involving political and other rights).

17. John Morton Blum, *V Was for Victory: Politics and American Culture during World War II.* (New York: Harcourt Brace Jovanovich, 1976).

18. Greenspan and Wooldridge, *Capitalism in America,* 268.

19. In fact, Galbraith and some others may have had disdain for entrepreneurs as a whole. See, e.g., Robert D. Atkinson and Michael Lind, *Big Is Beautiful: Debunking the Myth of Small Business* (Cambridge MA: MIT Press, 2018), 7.

20. By the end of World War II, the country had 7% of the world's population but 42% of manufacturing output and produced 80% of all automobiles. The economy grew at a 3.8% annual growth rate between 1946 and 1973. Greenspan and Wooldridge, *Capitalism in America,* 274.

21. By 1956, there were 7.8M veterans in the workforce, including 450,000 engineers, 360,000 teachers, and 180,000 doctors. Greenspan and Wooldridge, *Capitalism in America,* 274; and Gordon, *An Empire of Wealth,* 364. See also David Hart, *Forged Consensus: Science, Technology, and Economic Policy in the U.S.,* 1929–1953 (New Jersey: Princeton University Press).

22. Michael Lind, *Land of Promise,* 347.

23. See Appleby, *The Relentless Revolution,* 289 (post–World War II socialist bureaucracies in Great Britain, Italy, and France led to economies that were "government-directed"; and nationalized railroads, banks and utilities; Soviet Union – "imperative"; U.S. – "informative" – private but some attempt to address inequality), 295 ("Continental Western European countries adopted a corporatist economic form. Government guided growth with fiscal and monetary policies, central banks virtually monopolized venture capital, and unions secured worker representation on corporate boards"), 297 ("Unlike American efforts to level the playing field through antitrust litigation, European countries tended to foster a front-runner in its industrial sectors, thinking more in terms of industrial growth than internal competition.").

24. See, e.g., Niall Ferguson, *Civilization: The West and the Rest* (New York: Penguin, 2011), 243 (discussing the "kitchen debate" and the role of consumer goods such as blue jeans and appliances in fighting the Cold War) and Daron Acemoglu and James A. Robinson, *Why Nations Fail: The Origins of Power, Prosperity and Poverty* (New York: Crown Business, 2012), 124 (the fall of the Soviet Union was due to an extractive political system, lack of economic incentives, resistance to change by elites, challenges of centrally planned economy, lack of technological change and zero-sum rivalries at the top).

25. The "Treaty of Detroit," concluded in 1950, secured health care and pension benefits for employees of the Big Three automakers, for example. The U.S. pushed companies to adopt strong programs for their employees but gave corporations and executives a "freer hand" compared with the welfare state of Europe or the managed economy governed by the Japan Ministry of International Trade and Industry. Greenspan and Wooldridge, *Capitalism in America,* 274, 288.

26. Lynn, *Cornered,* 165 (40,000–50,000 patents were covered under compulsory licensing arrangements).

27. Nitin Nohria, Davis Dyer, and Frederick Dalzell, *Changing Fortunes: Remaking the Industrial Corporation* (Hoboken, NJ: Wiley, 2002), 64–65; G.F. Davis, K.A. Dieckmann, and C.H. Tinsley, "The Decline and Fall of the

Conglomerate Firm in the 1980s: A Study in Deinstitutionalization of an Organizational Form," *American Sociological Review* 59 (August 1994): 547–570.

28. See, e.g., Walter Kiechel III, *Lords of Strategy: The Secret Intellectual History of the New Corporate World* (Cambridge, MA: Harvard Business Review Press, 2010).

29. Peter Drucker cautioned companies to outsource as early as the late 1940s and to decentralize if they got too big. See, e.g, Peter Drucker, *The Concept of the Corporation* (New York: John Day, 1946).

30. On the development of corporate strategy and structure through the first half of the 20th century, see especially Alfred D. Chandler, *Strategy and Structure: Chapters in the History of American Industrial Enterprise* (Cambridge, MA: MIT Press, 1969).

31. See, e.g., Edward B. Roberts, *Entrepreneurs in High Technology: Lesson from MIT and Beyond* (New York: Oxford University Press, 1991); and Tracy Kidder, *Soul of a New Machine* (New York: Little, Brown and Co., 1981).

32. David Grayson Allen, *Investment Management in Boston: A History* (Amherst: University of Massachusetts Press, 2015), 169–191.

33. Virginia State Pharmacy Board v. Virginia Citizens Consumer Council (1976). See also Narain D. Batra, *The First Freedoms and American's Culture of Innovation* (Lanham, MD: Rowman & Littlefield Publishers, 2013).

34. David Halberstam, *The Reckoning* (New York: William Morrow & Co., 1986) and Maryann Keller, *Rude Awakening: The Rise, Fall and Struggle for Recovery of General Motors* (New York: William Morrow & Co., 1989).

35. See Thomas K. McCraw, *Prophets of Regulation* (Cambridge, MA: Belknap Press, 1984), chapter on Alfred Kahn.

36. Rudolph J. R. Peritz, *Competition Policy in America: History, Rhetoric, Law* (Oxford, UK: Oxford University Press, 2001), 260.

37. Revlon, Inc. v. McAndrews & Forbes Holdings, Inc. (Delaware, 1986).

38. Allowing ConAgra to buy Beatrice was itself a sign of the times. With heightened competition, regulators no longer worried about horizontal combination. George Baker, "Beatrice: A Study in the Creation and Destruction of Value," *Journal of Finance* 47, no. 3 (July 1992): 1081–1119.

39. The changes to the Employee Retirement Income Security Act in the 1970s gave pension funds latitude to invest up to 10% of their assets in venture capital. See, e.g., Paul A. Gompers, "The Rise and Fall of Venture Capital," *Business and Economic History* 23, no. 2 (Winter 1994): 1–26.

40. AnnaLee Saxenian, *Regional Advantage* (Cambridge, MA: Harvard University Press, 1996).

41. See, e.g., Michael A. Hiltzik, *Dealers of Lightning: Xerox PARC and the Dawn of the Computer Age* (New York: Harper Business, 1999).

42. Alan Murray, "Myth-Busting the Fortune 500," *Fortune,* June 15, 2015.

43. Justin Fox "The Disruption Myth," *Atlantic,* October 2014 (online reference to "What Does Fortune 500 Turnover Mean?" Dane Stangler and Sam

Arbesman, Ewing Marlon Kauffman Foundation, June 2012). The authors identify sectorial change and greater efficiencies as causes of the churn.

44. Nohria, Dyer, and Dalzell, *Changing Fortunes,* 35–60. This study notes the shift from manufacturing to services and the variations by industry, with certain new industries growing (computers, electrical equipment, specialty chemicals, materials and defense contractors, and pharmaceuticals) while other industries were experiencing maturity and consolidation (metals, aerospace, food).

45. Thomas K. McCraw, *Prophets of Regulation,* 74–77, citing Alfred Chandler, *The Visible Hand* (Cambridge, MA: Belknap Press, 1977) and subsequent research (see list of the largest 200 manufacturing firms between 1917 and 1973). See also Innosight 2021 Corporate Longevity Forecast.

46. It should be noted that the list included only manufacturing firms until 1995, when services and other types of businesses were added. (In 1969, one-third of the S&P 500 were industrial firms; by 2021 that number was 68).

47. Richard Foster and Sarah Kaplan, *Creative Destruction: Why Companies That Are Built to Last Underperform the Market and How to Successfully Transform Them* (New York: Doubleday, 2001), 7–8, 11–13, 28–30 and Richard Foster, *Innovation: The Attacker's Advantage* (New York: Simon & Schuster, 1986). But see Leslie Hannah and Neil Fligstein, who suggest churn is not a new phenomenon.

48. Innosight 2018 Corporate Longevity Forecast.

49 Alan Murray, "Myth-Busting the Fortune 500," *Fortune,* June 15, 2015.

50. Philippe Aghion, Celine Antonin, and Simon Bunel, *The Power of Creative Destruction: Economic Upheaval and the Wealth of Nations* (Cambridge, MA: Belknap Press, 2021).

51. Thomas K. McCraw, *Creating Modern Capitalism* (Cambridge, MA: Harvard University Press, 1995). See also Aghion, Antonin, and Bunel, *The Power of Creative Destruction,* 239 (comparing France with the U.S.).

52. Peter Marsh, "Virtues and Foibles of Family Values," Corporate Longevity, special report, *Financial Times,* November 10, 2015.

53. Rita McGrath, "Churn, Longevity the FTSE 100," August 28, 2012. See also "Why Corporate Longevity Matters," Credit Suisse Global Financial Strategies, April 16, 2014.

54. An alternative approach to comparing the United States with other countries can be found by looking at the longevity of family businesses across country. The Henokiens Association is comprised of family businesses that are over 200 years old. Today, there are only 47 members worldwide, with most of them in Europe (Italy, 12; France, 14; Japan, 4; Germany, 4; Switzerland, 3; Belgium, 2; England, 1; Austria, 1).

55. Foster and Kaplan, *Creative Destruction,* 291–293. See also Carlos Garcia Pons, "Business Longevity or the Business of Survival," thenewbarcelonapost.com, February 27, 2018 (noting the UK's Tercentarians and Les Henokiens

societies; Spain has 100 companies over 100 years old, Germany 800, France and The Netherlands, 200).

56. Bryan Lufkin, "Why so many of the world's oldest companies are in Japan," BBC.com, February 12, 2020; Tsukasa Morikuni and Mio Tomita, "Corporate Japan struggles to scale up as longevity limits dynamism," NikkeiAsia, November 8, 2018. See also Robin Harding, "Deep Roots in Need of Tonic: Japan's leader wants more companies to die and give way to start-ups," Corporate Longevity special report, *Financial Times,* November 10, 2015.

8

The Entrepreneurial Revolution

The stock opened at \$28, but it rocketed to over \$75 before closing at \$58 for the day. For both the company and the rest of the world, the \$3 billion market cap signaled that a new era had arrived. Netscape's public offering in February 1995 – dubbed "The IPO That Inflated the Dot-Com Bubble" – sparked the imagination of entrepreneurs and investors alike.

The upstart soon found the incumbent a powerful foe. Microsoft had itself outmaneuvered IBM as a scrappy upstart 20 years earlier to establish the dominant operating system for personal computers. Now it quickly responded to the threat from Netscape's internet browser. By bundling Internet Explorer into its ubiquitous Windows software, Microsoft soon supplanted Netscape and protected its position as the gateway for computer users. Netscape's share of the browser market plummeted from over 90% to below 10%, and the company was eventually sold to AOL, another high-flying-upstart-turned-incumbent that would be undone by the dynamism of the era a few years later.

Microsoft's success in fending off the challenge from Netscape was both ironic and instructive. A model of upstart entrepreneurship, it had created thousands of "Microsoft millionaires" after its own IPO in 1986. Despite Netscape's difficulties, its public offering a decade later unleashed a new and greater wave of enthusiasm among aspiring entrepreneurs. Both helped generate increased investor interest in venture capital investing and technology public offerings. The result was an explosion of entrepreneurship that has continued to the present, despite the collapse of the "dot-com" bubble that threatened to stop everything in its tracks before it really started.

Netscape's challenge to Microsoft and the latter's response is also important in highlighting both the new source of competitive advantage for incumbents – "network effects" – and the new risks of "disruption" from emerging platform technologies in the digital age. Reminiscent of economies of scale from earlier eras, the essential concept around the former is that having large numbers of users creates barriers to entry through usage patterns that are hard to switch (akin to the "QWERTY" keyboard layout). These barriers rise with more users and additional features, which makes it easier to lock customers in and keep potential competitors out. Companies and their networks become more valuable with each incremental user, each of whom adds little cost while making the network deeper, more robust, and harder to abandon. As these companies gather data and turn it into proprietary insights, the advantages become even stronger.[1]

This advantage isn't ironclad, however, and incumbents such as Microsoft have needed to constantly copy or acquire new applications to maintain relevance, using its control of operating systems to facilitate the deployment of its own versions. Early "killer apps" such as the spreadsheet, word processing, and email threatened Microsoft, and the company had to come to market quickly with copycat versions to fend off these threats, or else acquire nascent firms to preempt the risk. This was essentially the same strategy it deployed against Netscape. It would be the blueprint for maintaining competitiveness in the software era.

Microsoft's victory in the "browser wars" also challenged regulators. The U.S. Department of Justice (DOJ) brought a civil antitrust case against the incumbent in 1998, arguing that its Windows arrangement with computer manufacturers was unfair and that bundling of the Explorer browser within Windows was illegal. For its part, Microsoft claimed its approach reflected continued innovation and asserted, in effect, its own right to compete in product development. The lower court found in favor of the government but Microsoft appealed, eventually settling by agreeing to provide greater access to its operating system. Yet by the time the case was decided, Microsoft had already in effect won the real war against the upstart competition. The regulators would not stop, however, and Microsoft has continued to face scrutiny from the DOJ and especially from European regulators.[2]

Indeed, the second element in the Netscape IPO story has proved the more important one. As with incumbents in past eras, Microsoft's biggest threats ultimately came from new firms. For all its vaunted network effects, the company has also had to stay innovative in order to thrive. The company initially faced challenges to its operating system from "open systems" like Linux, where developers freely shared source code, and it was slow to address the smartphone market, where Apple iOS and Google's Android grabbed market share. IPO riches have attracted abundant entrepreneurs and risk-tolerant venture capital, so incumbents have faced a continual flow of new ideas and innovation. And playing catch-up did not always work. Upstarts such as Google, Amazon, and Facebook, as well as a resuscitated Apple, came to dominate emerging areas such as search, e-commerce, and social media, and then each sought to broaden and deepen their engagement with consumers, thereby clipping Microsoft's preeminence while joining its ranks as powerful incumbents. While these companies indirectly challenged Microsoft, they could not unseat it, and all of these behemoths topped the astounding $1 trillion market valuation by 2021.

While Microsoft maintained its position, many established companies would not be as smart or as fortunate. Ambitious entrepreneurs, new technologies, a growing venture capital industry, a robust stock market, and acquisition-hungry incumbents needing to stay ahead all created a virtual cycle of innovation and entrepreneurship that came to define the era. And this climate spilled over into other more traditional industries, in which traditional incumbents found themselves forced to respond to entrepreneurs with new ideas and technologies or else face the consequences. The balance between upstarts and incumbents was recalibrated.

The Revenge of the 1960s

The Netscape IPO was the clarion call that unleashed the internet economy, bringing with it waves of technological innovation and establishing the venture capital industry as a potent force in driving economic growth. Yet many of the underlying forces that enabled it had been well underway by that time. The entrepreneurial surge that led to the internet and digital economy of the late 1990s and into the first two decades of the 21st century was, in fact, a generational one. Having grown up with the Civil Rights struggles, the Vietnam War, environmental pollution, and Watergate, the postwar Baby Boomers had no reverence for big institutions.

Social rebellion against the Establishment went hand-in-hand with the willingness to challenge or outmaneuver economic institutions that earlier generations had treasured. Along with their anti-authoritarian streak, many tech pioneers dabbled in drug use and had close ties with the anti-war movement and cultural renegades such as Ken Kesey.[3] Even at traditional MIT on the East Coast, a longtime bastion of military contracts, a deep-rooted "hacker" culture celebrated challenges to authority. There was something Emersonian in their story, reminiscent of Benjamin Franklin, too, and of Thomas Edison. John Perry Barlow, the Grateful Dead lyricist who published his "Declaration of the Independence of Cyberspace" in 1996, was fond of quoting Thomas Jefferson.[4]

Over the next several decades, these challengers and ensuing waves of successors launched visionary ventures that disrupted incumbents, reshaped the economic landscape, and overturned long-held assumptions about how business worked. It was an extraordinary reversal of the conventional wisdom that said the American economy could succeed as a comfortable oligopoly of big business, big unions, and big government. A new consensus emerged, lauding individualism, innovation, creativity, and entrepreneurship. In fact, many of the successful pioneering upstarts would find themselves disrupted within a few years, as the velocity and intensity of innovation and competition and the adoption of new technologies accelerated.

By the early 2020s, virtually all facets of the American economy were transformed. The country enjoyed more than three decades of growth, innovation, and prosperity, despite challenges such as the "dot-com crash" of 2000, 9/11 terrorist attacks, 2008 financial crisis, and costly wars in Iraq and Afghanistan. Low consumer prices, high stock prices, and a vast array of new products and services made America the envy of much of the world, and nearly every other country sought to emulate American entrepreneurial capitalism, racing to create "the next Silicon Valley."

At the same time, persistent issues remained around income inequality, the challenges of small businesses, climate change, and the dominance of large companies – particularly the now massive Big Tech firms. Many of the social issues that the hippies fought for were now landing at their own New Establishment doorsteps 50 years later. With the outbreak of the COVID pandemic, many of the questions regarding American entrepreneurial capitalism gained momentum, led mostly by a new generation.

Bringing Down the Barricades

In many respects, the fall of the Berlin Wall in 1989 was the signalling event of the era. Most saw it as validation of the American economic model and a new consensus around freedom, though what that meant going forward was open to interpretation. Ronald Reagan, who denounced college protesters when he was California governor in the late 1960s (famously calling them "communist sympathizers" and "sex deviants"), pushed for greater military spending and deregulation when he was president. Ironically, he opened the way for the billionaire generation, some of whom in fact had been communist sympathizers in their student days.

The Reagan and Bush administrations' embrace of free markets in the 1980s gave a green light to free enterprise, and their approach largely continued through successive administrations, both Republican and Democrat. Deregulation assisted incumbents by reducing costs and helping them to compete globally, but it also enabled upstarts and eased market entry. Antitrust enforcement fell substantially as "consumer welfare" rather than market share became the standard, and companies could restructure and vertically integrate so long as they had a path to share some of the savings with consumers.

Though Bill Clinton ran as a new-generation candidate, he adopted this consensus, changing the way the Democratic Party engaged in economic matters. In much of his economic policy he acted like a traditional Republican – reducing capital gains taxes, shrinking the deficit, "reinventing government," and allowing the market to act with little intervention. As in the previous administrations, regulations were limited and antitrust policy was light. The federal government gave companies latitude to transform themselves.

The Clinton Administration also took important steps to encourage new technologies to develop, particularly the internet and communications. The most noteworthy legislation was the Telecommunications Act of 1996, which sought to update or dismantle New Deal restrictions. The legislation allowed firms (including the Baby Bells) to combine as well as to cross into new areas, leading to substantial consolidation in the telecommunications, radio, cable, and other industries, despite state and local regulations.[5] But while expanding property rights, it also bolstered the right to compete by requiring incumbents to give new entrants access to their networks, encouraging interoperability, new technologies, and choice. One important feature of the legislation was telephone number "portability," which allowed consumers to switch carriers without the loss of personal numbers.[6]

Aside from transforming the telecommunications and media industries – while maintaining the entrepreneurial balancing act, several of the act's provisions remained at the center of controversy for decades.

Section 230 of the Communications Decency Act (part of the 1996 Act) gave immunity to online service providers related to third-party content, a provision that supported the nascent industry but became ripe for review as Facebook and Twitter became powerful incumbents 20 years later. Similarly, as digital access became critical and bandwidth providers consolidated and sought differential prices for speed, the issue of "net neutrality" under the Act became the subject of heated debate and litigation in the 2010s, a modern riff on the price discrimination furor of the Standard Oil era.[7]

The Telecommunications Act was criticized by some as going too far in enabling consolidation.[8] But the result of the act was that many incumbents found themselves on the defensive, while consumers saw increased innovation and choice and lower costs. More broadly, the act helped to recalibrate the tension between upstarts and incumbents in an era of lesser government intervention and in which the nature of both property and competition was changing. Incumbent property rights morphed into an incumbent's right to compete and innovate without government intervention, while an upstart's right to compete focused on market entry and access. Key questions emerged on the boundaries between technology and the products or services it enabled, the rights and ownership of data, and the nature of competitive advantage.

The Supreme Court and other courts also wrestled with how to address new technologies. With e-commerce, for example, it wasn't clear where companies were transacting business, especially for tax purposes. In *Quill Corp. v. North Dakota* (1992), the high court ruled that a company cannot be taxed at the state level if it lacked a physical presence in that state, a decision that helped spawn Amazon; the decision was effectively overturned 26 years later as e-commerce became a pervasive way of shopping.[9] The ease of copying and distributing digital information also created issues around the bounds between information platforms and property rights for digitized content such as music, books and print media, videos, and eventually movies and TV shows. An early test case involved Napster, which presented itself as a peer-to-peer file sharing system meeting the definitions of "fair use" and thus exempt from copyright liability. The courts, however, ruled that it infringed on copyright by abetting piracy.[10] Yet Uber, Airbnb, and other companies used a similar argument about information platforms to claim exemption from local regulations, and they were often successful. Traditional legal areas such as franchise law had to adjust as well, as courts ruled that companies could offer products over the internet despite franchising agreements that required them to work through local distributors, a rebalancing of property rights in order to facilitate innovation and competition.[11]

As the "innovation economy" took off, new ways of doing business became prized business assets, and the patent law system tried to adjust accordingly. The lines between technology and processes became murky, and the Patent and Trademark Office relaxed the standard limiting "methods of doing business." This move triggered an explosion in business creativity, but also a flood of patents designed to protect existing advantages or claim broad powers.[12] Those moves engendered a counterreaction as regulators worried about entrenching incumbents, so the Patent Office sharply limited these patents in 2005.[13] Meanwhile, under President Barack Obama, Congress updated the patent laws more broadly, including a provision that modified the review process for patents that were already issued, in part an early effort to rein in "patent trolls" that had been acquiring pools of intellectual property and suing large companies.[14]

The most complex issues involved antitrust and centered on software companies with network effects, but successive administrations preserved a largely hands-off approach. Government efforts that did try to limit the power of new firms were not especially effective. The high-profile case against Microsoft defined the issue well, as the company settled with the government in 2001 by modifying some practices while securing its own right to continue to innovate. The case and the oversight nonetheless distracted the company and slowed its entry into new areas, notably its attempted acquisition of Quicken and its efforts in the smartphone market. It would take almost two decades before the U.S. government would reassert itself aggressively against the new platforms; the European competition authorities, however, continued to challenge not just Microsoft but the other large American digital firms.

The New Consumer Market

The entrepreneurial ferment went far beyond high tech, into airlines, steelmaking, and stock brokering. A common path to disruption was targeting price-sensitive customers willing to forego some amenities. Thus JetBlue, Charles Schwab, and other discount providers gradually moved along the learning curve, gained scale, and added many of those amenities. Incumbents were often quite rationally stuck in an "innovator's dilemma," hesitant to match the discounters or switch to new technologies lest they antagonize their core, high-paying customers. U.S.

Steel lost so much market share to Nucor, which started out 1968 as a steel recycler, that it dropped out of the S&P 500 altogether – an amazing fall for Carnegie's seemingly unstoppable creation.[15]

Other upstarts attacked or developed the high end of the market, offering affordable luxuries for niche markets with a dash of cultural cachet. Trendy coffeeshops, craft beers, boutique hotels, "fast fashion" labels, and organic food purveyors first established themselves, then gradually challenged the great mid-market brands that had dominated consumer products for most of the 20th century. The era's culture of individuality played a role, as people rebelled against the uniformity that had built the incumbent brands. Niche providers enabled consumers to better express themselves, while the internet and alternative media outlets such as Etsy greatly reduced the cost of marketing for artisans and others. It was easier than ever to scale up a business model focused on the "long-tail" of niche offerings.[16] Rising social concerns about environmental pollution, diet-based diseases, and exploitative supply chains gave upstarts many openings for products and brands, at least in consumer goods.

Established companies that became nimble or mastered new technologies could also play this game, either by expanding from regional to national markets, or by exploiting capabilities that their larger rivals ignored. New database marketing and the use of information became a particularly important new core competency for some. Capital One in banking, Progressive in insurance, and Enterprise in rental cars combined new technologies and innovative practices to challenge their dominant rivals both old and new. Many national brands tried to establish sub-brands geared to these concerns, but with mixed success because these had questionable authenticity.

In retail, the rise of new "big-box" companies as well as specialty retailers created a barbell effect, essentially squeezing out department stores in the middle. Companies such as Walmart and Starbucks embodied the newest generation of upstarts challenging traditional competitors, only to face new challenges as e-commerce and artisanal providers emerged later.

Founded in 1962 by former retail franchisee Sam Walton, Walmart grew initially in rural areas underserved by major retailers. As it gained scale, it relentlessly worked for lower costs, internally and with suppliers. Then in the 1980s, it committed aggressively to systems that integrated its logistics with suppliers. The new technology enabled another wave of cost-cutting and proved a major competitive advantage as the company entered other markets. By the 1990s its low prices were undermining

Sears and Kmart, as well as thousands of incumbent Main Street merchants that had survived previous onslaughts. The latter sought political protection but with little effect.[17]

Yet even Walmart's dominance proved only temporary. The company faced its own disruption as Amazon emerged and drove its own technological and platform advantages. Walmart struggled for years to compete on the internet – and ultimately realized it needed a more aggressive approach. It paid $3 billion for another e-commerce upstart, Jet.com, launched only two years earlier. Walmart survived and even thrived, largely a result of its ability to address this technological disruption and changes in consumer behavior. Other retailers were not as astute or as lucky.

Likewise, the coffee chain Starbucks gained popularity in the 1980s by championing individuality and a "cool factor" through beverages made to order by "baristas." By 2010 it had grown to 20,000 quite similar locations worldwide, the face of a new trend of mass affluence and affordable luxury. But over time that uniformity gave an opening for upstarts who claimed a more authentic environment than the global megacorporation. Starbucks responded to preserve its cultural resonance, expanding its menu with ever more specialized beverages, often fairtrade and organic, and offering itself as a replacement to offices in the increasingly distributed work environment of freelancers and flexible employees. Both paths helped, but neither amounted to the kind of entry barriers that incumbents in earlier eras had enjoyed.

Financial Engineering and Financing Engineers

Aside from new technologies and changing consumer and cultural norms, another powerful breakthrough occurred in finance. The august New York Stock Exchange came under challenge from Nasdaq, which in turn faced competition from new virtual trading networks. Discount firms, mutual funds, and then index funds such as Vanguard disrupted brokerages and money managers. Apps such as Robinhood are now disrupting those firms. New kinds of commercial paper freed firms from depending on large commercial banks, while the money market drained savings from stodgy local banks. Investment banks met their match in sophisticated institutional investors.[18]

The dot-com crash in 2000 put a temporary halt on some of the euphoria in the technology sector, with the Nasdaq index declining precipitously. Some notable start-up firms such as Webvan went out of business, but others used the opportunity to consolidate or enhance their positions. Large incumbent firms faced a similar challenge with the financial crisis of 2008. In an implicit recognition of the critical role of select big companies, banks deemed "too big to fail" were rescued, as were certain companies such as General Motors (in large part to protect workers and car dealers). The rescue sparked a populist outcry. The crisis hit small businesses particularly hard. Approximately 1.8 million small firms went out of business in the ensuing two-year period – but not some entrepreneurial "greenshoots" that drove growth through the period and beyond. Tesla was founded in 2003, Facebook a year later, and Uber in 2009. By 2013 the stock market had recovered, with technology firms becoming an increasing share.

Three main trends developed. The first overarching change was the continued growth of financial instruments and new capital sources to support growth, buyouts, and even takeovers. This put additional pressure on public companies to perform and also paved the way for increased shareholder activism. As noted in the previous chapter, deregulation in the 1970s had freed institutional investors to go beyond blue-chip firms, and by the mid-1980s high-yield "junk" bonds were heavily subscribed. Despite Michael Milken's legal troubles and dissolution of his firm, Drexel Burnham Lambert, the lessons and opportunities remained. Private equity firms and hedge funds grew exponentially in size and number, and much of their work proved critical in assisting larger companies that sought to restructure themselves in order to remain competitive. By 2020, private equity funds ($2T) and hedge funds ($3T) had record sums under management.

Even big companies that succeeded in staying strong took steps to change the way they competed. Under pressure from activist investors, many of them tightened their use of capital and reduced their empire building. They adopted a more short-term orientation that focused their operations and reduced investments in R&D and marketing, choosing to make acquisitions as a way to stay ahead. They initiated a wave of employee downsizing and outsourcing of all but the core functions. The result was faster growth rates, higher margins, and stronger balance sheets, but arguably at the cost of capabilities that could fuel long-term success. Indeed, the move toward doing things "virtually" and a dependence on third parties for key capabilities left many of them vulnerable to new entrants who could work with those same suppliers.

Some of the biggest names took the lead in transforming themselves, ever mindful of how new technologies might be changing the foundations of their industries.[19] IBM shed its once dominant hardware units, while ADP and Hewlett Packard split in smaller units to gain focus and flexibility. Cisco Systems, at one point among the most valuable firms in the country, developed a strategy of "spin-ins" to help keep itself and its innovation processes nimble.

General Electric at first seemed an exception, a vigorous incumbent that transformed itself before upstarts forced the issue. It moved aggressively into new industries while selling off mediocre divisions. Under CEO Jack Welch it worked on self-renewal with initiatives such as "destroyyourbusiness.com," an effort to preempt disruption. But much of its success in the 1990s actually came from short-term financial gains, which went south after 2000. In 2018 it fell off the Dow Jones index, after an astounding 110 years. By 2021 it was scaling back to focus on aerospace.

The second main force that transformed finance was the exponential growth of the venture capital industry. Here the Netscape IPO was indeed a signature event, demonstrating that risky start-up firms could generate exceptional payouts. Even the bursting of the dot-com bubble in 2000 only temporarily dampened the animal spirits. Investors plowed money into venture funds, eager to get in on the action. The industry raised $7 billion in 1995, topped $100 billion at the height of the internet boom in 2000, and then continued at an annual rate of $20 to 30 billion for several years. In 2014 the investment level grew again, and the industry raised $75 billion; by 2020, it topped $125 billion.[20] More important, the industry invested over $150 billion into U.S. firms that year, while "exit value" for venture-backed companies topped $230 billion.[21] And many of these numbers doubled in 2021. Aside from the growth of firms, individual angel investors became increasingly engaged; the America Jobs Act (2011) encouraged new sources of fundraising such as crowdsourcing in part to open up investment opportunities to more people. By 2020, venture capital firms had over $450B under management.

The third important trend in finance was the increase in stock ownership and the broadened range of choices for individuals looking to invest in the stock market. Important policy initiatives that began in the 1970s and continued through this period encouraged stock ownership, particularly automatic enrollment in 401(k) plans and the development of the IRA.[22] As a result, stock ownership increased significantly, from 13% of American households in 1990 to over 50% in 2020 (it reached a peak of over 60% in 2007 but retracted for several years after the financial crisis). This is substantially above the percentages in most other countries.[23] However, within this group there is significant disparity, particularly by race and ethnicity, which has exacerbated inequality as the stock market continued to rise.[24]

Finally, in the area of corporate law and governance, the Supreme Court decision in *Citizens United v. Federal Election Commission* (2010) essentially gave corporations the right to make financial contributions to political campaigns. A step in the long chain of cases involving corporate rights, including *Santa Clara* and *Virginia Pharmacy* described in early chapters, the decision brought with it the risk that large corporations would wield too much power. The backlash, however, sparked renewed debates about the role of corporations, their participation in the political process, and how they should be governed. These questions intensified with increasing calls for companies to give respect to environmental, social, and governance (ESG) issues.

Reinventing and Disrupting Government

Entrepreneurial enthusiasm spread beyond commercial business itself. The era's disenchantment with large institutions spurred some ambitious people toward "social entrepreneurship": using creative means to attack problems usually addressed by governments or conventional nonprofits.[25] Some of these enterprises were launched by pioneers who saw the opportunity to address issues with the same upstart mentality that made private-sector companies so valuable. Often, the leaders of these enterprises would partner with those who made early fortunes in the business world and sought a similar innovation or disruption in the philanthropic sector. While many of these organizations were focused on developing unserved areas or new technologies, some aimed at vested interests that they believed hindered more than helped in finding solutions.

The result was a flood of experiments and initiatives addressing everything from entrenched poverty in Africa to climate change in the Arctic. Efforts at addressing education through social entrepreneurship, such as Teach for America, mobilized thousands of talented young college graduates to spend several years teaching in schools in lower-income areas. Started by Wendy Kopp in 1989, the organization had nearly 60,000 alumni and was one of the most sought-after jobs for graduates of the country's elite colleges and universities by 2020.[26] Just as importantly, many new organizations addressing other social problems would be formed in its wake, inspired by the organization's success.

Another daring social entrepreneur was Paul Farmer, who cofounded Partners in Health. Among several innovations, he and colleagues succeeded in treating drug-resistant tuberculosis in Peru in the 1990s despite the health care establishment – both established nonprofits and government officials – telling them it was impossible. They delved into the economics as well as the medical treatments and found a sustainable solution.[27] Farmer, like many entrepreneurs in the social sector, showed that individual initiative, ability, and drive could solve important societal problems in new and creative ways.

Perhaps the biggest area of disruption was in public education itself. As cities wrestled with failed schools, some experimented with outsourcing schooling to third-party organizations (often reluctantly). The charter school movement started in Minnesota in 1992 and soon spread to most states. Though this effort was largely funded by state and local governments, the movement allowed flexibility, new energy, and performance management. Most importantly, charter schools introduced innovation, competition, and parent choice into the mix. By 2018, thousands of charter schools, mostly nonprofits, were teaching 3.3 million students, or 7% of all public-school enrollment. Many parents appreciated alternatives to the incumbent government-run schools and signed on to long waiting lists, even as teachers' unions fought back and slowed the spread. While some of their educational achievements were disputed, charter schools certainly forced accountability, dialogue, and a focus on results.[28]

Hybrid forms of social entrepreneurship also emerged. Venture philanthropy and impact investing addressed market failure while still aiming for a return on assets. Some companies even engaged in "social business," where they devoted a set amount of capital to activities that needed to only break-even, rather than cover the cost of capital.[29] Others promised to dedicate an agreed-upon percentage of revenue or profit to specific causes, and the "B Corp" was created to explicitly permit entities to serve not just shareholders but multiple stakeholders. In many cases, for-profit entrepreneurs simply began to recognize that addressing social goals through enterprise could make for a good business.[30]

Separately, universities, economic development agencies, and government officials also became more involved in trying to create technology or other clusters in their regions. The number of colleges offering programs and classes in entrepreneurship grew dramatically. States and towns worked to lure technology firms into their regions. Many began to see the link between entrepreneurial activity, regional development, and creativity more broadly, and they specifically sought to attract the "creative class."[31] Coffee bars and microbreweries seemed to open on every corner.

Silicon Valley Inspirations

Through it all, Silicon Valley became the era's iconic region. To earlier generations, it looked like a conventional industry cluster with numerous large- and mid-scale defense, electronic, and engineering firms in the area. Partnering with the government, they were designing rocketry, silicon chips, and other cutting-edge technologies aimed at continuing the momentum that IBM had gained with its popular mainframe computers. But "underground," engineers were experimenting, tinkering with projects assigned by their corporate employers or pursued on their own initiative. By the 1990s and 2000s, the rush toward entrepreneurial success was out in the open, and it continued unabated.[32]

Information technology moved from huge, capital-intensive machines to cheap, portable devices that start-ups could afford. With ever-more circuits on a computer chip, mainframes were superseded by minicomputers, then by personal computers, and ultimately by smartphones. The concept of "software as a service" and the growth of cloud computing dramatically reduced the amount of money needed to get a new venture off the ground, facilitating the "lean start-up" and speed.[33]

Established companies began to see the possibilities of new technologies as well as the risks of not keeping up. By the late 1990s, most businesses were becoming digital, and new opportunities often depended on information analytics as much as product breakthroughs. Companies focused on being nimble and agile and on avoiding "technical debt" that could slow down the ability to stay current. This enabled a virtuous cycle of greater interoperability, easier market entry for new technologies, and speedier returns on investment for innovation.

With computer power so cheap and consumers increasingly comfortable in using the technology, companies were finding that they could substitute software for hardware. The all-electric Tesla luxury car, for example, fixed many of its problems by sending customers a software update, rather than calling in the car for a mechanical repair. As early as 2011, Netscape cofounder Marc Andreesen – by now a venture capitalist – was saying that "software is eating the world." And the more things ran on software, the less capital you needed to disrupt them. Kids only recently out of school could improve on systems that engineers had spent their careers developing.[34]

Consumers also became more adept at using technology, especially as new generations grew up with access to computers, tablets, smartphones, and apps. This certainly made it easier for new products, services, and features to gain adoption. But it also helped established companies that were undertaking "digital transformation" themselves, as consumers were increasingly comfortable with online shopping, downloading apps for travel reservations, and using the smartphone to order services. Upstarts, nimble incumbents, and consumers all benefitted.

Steve Jobs as Hippie-Billionaire

A college dropout, Steve Jobs was hardly the sort of figure to inspire fear among big business incumbents. His favorite course was calligraphy. He hung out with hippies, tripped on LSD, ate a vegan diet, and studied Zen Buddhism. His engineering chops were good enough to get him a job at Atari in 1974, but he quit after a few months to seek enlightenment at an Indian ashram. A year later, he and a friend assembled circuitry to manipulate dial tones so they could access free long-distance telephone calls. The illegal device's (short-term) success convinced him that electronics could be profitable as well as fun – and that he could take on large companies and beat them. And so he did – to the point of building the most valuable company ever.

It helped that Jobs lived in Silicon Valley, which in addition to its military-funded innovation and research universities had been a symbol of the countercultural 1960s. Mainstream America first encountered his company in a 1984 Super Bowl ad introducing the Macintosh computer. Inspired by Orwell's dystopian novel, it depicted a woman smashing a computer monitor showing an overlord's speech to conformist drones. The meaning was clear: Apple and its products would liberate individuals and shatter the dreary incumbency of IBM. At least in those days, as Jobs said, it was "better to be the pirate than the Navy."

Marketing was only one side of the rebellion. Both geek and hippie, Jobs ignored computer conventions and offered a striking combination of high design and user-friendly interfaces. He was less able to handle success, and Apple struggled with growth in the late 1980s and early 1990s. The company fired him and then nearly went out of business. When he returned in 1997, he applied his ethos to new products and platform strategies that catapulted the company to astonishing levels of profitability. The hit parade included the iPod and the proprietary iTunes virtual store, as well as sleek new devices like the iPhone and iPad. Apple's stock appreciated 9,000% during Jobs's second tenure, and the company dominated the wireless telephone industry, displacing Motorola and Nokia. It then squeezed incumbents in music, photography, and media.

By the 2010s it had become a dominant incumbent itself, with enough market clout to maintain a closed system of apps for its users.[35] When he died in 2011, Jobs's net worth exceeded $10 billion, while the company he started had a market capitalization of $300 billion. By 2021 it was the most valuable company in the world, with a valuation approaching $3 trillion.

The Irony of Big Tech

Since the time of Steve Jobs's passing, the march of upstart technology firms into powerful incumbents only increased. Like successful upstarts in other eras and industries, these tech firms worked to become powerful incumbents themselves, erecting barriers to protect their accumulated customer base and ensure continued demand for their products, services, or intellectual property. Lobbying expenses rose markedly in the technology sector, as big firms pushed back against a range of adversaries that sought protection, from large companies to small. In the case of firms like Apple, with its "1984" commercial, and Google, which started off with the mantra "Don't Be Evil," the industry dominance and use of information to maintain competitive advantage seemed hypocritical.[36]

While these firms created enormous value for consumers, third parties that could take advantage of their platforms, and the economy as a whole, the increasing dominance of these firms in economic life was troubling. As these companies collected more and more data about users and suppliers and started to deploy emerging technologies such as artificial intelligence, it seemed that the competitive advantages they were building were becoming insurmountable. Moreover, the firms were increasingly using their position and insights to extract more value from third parties or to offer competing services of their own.[37] Finally, the power of many of these companies over information brought concerns that they might even be garnering control over American freedom and democracy itself.[38]

Staying ahead often required bold and aggressive acquisitions, as these firms learned the lessons of Microsoft. While the entrepreneurs who sold to these firms were happy and it often led to new products and services being deployed more quickly, others took issue. For instance, Facebook acquired more than 60 firms since it began in 2004; it paid $1 billion for Instagram in 2012, only to up the ante by acquiring WhatsApp for close to $20 billion in 2014. The rationale for these enormous prices was to stay in front of consumers, who were adopting these new services daily, and to avoid the risk of being disintermediated by these new firms over time. Critics complained that these acquisitions only furthered the company's lead and squashed nascent competitors.

While the tech platforms gained power, in certain cases content providers or other suppliers could push back. Artists or third parties with strong followings were particularly well suited to rebel, most notably Taylor Swift and gaming company Epic, the maker of the popular Fortnite.[39] In response to pressure, Apple eventually agreed to loosen certain restrictions.[40] Meanwhile newer companies such as Spotify attacked Apple's hegemony in music and TikTok challenged Facebook's in social media.

Arguably the most dominant of the Big Tech firms was Amazon, which not only drove its lead in e-commerce but also established leadership in cloud computing. In the retail area, the company combined efficient direct sales of items with a "marketplace" model that gave the third parties the ability to sell through its platform. As with other platforms, the company developed an enormous data advantage, which it could use to sell more goods directly as categories became large and popular. The company also developed proprietary warehousing and delivery capabilities, combined with enough user purchaser data to become a one-stop giant. Here, too, new competitors emerged, in categories ranging from furniture and pets, and in general e-commerce platforms such as Shopify.

The tidal wave of disruption that began in the 1990s and continued for the next three decades reshaped the economic landscape. It dramatically altered business strategies, structures, paradigms, and outlooks. Upstarts with innovative technologies or approaches were able to enter markets or disrupt them altogether, while incumbents were forced to transform themselves to stay competitive. Large companies that did not move fast enough could not rely on governments to save them, and those that were too slow or made the wrong moves suffered mightily. Consumers saw more choice and investors saw stock prices skyrocket. A consensus of sorts emerged around the virtues of entrepreneurial capitalism.

America's success had not gone unnoticed abroad. Entrepreneurship and venture capital began to expand markedly in other countries, with many reporting record levels of start-up activity and venture financings in 2021.[41] European policymakers sought to emulate aspects of America's open entrepreneurial capitalism, even as they maintained important aspects of their social contract and took the lead on corporate sustainability mandates in classic top-down ways. Japan, which had been the global darling at the beginning of the era, suffered from "lost decades" beginning in the 1990s, as an aging population, deflating asset prices, and lack of "creative destruction" took its toll. But many there also began to recognize the importance of entrepreneurship to reinvigorating its economy.[42] Countries throughout Asia and Latin America saw increasing activity, including record numbers of unicorns.

Meanwhile China emerged as a global powerhouse, on track to become the largest economy in the world. While it dismissed America's liberal political economic model, adopting instead an authoritarian version rooted in socialist ideology, it nevertheless tolerated entrepreneurship within limits. It even tackled inequality and climate change at the same time it limited individual liberties and human rights, including in the entrepreneurial enclave of Hong Kong.

By 2020, several decades of liberal economic policy, coupled with entrepreneurship, social entrepreneurship, consumer choice, and active shareholders, had demonstrated the ongoing power of the American political economy. At the same time important issues remained, with rising urgency. Workers, small businesses, and others left out clamored to get their fair share of the pie amid dramatic inequality, while issues such as diversity and climate change began to receive broad and overdue attention. How the country responded to these challenges would be critical both to continuing the country's long run of economic success, and to serving as a political and economic model for emerging entrepreneurial economies around the world.

Endnotes

1. See, e.g., Carl Shapiro and Hal R. Varian, *Information Rules: A Strategic Guide to the Network Economy* (Cambridge, MA: Harvard Business School Press, 1999), and Alex Moazed and Nicholas L. Johnson, *Modern Monopolies: What It Takes to Dominate in the 21st Century Economy* (New York: St. Martin's Press, 2016).
2. Andrew I. Gavil and Harry First, *The Microsoft Antitrust Cases: Competition Policies for the Twenty-First Century* (Cambridge, MA: MIT Press, 2014). See also Rudolph J.R. Peritz, *Competition Policy in America: History, Rhetoric, Law* (New York: Oxford University Press, 2001).
3. See, e.g., John Markoff, *What the Dormouse Said: How the Sixties Counter-Culture Shaped the Personal Computer Industry* (New York: Penguin Group, 2005); Katie Hafner and Matthew Lyon, *Where Wizards Stay Up Late: The Origins of the Internet* (New York: Simon & Schuster, 1996); Steven Levy, *Hackers: Heroes of the Computer Revolution* (Sebastopol, CA: O'Reilly Media, Inc. 2010); David Kaiser, *How the Hippies Saved Physics: Science, Counterculture,*

and the Quantum Revival (New York: W.W. Norton Company, 2011); and Robert X. Cringely, *Accidental Empires: How the Boys of Silicon Valley Make Their Millions, Battle Foreign Competition, and Still Can't Get a Date* (New York: HarperCollins, 1996).

4. "Governments of the Industrial World, you weary giants of flesh and steel, I come from Cyberspace, the new home of the Mind. On behalf of the future, I ask you of the past to leave us alone. You are not welcome among us. You have no sovereignty where we gather."

5. Telecommunications firms consolidated, including both local firms with one another and with long-distance firms. Radio stations consolidated from over 5,000 owners to less than 1,000, with iHeartRadio owning over 800 stations within a short period. Major media firms also consolidated, from over 50 in 1983 to 10 in 1996 and six by 2005. At the same time, new entrants in radio (SiriusXM) and internet-enabled media countered the effect of the consolidation by more mature companies.

6. The protections around consumer portability would help inform important data privacy law initiatives, including the California Consumer Protection Act (2018), the European Union's General Data Protection Regulations (2018) and Brazil's data protection law (LGPD).

7. At the heart of the issue of net neutrality is the question is how the Federal Communications Commission characterized internet service providers (ISPs). If "information services" under Title I of the act, they would have broader freedom to charge for their services. If "common carrier services" under Title II, they would have more limitations. In 2015, the FCC sought to classify ISPs under Title II, which withstood a challenge in U.S. Telecommunications Association v. FCC (2015), but ISPs were reclassified as coming under Title I in 2017.

8. The act was specifically called out in John Perry Barlow's "Declaration of Independence of Cyberspace" as "an insult to the dreams of Jefferson, Washington, Mill, Madison, De Tocqueville and Brandeis."

9. The case was effectively overturned 26 years later in South Dakota v. Wayfair, Inc. (2018).

10. A&M Records v. Napster, Inc. (2001), Ninth Circuit Court of Appeals. See also MGM Studios, Inc. v. Grokster, Ltd. (2005).

11. See Larry Downes, *The Laws of Disruption: Harnessing the New Forces That Govern Life and Business in the Digital Age* (New York: Basic Books, 2009), (discussing how digital disruption takes place across a range of areas and the challenges that regulators and courts have in keeping up).

12. State Street Bank v. Signature Financial Group (1998), (upholding USPTO position allowing business methods), and AT&T Corp v. Excel Communications, Inc. (1999).

13. Later USPTO or Supreme Court cases that pared this back include Ex Parte Lundgren (2005), Bilski vs. Kappos (2010) and Alice Corp v. CLS Bank International (2014).

14. See Steven Levy, "The Patent Problem," *Wired*, December 2012 ("non-practicing entities" cost the economy $29B in 2011), and Stefan Lederer, "The Growing Problem of Patent Trolls and What Should Happen Next," *Forbes*, July 22, 2021. See also KSR v. Teleflex (2007) and Alice v. CLS (2014), both of which made it easier to invalidate a patent.

15. See Chapter 2, discussing Clayton Christensen, *The Innovator's Dilemma: When New Technologies Cause Great Firms to Fail* (New York: Harper Business, 1997), and Richard Foster, *Innovation: The Attacker's Advantage* (New York: Macmillan, 1986).

16. Chris Anderson, *The Long Tail: Why the Future of Business Is Selling Less of More* (New York: Hyperion, 2006). See also Nicco Mele, *The End of Big: How the Internet Makes David the New Goliath* (New York: St. Martin's Press, 2013).

17. Charles Fishman, *The Walmart Effect* (New York: Penguin Books, 2006). As noted in the previous chapter, the Consumer Goods Pricing Act of 1975 effectively gutted the Robinson-Patman Act and Miller Tydings Act, enabling big-box retailers to offer much lower consumer prices but making it more difficult for mom-and-pop retailers to compete.

18. Michael Lind, *Land of Promise: An Economic History of the United States* (New York: HarperCollins, 2012), 363–391.

19. Richard Foster and Sarah Kaplan, *Creative Destruction: Why Companies That Are Built to Last Underperform the Market – and How to Transform Them* (Portland, OR: Broadway Books, 2001).

20. Statista.com; National Venture Capital Association Yearbook, March 2021.

21. National Venture Capital Association press release, January 14, 2021.

22. Assets for retirement plans have grown from $1.7T to over $7.2T between 2000 and 2021, with approximately 60 million participants. Investment Company Institute, October 2021. While 401(k) provisions were passed in 1978, an IRS ruling in 1981 that allowed payroll deduction sparked the increase in popularity. Similarly, Individual Retirement Accounts were created in 1974 as part of the Employee Retirement Income Security Act, but in 1981 legislation opened participation to more people.

23. "Population Participating in Stock Markets by Country," Twinkle Khandelwal, August 31, 2021. See also "Household Stockholding in Europe: Where do we stand and where do we go?" Luigi Guiso, Michael Haliassos, Tullio Jappelli, and Stijn Claessens, *Economic Policy* 18, no. 36 (April 2003), Oxford University (50% in U.S. and Sweden, one-third in UK, 15–20% in other countries).

24. Gallup Poll, Lydia Saad, and Jeffrey Jones, "What Percentage of Americans Own Stocks?" August 13, 2021. See also Kim Parker and Richard Fry, "More than Half of U.S. Households Have Some Investment in the Stock Market," *Pew Research Center*, March 25, 2020. In terms of disparities, the participation rate for white households with incomes above $100,000 is nearly 90%, while the rates among Blacks, Hispanics, and those making less than $40,000 is far less.

25. For a seminal article on the category, see J. Gregory Dees, "The Meaning of Social Entrepreneurship" (Duke University Fuqua School of Business case, 2001).

26. See, e.g., Wendy Kopp, *One Day, All Children: The Unlikely Triumph of Teach for America and What I Learned Along the Way* (New York: Public Affairs, 2003).

27. Tracey Kidder, *Mountains Beyond Mountains: The Quest of Dr. Paul Farmer, a Man Who Would Cure the World* (New York: Random House, 2003).

28. See, e.g., Luigi Zingales, *A Capitalism for the People: Recapturing the Lost Genius of American Prosperity* (2012), 142 (teachers unions as cronyism).

29. See, e.g., Ulrich Villis et al., "The Value of Social Business," BCG.com, October 14, 2014, and J. Gregory Dees and Beth Battle Anderson, "For-Profit Social Ventures," *Social Entrepreneurship*, Marilyn Kourilsky and William B. Walstad, ed. (Dublin: Senate Hall Academic Publishing, 2003).

30. See, e.g., Peter Diamandis and Steve Kotler, *Bold: How to Go Big, Create Wealth and Help the World* (New York: Simon & Schuster, 2015) (the quote "The Best Way to Become a Billionaire Is to Help a Billion People" is attributed to Peter Diamandis, the founder of the XPrize Foundation).

31. See Richard Florida, *The Rise of the Creative Class* (New York: Basic Books, 2002).

32. See, e.g., Everett M. Rogers and Judith K. Larsen, *Silicon Valley Fever: Growth at High Technology Culture* (New York: Basic Books, 1984), 48, 64, 79; Martin Kenney, *Understanding Silicon Valley* (Stanford, CA: Stanford Business Books, 2000); and AnnaLee Saxenian, *Regional Advantage: Culture and Competition in Silicon Valley and Route 128* (Cambridge, MA: Harvard University Press, 1996).

33. Eric Ries, *The Lean Start-Up: How Today's Entrepreneurs Use Continuous Innovation to Create Radically Successful Businesses* (New York: Crown Publishing Group, 2011). See also Mele, *The End of Big*.

34. See, e.g., Walter Isaacson, *The Innovators: How a Group of Hackers, Geniuses, and Geeks Created the Digital Revolution* (New York: Simon & Schuster, 2014); Markoff, *What the Dormouse Said*; Levy, *Hackers*; Lawrence Lessig, *Code and Other Laws of Cyberspace* (New York: Perseus Book Group, 1999); E. Gabriella Coleman, *Coding Freedom: The Ethics and Aesthetics of Hacking* (Princeton, NJ: Princeton University Press, 2013).

35. Walter Isaacson, *Steve Jobs* (New York: Simon & Schuster, 2011).

36. See Jonathan Taplin, *Move Fast and Break Things: How Facebook, Google, and Amazon Have Cornered Culture and Undermined Democracy* (New York: Little Brown and Company, 2017).

37. See, e.g., Lina Khan, "Amazon's Antitrust Paradox," *Yale Law Journal* 126, no. 3 (January 2017): 564–907. See also Barry Lynn, *Cornered: The New Monopoly Capitalism and the Economics of Destruction* (Hoboken, NJ: John Wiley & Sons, 2010) and Matt Stoller, *Goliath: The 100-Year War Between Monopoly Power and Democracy* (New York: Simon & Schuster, 2019).

38. See, e.g., Shoshana Zuboff, *The Age of Surveillance Capitalism: The Fight for a Human Future at the New Frontier of Power* (New York: Profile, 2019) and Tim Wu, *The Master Switch: The Rise and Fall of Information Empires* (New York: Alfred A. Knopf, 2010).

39. See, e.g., Hugh McIntyre, "Taylor Swift's Letter to Apple: Stern, Polite, and Necessary," *Forbes*, June 21, 2015, and Epic v. Apple.

40. The concessions were made in a settlement agreement in 2021 (Cameron et al v. Apple). Similar challenges were also made by Epic against Google. The Open App Markets Act was proposed in Congress in 2021 to limit, among other things, the ability of platforms to require in-app billing only.

41. In fact, 2021 marked the first time that the United States' share of global venture capital investment dipped below 50%, down from close to 85% (albeit of a much smaller pool) in 2001. National Venture Capital Association, *2021 Yearbook* (March 2021) and *Pitchbook-NVCA Monitor* (January 2022).

42. See, e.g., George Lloyd, "Will the 2020s be a decade of entrepreneurship in Japan?" *Japan Today*, August 7, 2021.

Travis Kalanick speaking at a conference in Germany in 2015. His entrepreneurially aggressive company, Uber, expanded rapidly in the startup-friendly United States, but faced heavy opposition in countries that favored incumbents.

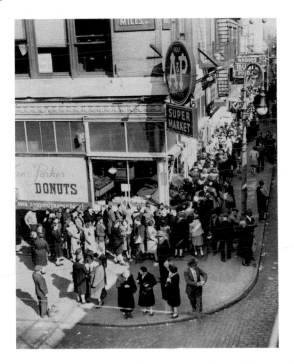

An early A&P supermarket opening in New York City in 1939. Small grocers tried to stop the innovator with government action, but consumers loved the low prices. Only competition from later supermarkets brought it down.

Jurist Edward Coke made breakthrough milestones for the right to compete in early 17th century England despite being enmeshed in monarchical politics.

Source: Mary Evans Library/Adobe Stock

The Baron de Montesquieu, in mid-18th century France, was the first major thinker to see businesspeople as distinct agents of progress.

Source: Achille Devéria/Wikimedia Commons

For all its openness, colonial America still favored incumbents culturally.
When Benjamin Franklin, later the paradigm for the self-made man,
first attained wealth in 1748, he commissioned this foppish painting to
help join the elite.

When James Madison led the framing of the U.S. constitution, he
emphasized not wise overall rule, but the competition of interests to
check both political and economic power.

John Marshall, chief justice of the U.S. Supreme Court from 1801-35,
led several rulings that checked government powers, established national
markets, and protected property rights while allowing competition.
(Statue in Washington, DC.)

After disrupting the Livingston monopoly in passenger ferries,
Cornelius Vanderbilt shifted platforms and became a relentless
cost-cutter in steamships and railroads, as in this 1869 cartoon.

View of the BRIDGE over CHARLES RIVER.

One of the most lucrative monopolies in early America, the Charles
River Bridge (engraved here in 1804) failed after the U.S. Supreme
Court ruled in 1837 for the right to compete.

Source: Hill, Samuel, approximately 1766-1804, engraver/Library of Congress/Public Domain

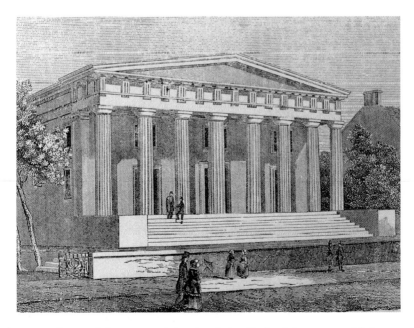

The grandeur of the Second Bank of the United States couldn't save it
from President Andrew Jackson's decisive strike in 1832 against
centralized finance.

Source: PRISMA ARCHIVO/Alamy Stock Photo

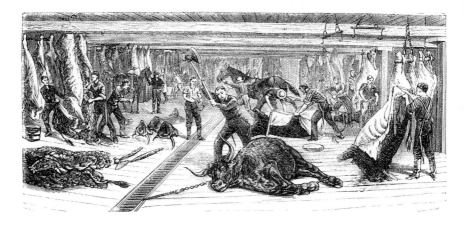

Slaughterhouses were a messy business in the 19th century (this drawing from Chicago in 1880), but that messiness may have led to important legal precedents involving entrepreneurship.

As in this 1902 drawing of President Theodore Roosevelt (left) and banker J.P. Morgan (second from right) discussing a coal strike, the federal government initially accepted big business and tried to induce good behavior.

David Sarnoff, here in a 1939 television broadcast, worked as an "intrapreneur" to innovate in telecommunications during the age of big business.

It's fashionable to say that Silicon Valley benefitted from abundant resources, but the powerhouse region emerged from Bill Hewlett and David Packard's humble garage in 1938.

Steve Jobs in his later years. The hippie entrepreneur challenged The Establishment in the 1970s, only to create what became the biggest incumbent in the world.

Source: Chuck Nacke/Alamy Stock Photo

Wendy Kopp in 2008: A daring social entrepreneur, she challenged the education establishment with Teach for America in 1989.

Source: WENN Ltd/Alamy Stock Photo

Marc Lore in 2017: Contrary to assumptions of Big Tech dominance, he sold his first big ecommerce company to Amazon, launched a startup that helped Walmart challenge the incumbent, and is now working on another new venture.

Source: Oscar Espaillat/Shutterstock.com

9

The Inflection Point?

After four decades of success, American entrepreneurial capitalism faced a critical challenge in the COVID outbreak that emerged early in 2020. At one level, the quick reaction to the crisis actually highlighted the strength of the nation's balanced economic system. The speedy vaccine development and rollout showed impressive collaboration between upstarts and incumbents, as new firms such as Moderna and established giants such as Pfizer and Johnson & Johnson all made important contributions. Retailers such as Target, CVS, and Walgreens led the mass distribution, alongside start-ups that helped identify locations and schedule appointments. The strength of America's mixed economy was on display. The consensus around entrepreneurial capitalism, with its ability to enable innovation, create opportunity, and challenge large incumbent companies to stay sharp, remained largely intact. Moreover, the quick and strong stock market rebound and increased consumer savings as a result of government payments and other measures helped alleviate the crisis for many, at least temporarily.

Yet the crisis amplified long-standing concerns over social issues that had bubbled below the surface for years. Some of these concerns had emerged with the fallout from the financial crisis in 2008 and the subsequent Occupy Wall Street movement. The divisiveness of President Trump, the George Floyd murder, continuing revelations from the MeToo movement, and intensified concern about climate change raised the tension markedly. The whipsaw effect of a near shutdown of the economy, followed just months later by a boom, labor shortages, and inflation, gave companies large and small as well as workers a topsy-turvy ride. The election of Joe Biden as president also signaled a shift in economic policy, at least in antitrust. The American entrepreneurial system, it seemed, was arriving at an inflection point in which the entrepreneurial revolution might give way to the next big reset, including a rebalancing of the right to property and the right to compete and the role of government in mediating it.

Meanwhile the rest of the world is confronting similar choices. On the one hand, the fall of the Berlin Wall led to a consensus around capitalism as the superior economic model, and many countries are now trying to replicate American-style innovation and entrepreneurship. Yet there also seems to be a global convergence around softening aspects of that system. How America navigates its way through this inflection point will be critical not only for its continued success but to maintaining its position as a model for other nations.

Social Concerns

The first and most important social issue is economic inequality. While the economy as a whole has grown significantly since the 1970s, the huge wealth created has not been shared equally; in fact, it became much more disparate. For the top 1% and even top 10%, particularly those who owned stock, the period was remarkable, with a sustained period of low interest rates rewarding holders of equities. For those at the very peak, such as technology titans, private equity and hedge fund partners, and corporate executives with hefty equity packages, it has been an extraordinary run. In the first two years of the coronavirus pandemic alone, America's billionaires added over $1 trillion to their collective net worth.[1] Meanwhile over 20 million people lost their jobs and the real wages of most workers remained flat, with opportunity increasingly limited to those with college degrees, especially elite ones. Even with the "Great Resignation" that began in spring 2021 and the reset in employee relations that followed, there is a sense that the rich simply have a disproportionate share of – and perhaps just too much – money.[2]

Traditional opportunities seem to be drying up. Only a few years recovered from the financial crisis and under pressure from e-commerce, small businesses suffered noticeably during the pandemic, as many customers stayed indoors and shopped online. Thousands of restaurant and hospitality firms were forced to close. And even when the situation eased temporarily between waves of COVID variants, worker shortages made it particularly difficult for smaller firms to compete on salaries and wages.

Along with inequality, lack of diversity and inclusion throughout the economy have come under scrutiny. Although laws, regulations, and corporate policies encouraged diversity and inclusion for decades with tangible results, many critics question the speed and extent of progress while noting uneven results in particular demographic segments. Female and minority participation in key executive positions, board representation, and other significant areas shows ample room for improvement. In the area of entrepreneurship, for instance, various studies have demonstrated that women and minorities receive far less venture funding and are also significantly underrepresented in the asset management firms that make investment decisions. (See Figure 9.1.) Beyond inequities involving class, race, and gender, the rewards are increasingly concentrated among a few groups, in a few cities, among people with degrees from a few select schools, though that is starting to change.[3] And while American history has demonstrated openness to immigrants, industries like manufacturing and small business that had afforded opportunity in the past no longer fill that role.

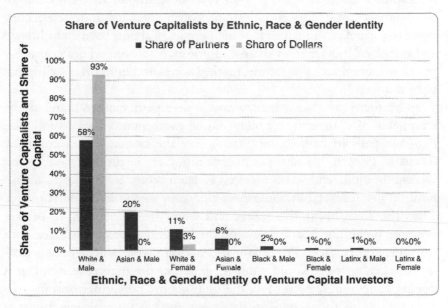

Figure 9.1 Share of venture capitalists by race, ethnic, and gender identity.

Source: Courtesy of Elizabeth Edwards, H Venture Partners; Richard Kerby, Equal Ventures; and Knight Foundation/Knight Diversity of Asset Managers Research Series, December 7, 2021.

Finally, increased evidence of climate change is dramatically changing the way people think about companies and their responsibilities. This was already underway in the consumer market, where organic foods, sustainable brands, and recycled goods had been gaining in popularity for decades. But climate worries also sparked an overall challenge to corporate governance. The environmental, social, and governance (ESG) movement is pushing companies to do more in all of these areas, prompting management to confront social and political issues as part of their responsibilities. ExxonMobil, one of the largest firms in the world, lost a very public proxy contest on climate worries, waking up many to the possibilities for changing the way public companies might be governed. Institutional investors, both of their own accord and as result of pressure from their clients, supported this change; it was not a government mandate.

Challenging Big Tech and Revisiting Antitrust

The rising power of the technology giants has galvanized many critics, with some arguing that the past 40 years of hands-off antitrust enforcement enabled vast concentrations of power in many industries. They point to dozens of industries in which big incumbents have consolidated and increased their market share and power. And even where consumer prices remained low, they argue, market access and entrepreneurship has been reduced.[4]

The focus on consumer welfare, rather than market share, as the barometer of competition policy has allowed incumbents to follow a two-step path to market domination, say the critics. First a company invests in growth. It keeps prices low, innovates in product quality and accessibility, and wins customers away from rivals. It gains a dominant position in a market, but consumers are happy so regulators don't object. Then the company shifts strategy and works on monetizing its market position, including creating new products and services that squeeze out suppliers and vendors. Prices rise and overall investment falls. In a normal market, upstarts would enter to undercut the market leader. But it doesn't happen here because of the incumbents' powerful position.

Once again, the tech giants have been the most prominent targets of criticism. The largest platforms of Facebook (Meta), Apple, Amazon, and Google (Alphabet), along with Microsoft, now dominate much of people's lives in areas such as media and e-commerce, and these companies collect so much data on users that they have an additional competitive advantage over upstarts. The range of services they provide raises the switching costs, while network effects from large numbers of users enable the companies to extract huge rents from third parties while creating barriers to new entrants. As the tech giants continue to gather and mine data, ranging from consumer preferences and user history to emerging product and service needs, the advantage continues to compound. The imbalance is so great that, instead of competing head-on, many upstarts now hope to simply to cash out to the incumbents for a hefty price. The continuing stream of upstarts may not be serious challengers but simply product development vehicles that can be absorbed into entrenched oligopolies as needed.

As with the natural monopolies of earlier eras, these critics call for supervision of Big Tech even though their competitive advantage is not directly a result of government privilege. Railroads, utilities, and even important patent pools were regulated or shared in prior periods, and some today claim we need a similar approach with the tech giants. After all, the now lightly regulated telecommunications companies are still closely watched.

Moreover, Microsoft's playbook from the 1990s remains a standard today: the other major platforms are also bundling offerings, quickly copying new features, and acquiring companies before they become threats. These incumbents argue that they are simply innovating or trying to stay current with competition or consumer taste, and that we need companies to stay nimble to compete in the global market. But both critics and some upstarts argue that the tech giants are essentially copying innovations and plucking off opportunities as soon as they ripen. As a result, they say, the incumbents are now not only preserving their dominant market positions, but also expanding in dangerous ways, far more than the industrial oligopolists of the early 20th century ever could. Facebook is influencing most of the media world. Google is leveraging its understanding of users to undercut advertisers and enter new businesses. Apple's closed marketplace is extracting hefty fees from app developers and content providers. Amazon controls an ever-larger portion of consumer wallets and is using that position to undermine its suppliers. Information technology, the great engine of economic revival in the late 20th century, threatens to undermine our entrepreneurial dynamism in the 21st.[5]

The only solution, according to these critics, is stronger antitrust action at the federal level. They claim that digital technology has overwhelmed market forces, and that only government intervention can save consumers and preserve the public interest.[6] Most of these critics call for dismembering or otherwise weakening the tech giants, such as by forcing them to spin off recent acquisitions or business units. And the Biden administration has listened, with many of the most prominent critics of Big Tech and large incumbents now heading antitrust enforcement.

Interestingly, much of the hostility toward Big Tech originates from incumbents both large and small in the same industries, under the theory that "the enemy of my enemy is my friend." Big-box retailers such as Home Depot and Target are making strange bedfellows with Main Street small businesses in arguing against the power of the tech giants. Big telecommunications companies, traditional newspaper and media firms, and many other traditionally strong firms also claim to be disadvantaged. To some outside the fray, it appears that antitrust, to the extent it is active at all, has become an arena of contest among interest groups and countervailing powers. In fact, proposed legislation to curb tech platforms from offering competing products seems to ignore the fact that large retailers such as Costco and Target have been doing this for years, to the delight of consumers.[7] Given the fluidity of industry definitions and range of interests, it is easy to see how consumer welfare became a standard that could cut through the complexity.

But this is starting to change. Given their size and power, Google, Amazon, and Facebook have each come under scrutiny for using their position and data to squeeze out rivals and limit new entrants, while Apple has faced a private action that argued many of the same principles. In its case against Google, the government alleged that the company was unfairly securing its position as the default search engine for computers and smartphones (including paying Apple $12 billion annually) and then using that position to increase leverage with digital advertisers. States also brought separate actions involving Google's use of its dominant position in the search field to parlay that into deeper engagement in specific categories, known as "vertical search." A new DOJ case in 2021 explored its control over digital advertising technology.

A case in the District of Columbia claimed that Amazon used its position to pressure third parties to set prices, the first major antitrust case against the company in the United States. With respect to Apple, third-party Epic Games argued that the AppStore ecosystem was too restrictive in requiring that all billing and enrollment take place within its marketplace. Finally, the case against Facebook related to its acquisition of "nascent" competitors, but the claim that its acquisitions of Instagram and WhatsApp were part of a "buy and bury" scheme was hard to support. The government lost this case in 2021, but the FTC modified the complaint in a new attempt a few months later.

Amid these calls for government intervention, entrepreneurial capitalism continues to demonstrate a more direct and potentially more effective way of responding to Big Tech, best illustrated in the story of Marc Lore. A "baby-buster" born in 1970, a math whiz from New Jersey, he had joined Credit Suisse's London office after college. He soon quit to start his own venture, "The Pit," an eBay rival focused on collectibles. He sold out to Topps in 2001 and joined that company. Then in 2005, as a time-starved new father annoyed with the hassle of getting supplies, he quit and cofounded 1-800-DIAPERS, later Diapers.com. The business grew rapidly with Lore's focus on membership-driven discounting, using algorithms to find low-cost suppliers. The success convinced him to expand to a portfolio of websites, called Quidsi, all catering to young families in urban areas.

Amazon noticed and offered to buy Quidsi in 2009, which Lore rejected. Spurned, it cut prices on diapers by 30%. Lacking the deep pockets to sustain a price war, Lore put Quidsi up for a sale a year later. Amazon beat out Walmart with $545 million bid, and Lore joined it as a high-level executive.

He could have accepted the embrace of Big Tech incumbency, but he soon quit to scratch his entrepreneurial itch yet again. This time he aimed at a kind of Quidsi on steroids, which became Jet.com in 2014. With his Amazon proceeds as the foundation, he attracted more than a billion dollars for the venture. It aimed to be "the Costco of the internet," with ever more sophisticated algorithms to reduce prices – unlike Amazon, which focused on convenience and cross-selling.

Meanwhile Walmart's stores were losing out to fast-growing Amazon, and its own online sales were sputtering. So it bought the two-year-old Jet in 2016 for a whopping $3.3 billion. Jet immediately became the center of Walmart's e-commerce operations, with Lore as its hard-driving head working to disrupt the incumbent.[8] Once he had the operation in place, he quit in 2019 to form a new venture, a food tech upstart he called Wonder Group to disrupt emerging incumbents DoorDash and Uber Eats. And Walmart.com is now a viable competitor in e-commerce, with its online sales growing faster than Amazon's.[9]

Lore's story counters the pessimism of antitrust critics who think entrepreneurs are helpless against tech giants. His success suggests that technology has enabled upstart competition just as much as it has undermined it. There is always room for innovation, speed, and fresh approaches. Despite two powerful incumbents in place, Lore found a way into the market and consumers responded favorably. And even when an innovator such as Lore sells out to a bigger firm, this assists in helping large firms to stay competitive. In fact, it is part of a virtuous cycle in which the strengths of both start-ups and established firms can benefit.

Building on this story, there are several reasons why aggressive antitrust may be problematic or even undesirable. The first is that the targeted platforms deliver real value to consumers. As in the case of A&P a hundred years ago and many antitrust cases since, the objections to the Big Tech platforms are not coming from consumers, who continue to buy goods on Amazon, conduct searches on Google, and download apps from Apple at record numbers. Moreover, these firms have facilitated consumer trust and adoption of new services by standardizing important marketplace rules and easing important functions such as billing.

Second, there is a strong argument that these platforms actually help new companies reach the market much more quickly and with greater scale. Despite the argument that Big Tech firms use their position to copy ideas, most new start-ups benefit greatly from being able to make their products known on Google, sold through Amazon or other e-commerce marketplaces, or downloaded on an app store. And in some cases, the brand recognition they achieve may give them leverage over the platforms themselves over time, as Epic and Jet.com have demonstrated. Similarly, many new service providers can quickly launch through service marketplaces and even establish direct customer relationships as a result. Here, too, it is often incumbent retailers, media firms, or taxicab medallion owners that are pushing back.

Third, it is important that large firms be allowed or even encouraged to evolve. In the 1970s and '80s, academics, corporate strategists, and policymakers worried about America's global competitiveness, fearing that companies did not move quickly enough; now, they seem to lament that corporations have become too nimble and too competitive. As noted in Chapter 2, companies have learned over the last several decades the importance of digital transformation and the need to be mindful of technology changes to survive, much less thrive. This is particularly the case when new technologies are developing quickly and venture capital is available.

Fourth, the major technology platforms themselves may be more vulnerable than many people first think.[10] Facebook overtook Myspace and other companies, but TikTok has grown quickly and now rivals it for attention. Apple has faced pushback from third parties who bristle at some of its rules and restrictions, and it commands a smaller market share in software for mobile devices than Google's Android. Amazon has faced challenges in categories such as home goods and pet supplies, not to mention marketplaces such as Etsy and Shopify and the Marc Lore–rejuvenated Walmart.com. While the tech giants' platforms look to lock in eyeballs, consumers may be more fickle than many critics imagine.[11]

Fifth, there is the issue of the corporate life cycle. Many great firms lose their energy when the founding entrepreneur leaves. A&P and U.S. Steel saw this happen, as did Apple when Steve Jobs left the company in 1985. Back in 2015, the *New York Times* reported that Jeff Bezos was creating a harsh work environment at Amazon. In meetings he would point in the direction of his Seattle corporate neighbor and tell managers he didn't want his organization to fall into Microsoft's complacency. He fretted that Amazon's success and market power would dull the organization to emerging threats. Boasting that the company's standards are "unreasonably high," he has the company follow "purposeful Darwinism" with annual culling of staff.[12] But this drive is extraordinarily hard to maintain, and it remains to be seen if the company can continue to operate at the same pace after Bezos's recent departure as chief executive.[13]

Even when entrepreneurs hand over the reins to able corporate executives, size and organizational dynamics can take a toll. Throughout American history, every company that became large eventually succumbed to stasis, complacency, infighting, and conservatism that rendered it incapable of keeping up with market trends. A glaring recent case is General Electric, which in the 1990s had seemingly reinvented itself for the 21st century. It was making all the right moves, transforming itself as a digital powerhouse, becoming the most valuable company at the height of the "New Economy" of 1999. But a mix of arrogance and insularity put it on the ropes by 2018.[14] Even companies that continue to survive often break themselves up voluntarily to remain competitive. The great icon of Silicon Valley, Hewlett-Packard, is a prime example.

Finally, antitrust and economic regulation are hard to get right. In an environment with lots of venture capital available and new technologies being developed constantly, even fast-moving and well-run companies that are on high alert for opportunities can find it hard to adapt, and this applies all the more so for governments, with political and special interests weighing in. While it is important to keep incumbents honest by peering over their shoulders from time to time, there are plenty of cases in which well-intentioned government action has led to unintended consequences. Government action to force Kodak to open its service market contributed to the company's decline, even if failure to move quickly on digital photography was the main cause. Recent efforts to

restrict book publishers from merging might actually help the tech platforms by limiting the potential for countervailing powers to develop.[15]

Good faith attempts to protect consumer privacy and control, such
as recent European and California regulations requiring consent for the
use of tracking cookies, can backfire; the regulations led to restrictions
on "third-party cookies" that hurt many small app providers.[16] As one
expert explains in his *Laws of Disruption,* lawyers, judges, and regulators
need to be mindful of intervening quickly or aggressively, because
"technology changes exponentially, but social, economic, and legal systems change incrementally."[17]

Perhaps the greatest evidence of the ability of American entrepreneurial capitalism to reinvigorate itself is the continued rise in the
number of unicorns, the success of countless smaller start-ups, unre-
lenting expansion in venture capital, and the new innovations that
come to market daily. In 2021, more than 5.4 million people in the
United States filed an application to start a business, higher than even
before the pandemic. All this is happening independent of the power
of Big Tech, or even arguably as a consequence of them. And while
there is merit in ensuring these giants do not overstep bounds, the
inherent dynamism of an entrepreneurial economy, coupled with the
virtue of a mixed economy that leverages both new upstarts and large
incumbents, argues against aggressive antitrust or regulation. Such
interventions risk impeding the economic successes that the country
has witnessed over the past several decades.

Assessing European Capitalism and Regulation

For many critics of the American entrepreneurial economy, particularly those focused on social issues, the economic model prevailing in
the European Union has broad appeal. Strong government administrative oversight in the E.U. has ensured more rights for workers, a
stronger social safety net, and protections for small businesses. This
model comes with expansive government, heavy regulation, and some
government ownership of stocks and industry. Banks, workers, and
governments have greater say over the corporation, sometimes referred
to as "co-determination," including workers councils that limit layoffs
or restrict innovation. There are also more assertive mandates for
addressing climate change. European competition policy is often a
misnomer, as noncompetition and protection are typically the actual
goals. The grand bargain between interests has created an environment

that tends toward stability and the status quo. The drawback, however, is difficulty for market entrants, less innovation, and higher consumer prices.[18]

Such drawbacks have attracted the attention of policymakers in Europe, many of whom have tried to liberalize their own laws to become more entrepreneurial. Emmanuel Macron of France is a prominent example, having publicly proclaimed a desire to open up the economy, though pushback from the "yellow vests" and challenges related to COVID have impeded progress toward that goal. Moreover, domestic politics continues to add roadblocks meant to deter innovators coming in from outside or disrupting traditional industries from within.[19] Institutional investment in new ventures also lags.[20] Even in Germany, the most productive economy in Europe, which has effectively managed liberalization along with coordinated government, feels pressure on its economic model. The ongoing move toward the knowledge economy is challenging the country's long-standing institutional consensus.[21] Meanwhile, the United Kingdom, which shares many of the features of the United States system, is also trying to increase its entrepreneurial ecosystem in the wake of Brexit.[22]

Because of these strong country-by-country interests, European entrepreneurs face a fragmented political marketplace. It takes them longer to access a large market and reach scale than in the United States, as illustrated by the difference between Uber and its European counterparts noted at the beginning of the book. While both the American and European competitors have fought to work through local regulations and political fallout on the Continent, Uber's and Lyft's start in the larger and relatively open American market allowed them to more quickly gain scale, develop technologies, and raise capital, an advantage that European firms are still struggling to achieve.

The European Union was founded in part to create a common market, but it is only decades old, much younger than the political and institutional histories of the constituent countries. As described in earlier chapters, the American structures took many decades to develop. While the federal government assured the triumph of a single market, the balance between national and local interests continued throughout. Similarly, the right to compete and the ability to challenge the status quo took time, even as the strong constitutional system ensured that rights obtained in a dispute in one state would carry through to the others. In Europe, each country maintains more control over swaths of their economies, deterring many features of a common market and leading to fragmented enterprises in many industries.[23]

Nevertheless, two features of the European model have received particular attention in the United States. The first is the approach of the European Commission to Big Tech. Over the past few years alone, the commission has brought actions against Apple (regarding app store streaming services), Amazon (over unfair use of sales data to favor in-house products over third parties), Google (alleging unfair use of advertising technology to the detriment of other advertisers and online publishers), and Facebook (involving use of advertising data to enhance its classified ads marketplace). The European Commission has also levied large fines on American digital companies. The commission has had a long history in fining Microsoft for alleged abuses involving its market dominance, while Google has had to pay large penalties for using its Android app to enhance its position in general search and for restricting third-party websites from showing competing advertising.[24] Other noteworthy actions have penalized Amazon (fined by the Italian government for favoring its own logistics service) and Facebook (for violating privacy rules). Similarly, regulations such as digital service taxes in certain countries and the European Union's proposed Digital Services Act and Digital Markets Act seek to limit the power of Big Tech, even at the cost of discouraging innovation and deterring new entrants.[25]

The common feature of many of these actions appears to be an effort to limit disruption by primarily American digital firms of the European market, protecting large incumbents and small firms. Because apps and similar technologies are so easy to access, the new technology platforms have been able to cross geographic and political boundaries more readily than innovators from prior eras. In doing so they have upset the political and institutional compromises that protected the status quo relationships among the participants. Much of the European regulators' attention has been focused on preserving and even protecting those compromises and their local industries, rather than in expanding the market, increasing innovation, and enabling competition or new upstarts. Yet this may be changing, as the number of domestic unicorns has been increasing.[26] This trend may increase pressure to open up markets to competition.

European regulations involving data privacy are more promising and have encouraged critics of the American model, as these regulations tend to promote transparency and even consumer choice. For instance, the General Data Protection Regulations (GDPR) passed in 2016 have given consumers more control over their data. The act is similar to legislation in certain states, notably California, as well as several other countries. While the concept behind the regulations makes sense, they will need to be monitored to ensure that they achieve the desired objectives and do not result in unexpected outcomes, as noted earlier.[27]

The second area in which European governments are taking a more active role than their American counterparts is in managing climate change and social responsibility. The EU began its foray into corporate governance in 2013 and by 2020 had passed the Sustainable Finance Disclosure Regulation (SFDR) to require disclosures regarding social and environmental measures, including penalties for noncompliance. This has been quickly followed by Corporate Sustainability Reporting Directive (CSRD) for nonfinancial firms.[28] These provisions are stronger and more assertive than those found in the United States, which remains focused on reporting and accountability to shareholders rather than "stakeholders" broadly. As a result of these disclosures, more executives are paying attention to climate change and in many cases compensation is in part tied to progress on those goals. In several countries, directors are even being held accountable for addressing sustainability as part of their fiduciary duties.[29] Of course, many American companies also report on sustainability and corporate social responsibility, but such reports are voluntary and critics often view them skeptically as "greenwashing."[30]

While disclosure and transparency are essential, the European approach of more assertive government involvement in corporate governance brings with it great risks both to entrepreneurship and innovation as well as to sustainability. As noted in earlier chapters, heavy direct political involvement frequently leads to the misallocation of resources, inefficient use of capital, and reduced global competitiveness.[31] It can also make it more difficult for activist shareholders to push for change or hold management accountable.[32] One can easily imagine initiatives in the boardroom leading to decisions that are geared simply to meeting measurements that may prove inappropriate, unable to gain traction in the market, or susceptible to regulatory capture or cronyism. Moreover, heavy mandates may discourage innovators or investors from finding new approaches that might be quite effective but are not within specific guidelines. They may also deter the adoption and spread of new technologies, result in less choice and lead to higher consumer prices.

By contrast, America's more bottom-up and market-based approach may be more effective in making change, with less risk of cronyism or bureaucracy. In particular, while shareholder activism is often messy and uneven, it forces competing views and broader debate on important topics. It also enables firms, including management, boards, and diverse shareholders, to mediate among competing interests and find company- and industry-specific strategies to achieve sustainability goals. The United States also has a stronger tradition of securities class action litigation, an important enforcement mechanism related to shareholder activism.[33] The dramatic increase in ESG among both individual and institutional investors suggests that investors may be able to drive both sustainability as well as economic performance and find the right way to balance objectives. The recent success of the activist firm Engine No. 1 in winning a proxy contest involving ExxonMobil, as well as BlackRock CEO Larry Fink's letters to clients around the mission of corporations, demonstrate that change can happen without top-down mandates.[34] Certainly, more disclosure helps, but attempting to address the problems exclusively or even primarily through government mandates will shortchange the potential for entrepreneurial solutions.

Understanding China and Authoritarian Capitalism

Just a few months before the 1989 fall of the Berlin Wall, Chinese citizens gathered in Beijing's Tiananmen Square to protest against their autocratic government and to advocate for democratic reforms. The movement appeared as generational as the ones at the Brandenburg Gate. The outcome in the near term proved far different, however, as the Chinese government brutally suppressed the protests. Yet many of the forces that had fueled it remained and even accelerated in the following decades.

When Deng Xiaoping announced that "to get rich is glorious" in 1978, few would have anticipated how adeptly Chinese citizens would pursue that mission. Deng pushed hard for reforms that helped spur accountability and productivity and sought "capitalism with Chinese characters." The township and village enterprise initiative in the mid-1980s gave local towns and factories more latitude in managing facilities and operations. Deng's policy of "reform and opening," and his lifting of the "bamboo curtain," proved critical to the country's development, even if a strong authoritarian undercurrent remained.[35] It was Deng, in fact, who authorized the crackdown in Tiananmen Square.

But even Deng would have been surprised by the explosion of entrepreneurial activity he helped to unleash. Between 1980 and 2020, the country's economy grew more than 10% annually. By 2021, the country had enabled more than 172 "unicorns," as befitting what is now the world's second largest economy.[36] The number of billionaires grew dramatically, and while poverty remains an issue in many parts of the country, the astounding rise of the middle class has created a stable base of consumers and educated workers likely to propel growth well into the future.

Nevertheless, authoritarianism dies hard. And just as America and other countries may be facing an inflection point, the events of 2021 suggest that a pullback of a different sort may be underway in China. Under paramount leader Xi Jinping, the country has recently been executing a remarkable redirection. Partly to cement his party's control over the country, Xi has reined in its high-flying tech leaders and cracked down on the entrepreneurial enclave of Hong Kong.[37] Instead of encouraging these would-be role models and national champions, he has forced them to retreat from world capital markets – making it harder for them to achieve global network effects for their platforms. While Xi's focus on "common prosperity" and his "new development concept," which includes efforts to reduce inequality and protect privacy, may appeal to some, many of the policies appear to be simply attempts at securing government control.[38] To get rich may still be glorious, just not too rich.[39]

Didi's recent travails, discussed briefly at the outset of this book, question whether entrepreneurship and authoritarianism can coexist over the long term. While entrepreneurship is continuing at a torrid pace, the economy is still in relatively early stages of development. The issue keeps coming back to creative destruction. Economists have long pointed to the "middle-income trap" as a risk many developed countries face. While countries ranging from Argentina to Japan have been able to jump-start their economies through assertive state actions, success also makes it easy for cozy oligopolies to settle in. Political institutions and economic actors tend to converge. Entrepreneurship becomes difficult and innovators become discouraged or even fearful.[40]

Perhaps the most interesting question is whether and how entrepreneurship might ultimately change the political institutions in the country and drive reform over time. As one observer has noted, China has a long-standing suspicion of entrepreneurship, viewing the economy as a "bird in a cage" that must be given room, but not released.[41] But once the successes are tasted, the entrepreneurial spirit is hard to contain, and many experts have noted how wealth and economic development can help foster democracy.[42]

The historian Niall Ferguson has painted several plausible scenarios in which China loses its momentum. The first involves natural stagnation from declining economic and political competitiveness, perhaps triggered by the collapse of a bubble (the recent Evergrande real estate debacle could be a harbinger). A decline in entrepreneurship may be a component, as the detention of high-profile executives such as Jack Ma and the crackdown on liberties in Hong Kong and elsewhere may scare off would-be innovators. The second scenario involves social unrest brought about by inequality, though here that very crackdown on excessive entrepreneurship may stem the tide. The third scenario is political unrest from the rising middle classes demanding more participation and other reforms – though if successful this movement could reverse the trend to authoritarianism and reignite entrepreneurship. Finally, China's aggressive foreign policy may lead to coalitions among neighboring countries and Western nations that halt the expansion and discredit the government.[43]

Regardless of how these or other scenarios unfold, the development of the Chinese economy and political system will clearly continue to be an important backdrop for America over the next several decades. Whether China picks up its entrepreneurial momentum again or retrenches into its authoritarian model, America's best path forward will be to keep its own entrepreneurial engine humming with enhancements to address its shortcomings.

The Only Thing to Fear

The United States is largely in control of its own economic destiny. As the long history of entrepreneurship has demonstrated, the country's unique political, institutional, and cultural forces are well equipped to evolve to meet changing needs and opportunities as they emerge. Closely linked with the country's form of democratic government and highly responsive to consumer preferences, the system has proved resilient and responsive, if also contentious and messy at times.

This entrepreneurial spirit has been leveraged continually throughout the country's history, both to identify and seize new opportunities as well as to serve as a natural check on incumbency. Many of the social issues that need to be addressed today are likely to have entrepreneurially driven solutions tomorrow. Many underserved markets remain untapped, while a whole range of sustainable solutions are just finding their way into the marketplace. Similarly, the natural forces of "creative destruction," spurred on by changes in demographics and consumer trends, paradigm shifts enabled by new technologies, and the natural limitations of large firms as they mature, will most likely limit power of now-dominant companies in ways that government action cannot or should not, keeping the country competitive along the way.

As the examples of Europe, China, and indeed most other countries show, addressing these issues through assertive government action can lead to stagnation, cronyism, and even worse. The challenge we now face is how to build on the country's unique strength to ameliorate the social costs and ensure that the balance between upstarts and incumbents, large firms and small, and property and competition remain in place. During certain periods, the country has swung in one direction or another, sometimes favoring upstarts or incumbents, big government or small, property rights or the right to compete. Yet the system has always largely self-corrected, thanks in large part to the open political arena. So long as policymakers understand the bounds of the system, and citizens–consumers–shareholders recognize when extremes are approaching, the system is well positioned to work through issues and remain strong in the years ahead.

Endnotes

1. Chase Peterson-Withorn, "How Much Money America's Billionaires Have Made During the Covid-19 Pandemic," Forbes.com, April 30, 2021.
2. For useful context on how wealth has been viewed in America, see Robert F. Dalzell, *The Good Rich and What They Cost Us: The Curious History of Wealth, Inequality, and American Democracy* (New Haven: Yale University Press, 2013), and Kevin Phillips, *Wealth and Democracy: A Political History of the American Rich* (New York: Penguin Random House, 2003).
3. See, e.g., "Beyond Silicon Valley: Coastal Dollars and Local Investors Accelerate Early-Stage Startup Funding Across the U.S., Rise of the Rest," Revolution.com/Rise of the Rest.
4. See, e.g., Barry Lynn, *Cornered: The New Monopoly Capitalism and the Economics of Destruction* (Hoboken, NJ: John Wiley & Sons, 2010), and Matt Stoller, *Goliath: The 100-Year War Between Monopoly Power and Democracy* (New York: Simon & Schuster, 2019).
5. David Wessel, "Is Lack of Competition Strangling the U.S. Economy?" *Harvard Business Review*, March–April 2018; Tyler Cowen, *The Complacent Class: The Self-Defeating Quest for the American Dream* (New York: St. Martin's Press, 2017).
6. Tim Wu, *The Curse of Bigness: Antitrust in the New Gilded Age* (New York: Columbia Global Reports, 2018), and Lina Khan, "Amazon's Antitrust Paradox," *Yale Law Journal* 126, no. 3 (January 2017): 564–907. See also Amy Klobuchar, *Antitrust: Taking on Monopoly Power from the Gilded Age to the Digital Age* (New York: Alfred A. Knopf, 2021).

7. Michael R. Bloomberg, "A Bipartisan Bad Idea: Congress's attack on tech companies would hurt consumers, workers and the economy," Bloomberg.com, January 28, 2022.

8. Ari Levy, "New Details on Amazon's Move to Shutter the Company It Bought for $545 million," CNBC.com, April 3, 2017, https://www.cnbc.com/2017/04/03/amazon-was-sucking-in-quidsis-inventory-over-a-year-before-shutdown.html. "Who is Marc Lore?" Yosuccess.com, January 7, 2016, https://www.yosuccess.com/success-stories/marc-lore-jet/.

9. Richard Kestenbaum, "Walmart Is Gaining on Amazon in Ecommerce," Forbes.com, October 20, 2021.

10. Jonathan Knee, The Platform Delusion: Who Wins and Who Loses in the Age of Tech Titans (New York: Penguin Random House, 2021).

11. See, e.g., "How Shopify Outfoxed Amazon to Be the Everywhere Store," Bloomberg.com, December 25, 2021; Ashley Gold, "TikTok Surpassed Google as the Most Popular Site in 2021," Axios.com, December 22, 2021.

12. Jodi Kantor and David Streitfeld, "Inside Amazon: Wrestling Big Ideas in a Bruising Workplace," New York Times, August 15, 2015, https://www.nytimes.com/2015/08/16/technology/inside-amazon-wrestling-big-ideas-in-a-bruising-workplace.html.

13. Andrew Ross Sorkin, "Bezos Departure Letter," Dealbook, April 16, 2021, and "Amazon After Bezos," Dealbook, July 2, 2021.

14. See, e.g., Thomas Gryta and Ted Mann, Lights Out: Pride, Delusion and the Fall of General Electric (New York: Houghton Mifflin Harcourt, 2020).

15. See Rudolph J.R. Peritz, Competition Policy in America: History, Rhetoric, Law (New York: Oxford University Press, 2001), 318; Eastman Kodak v. Image Technical Services (1992) (Kodak had 80–95% of the service market and the Court decided that the customer "lock-in" was too strong). See also U.S. vs. Apple Inc., 952 F.Supp. 2d, (S.D.N.Y. 2013) (case against e-book retailers, including Hachette and other major publishers); and Iain Murray, "DOJ's Case Against Publishers Is an Overreach," November 24, 2021, Competitive Enterprise Institute (challenging merger of Penguin Random House and Simon & Schuster).

16. Jessica Davies, "The Unintended Consequences of the shift from third-party to first-party cookies," Digiday.com, September 26, 2019.

17. Larry Downes, The Laws of Disruption: Harnessing the New Forces That Govern Life and Business in the Digital Age (New York: Basic Books, 2009).

18. See William J. Baumol, Robert E. Litan, and Carl J. Schramm, Good Capitalism, Bad Capitalism and the Economics of Growth and Prosperity (New Haven: Yale University Press, 2007), 188–227 (discussing "Eurosclerosis and Japanese Stagnation" and the Lisbon Agenda). See also Thomas K. McKraw, Creating Modern Capitalism: How Entrepreneurs, Companies, and Countries Triumphed in Three Industrial Revolutions (Cambridge, MA: Harvard University Press, 1998), 144 (noting the evolving role of the consumer in the U.S. compared with Europe).

19. Rebecca Rosman, "A new law in France aims to protect indie bookshops against outsized Amazon competition," *World,* October 27, 2021 (new law in France regulates book delivery fees to help counter Amazon's competitive advantage). See also Angelique Christafis, "French MPs pass bill to curb Amazon's discounts on books," *Guardian,* February 22, 2013, and Pascal-Emmanuel Gobry, "The Failure of the French Elite," WSJ.com, February 22, 2019.

20. Philippe Aghion, Céline Antonin, and Simon Bunel, *The Power of Creative Destruction: Economic Upheaval and the Wealth of Nations* (Cambridge MA: Belknap Press, 2021), 243 (U.S. has 84x the amount of investment by institutions going into young companies compared with France).

21. Sebastian Diessner, Nicolo Durazzi, David Hope, "Skill-based liberalization: Germany's transition to the knowledge-economy," University of Edinburgh, April 13, 2021.

22. "Why Have We Not Grown Any Giant Companies? The U.K.'s Attempt to Take on Silicon Valley," publicnews.in, September 23, 2021.

23. America also has more political change at the top than most European countries and certainly more than authoritarian countries such as China. This means less political monopoly and also higher stakes for regime changes in those countries. See, e.g., Niall Ferguson, *Civilization: The West and the Rest* (New York: Penguin, 2011), 47.

24. "Here are some of the largest fines dished out by the EU," CNBC.com, June 27, 2017.

25. Alke Asen and Daniel Bunn, "What European OECD Countries Are Doing About Digital Services Taxes," Tax Foundation, November 22, 2021.

26. "Europe has now created more unicorns than China" Sifted, August 20, 2021.

27. See also Joe Nocera, "How cookie bans backfired," *New York Times,* January 29, 2022.

28. Cary Springfield, "What Is the Sustainable Finance Disclosure Regulation?," International Banker, April 13, 2021, https://internationalbanker.com/finance/what-is-the-sustainable-finance-disclosure-regulation/#:~:text=According%20to%20the%20official%20wording,the%20provision%20of%20sustainability%E2%80%90related.

29. See, e.g., Financial Reporting Council U.K. Stewardship Code 2020 (more than 20 countries have signed on). See also "The Duty of UK Directors to Consider Relevant ESG Factors," Debevoise & Plimpton Report, September 2019.

30. See, e.g., Alex Edman, "What Stakeholder Capitalism Can Learn from Milton Friedman," ProMarket, September 10, 2020, and Lucian A. Bebchuk and Robert Tallerita, "Will Corporations Deliver Value to All Stakeholders?" *Vanderbilt Law Review* 75 (May 2022).

31. See, e.g., Mark Roe, *Political Determinants of Corporate Governance* (New York: Oxford University, 2006) ("politics can press managers to stabilize employment, to forego some profit-maximizing risks with the firm, and to use

capital in place rather than to downsize when markets are no longer aligned with the firms production capabilities").

32. For example, several high-profile boardroom battles in Japan and Italy show the challenges of making change at the corporate level in countries with traditions of fewer shareholder rights. See, e.g., Leo Lewis and Antoni Slodkowski, "Toshiba chief steps down abruptly," *Financial Times*, March 1, 2022 (discussing the turmoil at Toshiba and the clash between corporate governance and shareholder capitalism), and "Ciao, salotto buono," *Economist*, February 26, 2022 (discussing the struggle over governance at insurance company Generali).

33. See, e.g., John C. Coffee Jr., *Entrepreneurial Litigation: Its Rise, Fall, and Future* (Cambridge: Harvard University Press, 2015).

34. See "Business Roundtable 2019 Statement on the Purpose of a Corporation" (signed by 128 companies). See also Andrew Ross Sorkin, "BlackRock Chief Pushes Big New Climate Goals for the Corporate World," *New York Times*, January 26, 2021, and Adele Peters, "The inside story of how tiny hedge fund Engine No. 1 reshaped the Exxon's board," *Fast Company*, June 10, 2021.

35. "To Get Rich Is Glorious: How Deng Xiaoping Set China on a Path to Rule the World," *The Conversation*, July 9, 2021. See also Joyce Appleby, *Relentless Revolution: A History of Capitalism* (New York: W.W. Norton, 2010), 375–380; Daron Acemoglu and James A. Robinson, *Why Nations Fail: The Origins of Power, Prosperity, and Poverty* (New York: Crown Business, 2012); and Niall Ferguson, *Civilization: The West and the Rest* (New York: Penguin, 2011), 420–424, 437.

36. Tracxn, December 1, 2021.

37. George Calhoun, "What Really Happened to Jack Ma?" *Forbes*, June 24, 2021.

38. See, e.g., Li Yuan, "For China's Business Elites, Staying Out of Politics Is No Longer an Option," New York Times, July 6, 2021 and Li Yuan, "What China Expects from Business: Total Surrender," July 19, 2021.

39. See "China Economist Is Rare Voice of "Caution on 'Common Prosperity,'" Bloomberg, September 1, 2021 (discussing the warnings of liberal economist Zhang Weiyang of Peking University).

40. Aghion, Antonin, and Bunel, *The Power of Creative Destruction*.

41. See, e.g., Richard McGregor, *The Party: The Secret World of China's Communist Leaders* (New York: Penguin, 2013) and *Xi Jinping: The Backlash* (New York: Penguin Specials, 2019)

42. See, e.g., Acemoglu and Robinson, *Why Nations Fail*, 443. See also Seymour Martin Lipset, "Some Social Requisites of Democracy: Economic Development and Political Legitimacy," *American Political Science Review* 53, no. 1 (1959); Seymour Martin Lipset, *Political Man: The Social Bases of Politics* (New York: Doubleday & Co., 1960); and Marc F. Plattner, Larry Diamond, and Andrew Nathan, eds., "Will China Democratize?" *China Review International* 20, nos. 1–2 (2013): 145–150.

43. Niall Ferguson, *Civilization*, 319 (How Might China Stumble?), 422–424.

10

Maintaining the Entrepreneurial Advantage

A s we have seen over America's long economic history, entrepreneurial capitalism generates impressive innovation and renewal, as well as rising prosperity. Upstarts continue to develop new products and services, enter existing markets or create new ones, and challenge incumbents. Those that succeed in becoming industry leaders then face their own pressures to adapt. That process creates cycles of broad growth and productivity over a sustained period, as well as social mobility and even churn among politically powerful elites. Even if messy at times, this remarkable record has stood out globally for centuries, and has been in many respects the secret to America's economic success.

Since the fall of the Berlin Wall, and in the light of several decades of Silicon Valley's emergence as a global model, the consensus that entrepreneurship is a key driver of economic growth and development has taken root around the world. In fact, entrepreneurship and the benefits of investing in and encouraging start-up enterprises may be America's most powerful current export. Over the past several years, the growth in early-stage and venture capital investing has skyrocketed in many countries across the globe, and the number of unicorns based outside the United States has grown dramatically. Venture capital had a record year in 2021, including inside the United States, but it was also the first year in which more than half of all venture investments were made outside it.

Along with this success, another parallel consensus has emerged. This is the view that, however successful, capitalism as a whole and even dynamic entrepreneurial capitalism must be tweaked, adjusted, reimagined, or even saved.[1] Behind this view is the recognition that the system does not distribute opportunities, benefits, and rewards fairly, that some of the destruction from creative destruction is too severe, and that business contributes disproportionately to climate change without bearing enough of the costs. All these are serious social and economic challenges that both the private and the public sectors must work to address.

While some of the foregoing suggests a grand convergence across the world in acknowledging these issues, the manner with which each country encourages entrepreneurship while ameliorating the negative fallout is quite varied. As discussed in previous chapters, there are several different flavors of capitalism, each intertwined with the local political system. Countries vary in how they enable entrepreneurship while grappling with social issues. And, of course, in many cases the desire for political power and control trumps those goals altogether.

Fundamentally, America's strength is the result of its political economy and its supportive cultural factors. This includes an adversarial, competitive political and economic system and a liberal or relatively hands-off approach to government, which have largely enabled the upstart-incumbent dynamic, avoided prolonged cronyism, and allowed innovation to find its way into the marketplace. Alongside this is the country's reliance on the individual – not just as citizen but as entrepreneur, social entrepreneur, consumer, and, increasingly, as shareholder – to make decisions instead of government. While the effects are uneven and imperfect, individual interests rather than special interests largely determine outcomes. The drawbacks, as critics often point out, are that promoting economic growth and productivity gains can leave significant social challenges in its wake.

Americans instinctively distrust both big government and big powerful corporations, and efforts to limit one can often enable the other. The key challenge and opportunity in the United States is how to address issues such as inequality, inclusivity, and sustainability without killing the golden goose of entrepreneurial prosperity. The best approaches are those that require limited government involvement while leveraging America's inherent entrepreneurial energy. We can tackle key social issues either directly or as a byproduct of innovation, while counting on the broad tools available to individuals as consumers and shareholders. This is also especially critical in the current divisive political climate, in which extremes on both ends of the spectrum result in markedly different views on the role of government and a stalemate in many important areas. Much of the country still shares a common middle-ground understanding. America has always had a messy way of working through these challenges, but the balance that has led to the country's success may becoming harder to maintain.

The Continuing Balance

In order to maintain itself, the American institutional framework will need to continue to adjust to changes in the market brought about by entrepreneurially driven innovation and the dynamism between upstarts and incumbents. The balancing act between property rights and the right to compete has evolved with changes in the nature of property and competition over the past two centuries, and it will continue to do so. While property once meant only real property or government-issued charters, for example, it now includes limited corporate protections from regulation and even rights to a degree of political participation.[2] Similarly, as technology developed, the bounds of what could be patented morphed to include software menus and business methods.[3] The issue has become even more complicated as notions of property have merged into claims that incumbent companies possess their own inherent right to compete.

A thorny set of questions continually arises regarding "proprietary advantage," or the competitive advantages that firms seek to establish in the marketplace without any government support. This includes debates over whether manufacturers can dictate certain prices, distribution, use or repair of products downstream, or what a technology platform can require from third parties in terms of standards, billing, or fulfillment. The tension can even be seen in the employment market, as the use of confidentiality and noncompete agreements forces a balance between how far a company can assert property rights vis-à-vis former employees.

The ability of large technology platforms or marketplaces to collect enormous amounts of data from their networks has led to new questions about the classic balance between property and competition. One issue is the ownership and use of the data itself. Many of these firms have begun to look more like utilities, and consumers increasingly demand at least some ownership rights in their data. A related issue is the degree to which these firms can use the data from their platforms to create new products and services. In fact, many large firms such as Microsoft, Google, and Amazon have asserted their own right to compete or innovate to stay ahead of new market entrants, even if many of the ideas come as a result of the participation of third parties on their networks.

Finally, some marketplaces claim they are only intermediaries and use that position to isolate themselves from the liability of product or service providers themselves. Napster was unable to do this in the area of copyright infringement, but firms such as Facebook, Uber, and Airbnb have done this successfully to preserve their business model. In all these cases, the messy work of the American political economy continues.

The Foundations for Continued Success

Amid the internal divisiveness and external threats, it is easy to overlook the key features of American entrepreneurial capitalism and to seek reforms that might undermine it. Yet the building blocks to keep entrepreneurship thriving while also addressing the social issues more effectively are right in front of us.

Limited Government. America's separation of powers, federalist structure, independent judiciary, and individual rights have all combined to allow competing interests to balance themselves out over time and with some sense of process. The division of power, as well as the competition of interests articulated in Madison's *Federalist 10,* has not only kept political power in check, but it has also enabled upstarts to challenge incumbents. The danger is in allowing interest groups to become so powerful that they weaken the balancing act. Lobbying, whether from large companies or small business associations, not to mention financial institutions and private equity firms, continues to rise. The size of the American economy, along with the range of economic interests and political inputs, makes it harder for a small group to dominate here, as compared to many other countries. But the ability of certain groups to defend their interests with very specific policies still often results in protectionism or inequitable policies in areas such as taxation. One approach would be to reduce the role of money in politics; the better one would be to reduce the role of politics in money by limiting governmental involvement in the economy when possible.

As Jefferson reportedly said, "That government is best which governs least," but we still need state and federal governments to have some role in promoting economic activity. Most observers agree that government should not "pick winners" – favor specific companies through subsidies or ownership. On the opposite end, even libertarians recognize the need for strong government to apply the rule of law equally. In setting standards and enforcing contracts, governments are essential for properly functioning markets.

Between those extremes, governments have an enormous field of action. Infrastructure development is one important area, as can be seen throughout U.S. history from the Erie Canal to the interstate highway system to the internet. These investments not only spawn growth generally, but they also upset vested interests and create new opportunities for upstarts to jump in. Basic research has been another significant area; the country's investment in science helped create pathbreaking innovation in areas ranging from telecommunications to genomics. These types of new technologies can often translate into commercial applications that alter the playing field and enable upstarts, setting the foundation for further growth.[4]

The more difficult areas are in fields such as regulation. The hard part is that these are the areas in which special interests are most active and unintended consequences can be most significant. Even the details of standard setting and contract enforcement may affect innovation and competition. Almost every law and regulation will have differing impact on upstarts and incumbents and may alter the balance in favor of one or the other. Licensing, taxes, bankruptcy, intellectual property, antitrust, employment, safety, environmental – even jurisdiction and federalism – the list goes on. When technology is changing rapidly, it is hard for government to keep up.[5] And the more the government is involved, the more interest groups get engaged.[6] In these areas, America's separation of powers may be its best attribute, because it helps create guardrails and allows issues to self-correct over time.

To the extent they have been involved in the economic sphere, policymakers have done best when they have leveraged the respective strengths of upstarts and incumbents to the needs of the time, especially with carrots rather than sticks. Upstart entrepreneurs were essential to building infrastructure and developing the country in most of the 19th century. The young republic needed to attract human and financial capital, and it focused on securing property rights to enable new endeavors. As the country and its companies grew in size, government facilitated new legal mechanisms to promote stability, consolidation, and efficiency. At certain break points, policy changed to enable new structures, platforms, or technologies – the right to compete. In the first three-quarters of the 20th century, the federal government took advantage of large-scale industrial capacity and managerial expertise to meet global imperatives. But here, too, a shift eventually occurred, and deregulation and other policy responses opened new forms of competition and innovation.

The more government can harness or unleash the power of both new and established companies, rather than solve problems itself, the better. One example of effective government policy to support innovation has been consumer tax rebates for electric vehicles, which helped jump-start new technologies while forcing incumbent companies to adapt. Incentives such as these not only helped launch Tesla, but they eventually made Ford and GM better as well. By the same token, once special provisions serve their purpose they need to be retired. Section 230 of the Telecommunications Act of 1996 is a good example of legislation that was effective in supporting the growth of the internet era but now may have run its course. Some incentives, such as those to invest in "opportunity zones," may be successful in generating investment but their effectiveness must continue to be monitored.

A Bias for Market Access and Consumer Choice. Since its beginning, the American legal system has favored   innovation and market access over stability and rent-seeking. By abolishing primogeniture and perpetual trusts, boosting the rights of debtors, setting time limits on patents, and allowing the careful use of eminent domain, legislatures and courts promoted vigorous competition – in essence, the right to compete. Innovations have found daylight, while incumbents have had to stay on their toes.[7]

Much of the current policy debate relating to regulation and market access involves innovation and competition at the local level, and it echoes the struggles seen in earlier times. Tesla fights states over dealer franchise laws, Uber and Lyft intrude on local taxicab privileges, and Airbnb tussles over local hotel rules. These battles look similar to those of Swift fighting local meat inspectors and Singer developing a captive service network in the late 19th century. When local stores, service providers, or artists complain about the dominance of Amazon or Google or Apple, we tend to support the underdog as a cultural preference, but that often changes when cost or convenience are at stake.

Antitrust policy is often thornier. To many Progressives, reading Robert Bork's *Antitrust Paradox* (1978) is akin to reading *Mein Kampf.* Some blame Bork and other members of the Chicago School for ignoring or even abetting corporate consolidation and concentration and their broader implications. Yet over the last few decades, Bork's emphasis on consumer welfare has resulted in lower prices and often more choice. And the notion of putting consumers first was at the heart of Ralph Nader's movement as well. In fact, reducing government intervention when new technologies are developing and venture capital is readily available should actually help achieve Progressive goals. When one considers that most antitrust actions are the result of well-heeled companies seeking either to pry open market access for themselves or to protect their own market positions from other large companies, it is hard to see antitrust as more than interest group politics writ large or to argue with consumer welfare being the ultimate standard. Similarly, many claims about incumbents killing off nascent industries are hard to back up when new innovations are launched and find their way into the market every day. And even when consolidation and concentration have appeared, new entrants have often shown up to disrupt them. The tension between barriers to entry and market access is at the core of the upstart-incumbent dynamic. While government has a role to play in making sure rules are followed and illegal behavior is addressed, it should tread lightly in this area, especially where technology change is happening quickly.

Whether or not consumer welfare remains the antitrust standard, however, more should be done to understand the real issues associated with consumer choice, ownership of data, and switching costs in the digital era – these are essential for the right to compete and consumer decision making. In the 2001 Microsoft case, the government won commitments from the company to enable some degree of market access for competitors; those proved ineffective, but at least they raised the issue. Meanwhile telephone number portability under the Telecommunications Act of 1996 proved enormously effective. In recent years, more thought is going to the subtleties in consumer choice. Opening up billing systems, increasing disclosure requirements and privacy regulations regarding web-browser cookies, understanding the impact of "opt-in" versus "opt-out" marketing, and making it easier for consumers to stop automatic app subscription renewal – all of these regulations appear to support consumer benefit and choice and should be developed further going forward. But, as noted earlier, policymakers should be mindful of unintended consequences and be ready to adapt.

Inclusive Entrepreneurship. The success of the entrepreneurial economy has brought with it increased demands to broaden opportunity. Women, veterans, Blacks, Hispanics, and other groups are significantly underrepresented in the boardroom at the executive level, in the investor world, and in the start-up community, though this is beginning to change. Companies are increasingly recognizing the wealth of talent within these groups and their responsibility in leading change, and consumers, employees, and investors are demanding it. Similarly, the lion's share of technology ventures has been concentrated in San Francisco, Boston, New York, Austin, and a handful of other cities. And the graduates of a small number of colleges and universities tend to lead most of the biggest companies.

The opportunity here is not just about making the system fairer. There are many underserved markets throughout the country, and founders with diverse backgrounds are most likely to be able to find them. And, as new products and markets develop, many large incumbents might also get on the bandwagon, as we have seen in areas such as organic foods and electric vehicles.

One persistent issue has been the challenges faced by small business. For most of the country's history, starting a small business was the path to a good life, and it was an inclusive affair. Over the years, many first-generation immigrants got their start with local enterprise. With technology firms increasingly dominating commerce and service industries, however, many traditional small business opportunities are waning.

In fact, a new set of opportunities is emerging. Many of the platforms, from Amazon and Etsy to Uber and Angie, create marketplaces for third-party providers, and therefore open windows for small entrepreneurs. Similarly, the "gig economy" allows individual workers to sell directly to consumers rather than through traditional intermediaries or employers. During the pandemic alone, more than one million new businesses opened on Shopify, and 2021 was a record year for new business applications in the United States. Uber has disrupted the owners of taxicab medallions but has given many more drivers control of their destiny and better working conditions. By encouraging continued innovation and competition, we may continue to find unexpected new channels for entrepreneurship to flourish.

Decentralized Access to Finance. America has a strong tradition of supporting enterprises of all sizes with capital, and access to funding has generally been available across the full corporate life cycle. Small businesses, start-up innovators, growth companies, and big corporations have all generally been able to secure financing to commence, expand, innovate, and improve their efficiency and profitability, supported by a robust stock markets with the promise of liquidity for investors. The financial system's most important feature has been its decentralized nature – not relying on a handful of dominant institutions – and its ability to raise equity capital rather than relying on debt.

The United States has many of the largest money-center banks in the world ready to lend to large corporations, and during J.P. Morgan's heyday they were especially powerful. But the country also has a long history of small banks helping local enterprises to form and grow. While small banks can be inefficient and risky, they have been vital in enabling small companies to develop and thus open opportunities to more people. Though the number of local banks has declined steadily over the past decades, there has been recent attention to community banking, particularly in underserved communities, and other new sources of capital and microfinance have been increasing. The tradition of decentralized banking started early in the country and it remains important.[8]

America's public credit markets are often overlooked, but they also play a crucial role in helping innovators to scale. Civil War and railroad finance depended on public markets in the 19th century, while the development of the money market in the 20th century helped take control of the credit supply out of the hands of powerful banks. It also facilitated capital flowing in from abroad. Even more significant was the high-yield "junk bond" market in the 1980s, which enabled a degree of entrepreneurship unlikely in countries dominated by such banks. Companies such as MCI would probably not have been able to challenge AT&T without this market.

The relative abundance of equity capital and the strong public equity market in the United States is especially significant. The New York Stock Exchange is nearly as old as the country itself and has been a key enabler of the American entrepreneurial economy. The dream of an IPO has special allure for entrepreneurs and it ensures that investors will have the ability to sell their shares eventually. It also helps young firms raise more capital to grow and provides opportunities for the broad public to participate in the innovation economy. Strong equity markets also induce companies throughout the world to either locate in the United States or use it as base for its financial operations. It has helped make America the place where foreign technology ventures want to test and scale up their innovations and find an exit for their equity stakes.

Finally, readily available, risk-tolerant, early-stage equity has been essential to funding entrepreneurship, and it is one America's greatest features. While the venture capital explosion since the 1990s is the most obvious example, this tradition dates back much longer. Early investors included the Brown family of Rhode Island, who moved capital from shipping into manufacturing, and the China traders of a century later who helped develop the American West. The Whitneys, Cabots, and other wealthy families in the early 20th century, motivated to keep their capital active, funded a great many new industries, including aviation. But the phenomenon is more than just successful entrepreneurs moving their resources to the next big thing. America's legal and financial systems have also been effective in enabling this type of investment. This includes the broad definition of fiduciary duty and the "prudent man standard" that was adopted in the 19th century, and flexibility in the pension system to allow risky equity investments in the 20th.

As noted earlier more must be done to broaden access to capital even further. Women, certain minority groups, veterans, people with disabilities, and towns and cities off the beaten venture capital path obtain far less financing than the primarily white and Asian males on both coasts and in Texas. Meanwhile, most venture capital firms lack diversity. Fortunately, institutional investors and venture capital firms are beginning to prioritize closing this gap – less because of dictates and more because they recognize the enormous untapped talent and that diverse perspectives often lead to better outcomes.[9] Policymakers may also have a role to play here and some incentives might help, but in most cases this dawning understanding of the market opportunity may be the most potent tool for making progress in this area.

Evolving Shareholder Capitalism. Beyond entrepreneurship per se, critics are challenging the nature of corporations themselves, including their purpose and mission, involvement in the political sphere, and how they are governed. America has a strong tradition of shareholder control, rather than control by banks or the government, and this has been essential to enabling dynamism. Thus, it is important that changes to corporate missions and governance come through shareholders, not government directives.

For most of the 20th century, it was actually managers and not shareholders who controlled these entities. They weren't seriously challenged until the 1970s, when Milton Friedman argued that the social mission of the corporation is to make money for its owners and Michael Jensen highlighted the "agency costs" of corporate management.[10] Those owners regained power in the 1980s with the emergence of corporate raiders, private equity firms, and hedge funds that could concentrate shareholding to force changes. Most recently, activist shareholder groups have become successful in influencing large companies to become more competitive – and thereby more productive and dynamic.

The objectives of shareholder-centered capitalism are now being questioned, as new activists push for greater corporate attention to environmental, social, and governance (ESG) issues. As noted in the previous chapter, the recent proxy contest involving ExxonMobil shows how activists with experience and a plan to make the company better can garner votes. A series of public letters from Larry Fink, the CEO of asset manager BlackRock, have suggested that social concerns should become central to corporate governance. These letters are particularly noteworthy because his firm is one of a handful that hold large positions in many firms. BlackRock and other intermediaries have shown themselves to be thoughtful in balancing investor interests with those of other stakeholders and the community more broadly. The debates around corporate mission and the trade-offs around certain ESG goals are healthy and will become more heated. Ultimately, management teams will become more responsible for balancing these goals and accountable for delivering on them. America's emphasis on shareholder control of the corporation is likely to prove more effective than bank or government mandates in the boardroom in balancing economic and social goals in the marketplace.

One area to be careful about is the increasing intersection of politics and corporations. Many on the left have been concerned about the *Citizens United* Supreme Court decision, which allowed large firms to spend money in areas related to campaign finance. Similarly, many on the right are concerned about the "woke corporation," with companies aggressively pushing state or local governments on political issues like voting rights. The net result is the rise of what has been characterized as the "political CEO," and predictions that companies will need to choose between being "red" or "blue." In the current divided political environment, companies can help to navigate the various issues, including leading progress in both economic and social outcomes. But they should avoid being dragged into politicized areas – we need them to focus on their main role of propelling or supporting dynamic growth.[11]

Workforce Development, Flexibility, and Broadened Equity Ownership. A knowledgeable and flexible workforce is a country's most important asset, and government can play a more direct role in developing the future workforce. Both upstarts and incumbents depend on capable employees and contractors to deliver on their strategies. And with technology changing rapidly, a broadly capable workforce will both support unknown future businesses and suffer less from the creative destruction that upstarts cause. Moreover, an educated consumer population will enable quicker adoption of innovations and new technologies, which will not just help them as individuals but benefit the economy as a whole.

The federal Morrill Act of 1862 and the GI Bill in the 1940s and '50s were both instrumental in developing an entire generation of well-trained workers and professionals. Beneficiaries of the latter act fed into the core of engineers and scientists that drove technological development for decades, and the bill itself has been characterized as the "Erie Canal of the new, post-industrial economy."[12] State governments added to the Morrill subsidies to develop public universities that greatly expanded higher education. Government-subsidized community colleges and vocational schools expanded access still further. With the costs of a college degree having exploded in the past few decades, reforms are again on the agenda. There are also opportunities to do more in areas such as community colleges and vocational and trade schools, especially through partnerships with the private sector.

On the flip side, a workforce that is not flexible and adaptive may constitute a barrier to growth and innovation. The fear of "technological unemployment" goes back centuries to the infamous Luddites in England, who destroyed textile machines. With artificial intelligence, robotics, and other new technologies this fear has resurfaced. Ameliorating this risk with concepts such as guaranteed income can go only so far. We need to continue to test and explore education systems and limited incentives for apprenticeships, continued training, retraining, and mid-career "re-skilling." This is one area in which some European countries may offer useful examples.[13]

The most powerful tool in generating wealth and alleviating inequality is stock ownership, and the workplace has proven to be an important context for this. Silicon Valley's success has come partly from equity-based compensation, which kept costs low for upstarts as they built their businesses and then shared some of the wealth if they succeeded. Microsoft purportedly created over two thousand millionaires a few years after its 1986 public offering, with similar stories at other companies. Since that time options have become the norm in venture-backed firms, and millions of employees have benefitted. Government should encourage the practice through additional tax incentives.[14] But start-ups are not the only ones that have used to stock ownership to assist employees in wealth creation. Fourteen million people now have stakes in employee stock ownership plans, and participation in "broad-based equity grants" has risen from one million people in 1990 to nine million today.[15] Simple innovations, such as automatic enrollment and payroll deduction for contributions to 401(k) plans, have had a powerful impact in this area.

America has a great tradition of stock ownership, and the percentage of Americans who own stock is among the highest in the world. Firms such as Merrill Lynch, Charles Schwab, Fidelity, and Vanguard have made investing easy and low cost, and new companies such as Robinhood are doing the same today with new technology for a younger demographic. But stock ownership needs to be dispersed more broadly, particularly for people not working in start-ups or for large corporations. With the rise of the gig economy, we need portable and flexible savings and investment vehicles to assist these groups. A combination of government policy and entrepreneurial energy might do the trick. Boosting the earned income tax credit, creating incentives for individual investment among certain underrepresented groups, and utilizing ideas such as "baby bonds" or "birthright funds," are a few other areas to explore.[16]

Finally, the balance between property rights and the right to compete is always tricky in the workplace. One current area of controversy is noncompete agreements, with good arguments on both sides of the debate. Upstarts and venture capital firms oppose these agreements, which discourage employees of established companies from launching or joining competing ventures. Incumbents argue on the basis of property rights, saying they have invested in their workforce and much of the knowledge or contacts developed or shared during the employee's tenure would be transferred at no cost to competitors. The impact of these agreements on trade secrets is also an important factor. Several states, including California, have prohibited these agreements, but it is unclear whether other states will or should follow that lead. A similar debate in many states involves "the right to repair," as independent shops seek access to critical technology in areas such as automobiles and cell phones, while manufacturers limit those activities to select dealers.

Social Entrepreneurship and Philanthropy. Successful entrepreneurs are increasingly applying their resources and experiences to tackle challenges in the social sector. Rather than resist this "social entrepreneurship," policymakers should help direct these energies creatively in areas such as education, environmental sustainability, and poverty relief.

America is already witnessing the largest wealth transfer in history, with $68 trillion in assets likely to be transferred between generations over the next 25 years.[17] Some politicians see that as an opportunity to increase revenues and level the playing field through larger inheritance taxes and even a wealth tax. But positive approaches that reward philanthropy and socially minded investments are more likely to both foster growth and reduce inequality. Policymakers might look at concepts such as Warren Buffett's "Giving Pledge," and encourage the new generation of entrepreneurs to donate ever larger portions of their resources to charity.

An important corollary is that more needs to be done to make sure philanthropy is effective and public-spirited. Today, a meaningful amount of philanthropic dollars goes to support either political causes (indirectly) or ego agendas. One area that warrants more attention is community foundations, as they combine a clear public purpose with less political or bureaucratic friction. There are roughly 700 community foundations nationwide, including in many big cities and Silicon Valley. These organizations connect donors with changemakers to channel resources for local needs, and in some cases they help develop entrepreneurial approaches to issues that complement government. Finding ways to encourage or entice donors to work with or through community foundations or similar intermediaries will increase the likelihood that our country's growing philanthropic resources will be deployed efficiently, effectively, and with a clearer public purpose.[18]

The Culture of Success – and Respect. Americans on both the left and the right value entrepreneurship, and its importance in our country is one of the few things that almost everyone agrees on. The nation's culture embeds a deep appreciation for the "underdog" and the achievement of the American Dream, particularly the small business variety. At the same time, there is grudging respect for mega-wealthy entrepreneurs such as Vanderbilt, Gates, Musk, and Bezos, especially when they begin as small upstarts and challenge incumbents. As a result, the country's political, legal, and institutional mechanisms have supported entrepreneurship and allowed it to reach its highest levels. These engrained elements of the culture and institutions enabled upstarts to strive and thrive even in the era of big business and "company men," and for innovation to find its way into the market. As we have seen, this sets America apart from most other countries, where people hesitate to start businesses, to challenge incumbents, or even to be too successful lest they generate jealousy or ire. This holds them, and their economies, back.

This culture cannot be taken for granted, especially now with widespread resentment brought about by heightened economic inequality and disruption impacting many workers and small businesses. Respect for entrepreneurship is closely tied to the egalitarian nature of American society and the sense that opportunity is open to anyone, and some see that as waning. As a result, instead of celebrating entrepreneurs, some are beginning to exude disdain toward them. Extremes on both the left and the right are guilty of unproductive rhetoric. In order to sustain a system that has proven effective in generating wealth and progress over generations, successful entrepreneurs, corporate leaders, policymakers, and others must lead in ways that unite the country around the long-standing values of success and opportunity and leverage those strengths to solve challenges, rather than engage in divisive posturing.

The Entrepreneurial Future

America has been a nation of entrepreneurs from the very beginning, but many of the most exciting opportunities lie ahead. Energy, materials, and health care, for instance, are a few areas that continue to show great possibility for major innovation, while new approaches in education and social services are addressing important needs. New fields, from space travel to stem cell research and development, are still in the early stages of attracting upstarts. Entrepreneurial approaches to such areas as privacy, security, environmental sustainability, and food supply security are highly promising. And there continue to be many large, underserved markets and segments of the population waiting to be fully addressed. We are just starting to see the range of opportunities that might come about by making the system more inclusive. Globally, the developing world offers vast opportunities both in markets and in talent.[19]

The country is well positioned to succeed, and the experience of the past 250 years, and the last four decades in particular, should be a reason for optimism about the future. But a dynamic economy by its nature results in winners and losers, and that is never easy. At the same time, America's democracy is at times messy and difficult. This combination of ever-changing economic competition and imperfect political and legal mechanisms can cause frustration, but it is also our greatest strength. While some countries can play catch-up or even outperform for some periods, our reliance on competing interests, and ultimately on consumers, generally prevails over time.

Perhaps the most encouraging sign is the increasing power of individuals not just as citizens but as commercial entrepreneurs, social entrepreneurs, consumers, and shareholders. At a time when the political climate is divisive and in spite of the pandemic, Americans continue to find ways to move forward. Few countries around the world have shown an ability to replicate this spirit and energy, and it is why our political system is the most durable and our economic progress the most sustained.

Nevertheless, America must address the social issues more effectively to keep the system intact and to enhance its moral authority and global leadership. As noted earlier, this does not mean big government stepping in to solve the problems. In fact, one should be wary of relying on government intervention beyond a certain point. Instead, we should continue to look to entrepreneurs to solve problems and to citizens-consumers-shareholders to play important roles in driving change. Leveraging the country's great tradition of entrepreneurial energy to address challenges will not only ensure the country's future success but build on the entrepreneurial revolution that it has sparked around the world.

Endnotes

1. See, e.g., Rebecca Henderson, *Reimagining Capitalism in a World on Fire* (New York: Public Affairs, 2020), and Robert Reich, *Saving Capitalism: For the Many Not the Few* (New York: Knopf, 2015).
2. Adam Winkler, *We the Corporations: How American Business Won Their Civil Rights* (New York: Liveright, 2018).
3. Gary Reback, *Free the Market! Why Only Government Can Keep the Market-place Competitive* (New York: Portfolio, 2009).
4. But see, e.g., Josh Lerner, *Boulevard of Broken Dreams: Why Public Efforts to Boost Entrepreneurship and Venture Capital Have Failed and What to Do About It* (Princeton, NJ: Princeton University Press, 2012).
5. See, e.g., Larry Downes, *The Laws of Disruption: Harnessing the New Forces That Govern Life and Business in the Digital Age* (New York: Basic Books, 2009).
6. The level of involvement of consumers also makes a difference. For instance, one antitrust scholar notes that "interest groups are stronger in patent law and consumers are stronger in antitrust law," explaining why patent terms keep getting longer (e.g. the Copyright Term Extension Act of 1998, also known as the "Mickey Mouse" Patent Act); Herbert Hovenkamp, *The Opening of American Law: Neoclassical Legal Thought* (New York: Oxford University Press, 2015), 187.
7. Rudolph J. R. Peritz, *Competition Law in America: History, Law, Rhetoric* (New York: Oxford University Press, 2001) ("A competition policy of opening access seeks to braid strands of liberty and equality, fairness and efficiency, into a political economy of free markets").
8. See, e.g., Louis Zingales, *A Capitalism for the People: Recapturing the Lost Genius of American Prosperity* (New York: Basic Books, 2012), 48–59.
9. See Knight Foundation Report, "Diversity of Asset Managers," Research Series.
10. See Milton Friedman, "A Friedman Doctrine: The Social Responsibility of Business Is to Increase Profits," *New York Times*, September 13, 1970, and Michael C. Jensen and William C. Meckling, "Reflections on the Corporation as a Social Invention," in *Controlling the Giant Corporation: A Symposium*, edited by Robert Hessen (Rochester, NY: University of Rochester, 1983).
11. See, e.g., Dorothy S. Lund and Leo Strine, "Corporate Political Spending Is Bad Business," *Harvard Business Review* (January–February 2022).
12. John Steele Gordon, *An Empire of Wealth: The Epic History of American Economic Power* (New York: HarperCollins, 2004), 364.
13. See, e.g., Tamar Jacoby, "Why Germany is So Much Better at Training Its Workers," *Atlantic Monthly*, October 16, 2014.

14. Marjorie Kelly, "A Powerful Under-Used Tool for Addressing the Roots of Inequality: Inclusive Ownership," *Stanford Social Innovation Review* (September 28, 2016).
15. National Center for Employee Ownership, "Employee Ownership by the Numbers," March 2021.
16. See Shahar Ziv, "Bill Ackman: Give Every Child $6,750 So They Can Retire Millionaires," *Forbes*, December 7, 2020.
17. Cerulli Associates, U.S. High Net Worth and Ultra High Net Worth Markets 2018: Shifting Demographics of Private Wealth.
18. "Silicon Valley Community Foundation supported non-profits with over $2 billion in grants in 2021," siliconvalleycf.org, January 19, 2022.
19. Tarun Khanna, *Billions of Entrepreneurs* (Cambridge, MA: Harvard Business School Press, 2013); Steven R. Koitai and Matthew Muspratt, *Peace Through Entrepreneurship* (Washington, DC: Brookings Institute Press, 2016); and C.K. Prahalad, *The Fortune at the Bottom of the Pyramid: Eradicating Poverty Through Profits* (Philadelphia: Wharton School Publishing, 2004).

Index

401(k) plans
  contributions, payroll
    deductions, 200
  enrollment, 157–158

A

Adams, Charles Francis, 105
Adams, John, 49, 63–64, 66, 88
  incumbent support, 84
Adams, Samuel, 56–57, 63
ADP, division, 157
Agency theory (Jensen), 118–119
"Age of Oligopoly," 131
Agricultural Adjustment Act, 129
Airbnb
  intermediary perspective, 192
  local regulation exemptions
    claim, 152
*A.L.A. Schechter Poultry Corp v. United
  States* (1935), 129
Alger, Horatio, 111
Alibaba, investment, 2
Allein, Thomas, 43
Almy, William, 82
Alphabet (Google), dominance,
  172
Amazon
  challenges, 176–177
  competition/innovation right,
    assertion, 191–192
  control, increase, 173

dominance, 172–173
European Commission actions, 180
pressure, application, 173
technological/platform
  advantages, 155
work environment, harshness, 177
Amendments
  Fifth Amendment, 70
  Fourteenth Amendment, 70,
    103–104, 108
  Sixteenth Amendment, 114–115
American Capitalism (Galbraith), 130
American capitalism, corporate
  reconstruction, 115
American Dream
  achievement, 202
  opportunity, 17
American individualism, 87–88
American Revolution, 57, 73–76
American Telephone and
    Telegraph (AT&T)
  government-sanctioned
    monopoly/power, 126
  MCI/DOJ antitrust
    lawsuits, 126–127
  patents, ownership, 133
  regional operating companies,
    spinoffs, 126–127
American Telephone and Telegraph
    (AT&T), size/control, 125
American Tobacco, Roosevelt
    actions, 114

Amoco, 126
Anchor customers, importance, 27
Andreesen, Marc, 160
Android (Google)
    impact, 149
    market share, 176
Anglican Church, dissenters
    (impact), 50–51
Antebellum investments, 105
Ant Group, crackdown, 4
Anti-Federalists, warnings/
    opposition, 66–68
Antitrust enforcement, 172–178
    action, increase, 173–174
    decrease, 151
Antitrust legislation,
    requirement, 119
Antitrust Paradox, The (Bork), 136, 194
A&P. *See* Great Atlantic and Pacific
    Tea Company
Apple
    closed marketplace, fees
        (extraction), 173
    dominance, 172–173
    European Commission actions,
        180
    growth, struggle, 161
    market capitalization, 162
    resuscitation, 149
    Spotify, attack, 163
    vulnerabilities, 38–39
Aristocratic class, creation
    (worries), 83
Arkwright, Richard, 82
"Arsenal of Democracy," 130
Articles of Capitulation, property
    rights assurances, 51–52
Articles of Confederation,
    weakness, 65
Artificial intelligence, impact, 200
Astor, John Jacob, 85
    wealth, 94
Authoritarian capitalism,
    understanding, 182–184

Authority, challenges/limitations,
    8–11
Autobiography (Franklin), 55, 87
Automatic enrollment, usage, 200
Automobile industry
    changes, 135
    Ford transformation, 128

B

Baby Bells, creation, 126–127
Baby bonds, 201
Baby Boomers
    social rebellion, 149–150
Baby Boomers, prominence/
    power, 141
Bank-controlled corporations,
    stability, 117
Bank of England, government
    establishment, 48
Bankruptcy code, Congress
    establishment, 83–84
Banks, proliferation, 95
Barlow, John Perry, 150
Barriers, incumbent creation, 107
Bayh-Dole Act of 1980, 135
B Corp, creation, 159
Beat Generation, impact, 137
Beatrice Foods, profitability
    (decline), 137
Bell, Alexander Graham, 111
Berle, Adolph, 118, 130
Berlin Wall, fall, 95, 141, 150,
    170, 182, 189
Bessemer process, 109–110
Bethelem Steel
    dominance, preservation, 127
    investments, 115
Bezos, Jeff, 13, 202
    work environment, harshness, 177
Biddle, Nicholas, 91
Biden, Joe (election), 169–170
Big-box companies, rise, 154
Big businesses
    dethroning, 133

rights, changes, 108–109
small business evolution, 103
Big companies, role, 156
Big corporations, distrust, 190–191
Big government, distrust, 190–191
Bigness
deregulation, 136
entrepreneurial activity,
    continuation, 132–133
push, 127–130
Sarnoff, impact, 133–134
test, 128–129
Big science, corporate conglomerates
    (relationship), 130–131
Big Tech
antitrust challenges, 172–178
complaints, 38–39
European Commission,
    approach, 180
hostility, 174
irony, 162–164
power, limitation, 180
supervision, calls, 173
Bill of Rights (England), 10, 47–48
Bill of Rights (US)
inclusion, 68
individual liberty, 70
Birthright funds, 201
BlaBlaCar, success, 2
Black laborers, reliance (South
    expansion), 96
BlackRock, social concerns, 198–199
Blackstone, William, 49
Boardrooms, political factors
    (impact), 117
Bolt, expansion, 2
Bork, Robert, 136, 194
Boston Massacre (1770), 56
Brandeis, Louis, 112–114, 129
Brexit, impact, 179
Britain
colonial markets, postwar access
    (loss), 82
"socialist lite" models, 131

British East India Company
Queen Elizabeth charter, 47
tea, sale (absence), 56
Brown, John, 56–57
Brown Shoe Company v. United States
    (1962), 132
Bryan, William Jennings, 113, 114
Buffett, Warren ("Giving
    Pledge"), 201
Bureau of Corporations,
    establishment, 114
Burke, Edmund, 64
Bush, Vannevar, 130–131
Business
shutdowns, cost, 17
War Industries Board powers, 128

C

Calvert, Cecil (Lord Baltimore), 52
Cantillon, Richard, 49
Capital
allocation, decisions (changes), 72
costs, reduction, 132
formation, 90
requirement, 105
sources, usage, 156
Capital gains taxes
code changes, 136
reduction, 151
Capitalism
authoritarian capitalism,
    understanding, 182–184
market-based capitalism, 46
shareholder capitalism, 130, 198–199
softening, 18
varieties, 3
Carnegie, Andrew
entrepreneurial achievement, 110
entrepreneur of scale, 109–111
J.P. Morgan & Company,
    assistance, 110
Pennsylvania Railroad,
    support, 109

Carroll, Charles, 52
Carter administration, deregulation
    efforts, 136
Carter, Robert "King," 53–54
Celler-Kefauver Act (1950), 132
Central administration,
    problems, 72–73
Central banks, aversion
    (continuation), 92
Central planning, resistance,
    131–133
Charles River Bridge v. Warren Bridge,
    93
Charles Schwab
    investment ease, 200
    scale, gaining, 153–154
Charter of Freedoms and
    Exemptions, securing, 51–52
Chevron, 126
China
    authoritarian capitalism,
        understanding, 182–184
    central planning, impact, 131
    common prosperity, focus, 183
    dominance, 164
    momentum, loss, 183–184
    natural stagnation, 183–184
    political unrest, 184
    public sector investments,
        percentage, 117
    social unrest, 184
    start-ups, increase, 7
Christensen, Clay, 28, 36
Churn rate (US), 6, 93, 139–140
Cisco Systems, spin-in strategy, 157
Citgo, competition, 126
*Citizens United v. Federal Election
    Commission* decision, impact,
    12, 158, 199
Civil Aeronautics Act (1938), 129
Civil Rights struggles, impact, 149
Civil War, 95–97, 109
    outcome, 104

post-Civil War economy,
    transformation, 119
pre-Civil War local/regional
    businesses, emergence, 106
public market dependence, 197
racial undercurrents/scars, 103
Clayton Antitrust Act, 115, 132
Climate change, evidence
    (increase), 172
Clinton Administration, technology
    encouragement, 151
Clinton, Bill, 151
Clinton, DeWitt, 84
Clinton, George, 67
Cloud computing, growth
    (impact), 160
Co-determination, 178–179
Coke, Edward, 43–44, 57
Colbert, Jean-Baptiste, 48
Cold War, 120, 125, 134–135
    fighting, 140
Collateral damage, toleration,
    16–18
Colonial foundations, 43
Colonial openness, 50–52
Combined trusts, development, 107
Commentaries on the Laws of England
    (Blackstone), 49
Commerce
    "dormant" commerce clause, 89
    Supreme Court viewpoint, 109
Commercial activity, contract law
    (impact/importance), 71
Common law, 70–71
    evolution, 89
    inconsistency, 49–50
Common prosperity, focus, 183
Common Sense (Paine), 63, 83
Communications Act of 1934, 129
Communications Decency Act,
    Section 230 (impact), 152
Companies
    big companies, role, 156

external constraints, 28–29
investors, company-level
    categorization, 119f
layoffs, cost, 17
lifespan (S&P Index), 139f
oversight, cessation, 129
revenue ranking, 138
Competing interests
balance, problem, 12
political economy, 11–13
Competition
property, balance, 88–90
rationalization, 113
rights, property rights
    balance, 201
    contrast, 92–932
Standard Oil, impact, 106
ConAgra Foods, acquisitions,
    137
Concentrated ownership,
    independence, 118–119
Conglomerates
corporate conglomerates, big
    science (relationship), 130–131
problems, 136
Congress. *See* United States
Consolidations, 111
losses, 112
Constitution. *See* United States
    Constitution
Consumer choice, bias, 194–195
Consumer market
changes, 153–155
Consumer market, growth
    (acceleration), 133
Consumers, examination, 15
Consumer welfare, 151
antitrust standard, 195
Continental Congress
Crown loyalty, 63
function, 65
Contracts
law, importance, 71

"will theory," 89
Cooke, Jay, 107
war bonds, sales, 107
Coolidge, Calvin, 128
Copyright Law of 1710, 48
Copyrights, US Constitution
    protection, 86
Corporate-administered marketplace,
    approach, 116
Corporate autonomy (US
    tradition), 115–120
Corporate bureaucracy, problem, 7
Corporate conglomerates, big science
    (relationship), 130–131
Corporate consolidation/
    concentration, abetting, 194
Corporate dynamism (US),
    138–140
Corporate governance, impact,
    14–15
Corporate independence,
    disadvantages, 116
Corporate lifecycle, position
    protection, 25
Corporate lifespan
decline, 139
Standard & Poor's
    500 index study, 6
Corporate R&D, failings, 27
Corporate securities, government
    investment
    (discontinuation), 91–92
Corporate strategy
entry barriers, 30
public policy goals, clash, 31
Corporate strategy 2.0, 36–39
Corporate sustainability, 163–164
Corporate Sustainability Reporting
    Directive (CSRD), 181
Corporations
bank-controlled corporations,
    stability, 117
challenges, 198

Corporations (*Continued*)
  executives, concentrated ownership (independence), 118–119
  regulation, Roosevelt (activist approach), 114
Costco, impact, 174
COVID crisis, 27, 150, 169–170, 179
Coxe, Tench, 81
Creative class, attraction, 159
Creative destruction, 72
  absence, 164
  cycles, acceleration, 86
  impact, 190
  natural forces, 184–185
Credit Suisse, 175
Crescent City Livestock Landing and Slaughterhouse Company, operation, 103
Crony capitalists, vulnerability, 6
Cronyism, 93–94
  susceptibility, 15
Crowninshield family, business competition, 85
Cultural bias, 14
Cultural shift, 137–138

D

Darcy, Edward, 43–44
Database marketing, usage/core competency, 154
Data General, prosperity, 133
Declaration of Independence, 75, 83
Declaration of Independence of Cyberspace (1996), 150
Declaration of Rights (Virginia), 63–64
Default risk, investor overstatement, 136
Department of Justice (DOJ) antitrust lawsuit, 126–127

enforcement, aggressiveness (increase), 132
  Microsoft civil antitrust case, 148
Depression (trigger), Jackson (impact), 92
Derby, Elias (business competition), 85
Derby, Elias Hasket (wealth), 94
Deregulation, impact, 136, 151
Descartes, René, 46
Developed countries, middle-income trap, 183
Developing world, entrepreneurship problems, 7
Didi Chuxing
  market value, decrease, 3
  rebranding, 2, 183
Didi Dache, market leadership, 2
Digital Equipment Corporation, prosperity, 133
Digital Markets Act (European Union), 180
Digital Services Act (European Union), 180
Digital transformation, 161
Disintermediation, risk (avoidance), 163
Disruption, 163, 202
  risks, 148
Disruptive competition, 113
Distributive justice (argument), 113
Diversity, absence, 171
"Dollar-a-Year Men," 128
"Don't Be Evil" (Google), 16, 162
DoorDash, disruption, 175
"Dormant" commerce clause, 89
Dot-com bubble, 148, 157
Dot-com crash, 150, 155–156
Dow Jones Industrial Average, 6
Drexel Burnham Lambert, dissolution, 156
Drucker, Peter, 35–36, 132
Due process, deployment, 104

Duke, James, 106, 114
DuPont
  acquisitions, 132
  military business, growth, 128
Dutch East India Company, impact,
  47

E

Economic anarchy, 75
Economic elites
  churn rate, 93
  impact, 93–95
Economic growth, support, 104
Economic inequality (social
  concern),
  170, 202
Economic interests/attitudes,
  competition, 66
Economies of scale, 32, 37, 86
  Rockefeller exploitation, 106
  understanding, 109–110
Ecosystems, corporate strategy
  (relationship), 36–38
Edison, Thomas, 34, 105, 112, 150
Elizabeth I. *See* Queen Elizabeth I
Emerson, Ralph Waldo, 87, 150
Engine No. 1, proxy contest win,
  182
England, headright grants, 46
Engraver's Act of 1735, 48
Enlightenment, 73, 75
  impact, 8, 10
Entrepreneurial activity
  continuation, 132–133
  US leadership, 3–4
Entrepreneurial advantage,
  maintenance, 189
Entrepreneurial balance,
  115–117, 151–152
Entrepreneurial capitalism, 150
  ability, evidence, 178
  innovation/renewal
    generation, 189

Entrepreneurial dynamism, fostering/
  harnessing, 31–32
Entrepreneurial economy
  features (US), 13–15
  political system, balance, 11
  upstarts/incumbents/innovation,
    relationship, 34–36
Entrepreneurial ecosystem, large
  company contribution, 26
Entrepreneurial future, 202–203
Entrepreneurial nations, growth, 7
Entrepreneurial prosperity,
  impact, 190–191
Entrepreneurial rebels, 57
Entrepreneurial republic, building,
  81
Entrepreneurial revolution, 147
Entrepreneurial spirit
  (*Unternehmergeist*), 35
Entrepreneurs
  challenges/barriers, 5
  economic theory, 48–50
  emergence/rise, 73–76
  experience, 32–33
  opening, American law
    (impact), 72
  resistance/co-optation, impact, 5
Entrepreneurship, 150
  barometer, 4
  breakthroughs, 45–48
  expansion, 163–164
  factors, 14
  impact, 95–96
  inclusive
    entrepreneurship, 195–196
  long-term success, question, 4–5
  problems (developing world), 7
Entry barriers, construction,
  30–31
Environmental, social, and
  governance (ESG) goals, 199
Environmental, social, and
  governance (ESG),
  increase, 182

Environmental, social, and
governance (ESG)
issues, 158, 198
Environmental, social, and
governance (ESG)
movement, 172
Environmental, social, and
governance (ESG) oversight,
company factors, 15
Epic Games, AppStore
argument, 173, 176
Equal protection, deployment, 104
Equity capital, abundance, 197
Equity ownership,
broadening, 199–201
Erie Canal
completion (1825), 84
costs, reduction, 86
infrastructure development,
193
Erie Railroad, control, 91
Essay on the Nature of Commerce
(Cantillon), 49
Establishment, social
rebellion, 149–150
Etsy, impact, 177
European capitalism/regulation,
assessment, 178–182
European foundations, 43
European Union
disclosure/transparency,
importance, 181
founding, 179
Evergrande, financial crisis,
4, 183–184
Expansion, culture (creation),
4–5
Experience curve, 132
ExxonMobil, 126
Engine No. 1, proxy
contest win, 182
market capitalization, size, 139
public proxy contest, loss,
172, 198

F

Facebook
acquisitions, 162
"buy and bury" scheme, 174
European Commission actions, 180
founding, 156
intermediary perspective, 192
Meta (dominance), 172
power, 152
TikTok challenge, 163
Facebook, Apple, Amazon, Netflix,
and Google (FAANG),
scrutiny, 38
Fairchild Semiconductor,
founding, 137
Fair use, definitions
(meeting), 152–153
Farmer, Paul, 158–159
Favoritism, 14
avoidance, 11
Federal Aviation Administration,
129
Federal Communications
Commission (FCC), setup
(1934), 129
Federal government
nondemocratic elements, fading, 75
states, relationship, 68–69
Federalist No. 10 (Madison),
11, 67, 192
Federal Reserve System,
creation, 115
Federal Trade Commission (FTC)
challenges, 135
creation, 115
enforcement, aggressiveness
(increase), 132
Ferguson, Niall, 183–184
Fidelity, investment ease, 200
Fiduciaries, "prudent man" standard
(relaxation), 107
Field, Stephen, 104
Fifth Amendment, 70

Finance
  decentralized access, 196–198
  Jackson decentralization, 91–92
  transformation, 156–157
Financial crisis (2008), 169
  recovery, 170–171
Financial engineering,
  impact, 155–158
Financial instruments, growth, 156
Financial liberalization, impact, 137
Financial resources, risk, 5
Financing engineers,
  impact, 155–158
Fink, Larry, 182, 198
Firms
  domestic rivalry, 34
  efficiency, reduction, 135
  evolution, allowance/
    encouragement, 176
First Bank of the United States,
  building, 85
Five forces (Porter), 30
Floyd, George (murder), 17, 169
Forbes 400 members, aggregate net
  worth (increase), 94
Ford, Henry, 106, 128
Formalism, 96
Four Seasons Hotels, evolution, 33
Fourteenth Amendment (US), 70,
  103–104, 108
France
  corporate governance (state
    administration roles), 116–117
  monarchy, break (analysis), 72–73
  "socialist lite" models, 131
Franklin, Benjamin, 34, 54–55,
  65, 87, 150
Frederick the Great, reforms, 45
Free banking, era, 92
Free markets, embrace (Reagan/Bush
  administrations), 151
FREE NOW, Hailo merger, 2
French and Indian War, 53, 55

Friedman, Milton, 136, 198
FTSE 100, London Stock Exchange
  index study, 140
Fulton, Robert, 89
Fundamental Orders of
  Connecticut, 51

G

Gadsen, Christopher, 56–57
Galbraith, John Kenneth, 130
Gaspee (destruction), 56
Gates, Bill, 138, 202
General Data Protection Regulations
  (GDPR), 180–181
General Electric (GE)
  index drop, 6
  patents, ownership, 133
  size (S&P 500 index), 139
  survival, problem, 177
  transformation, 157
General Motors
  acquisition, 132
  rescue, 156
Gentlemen's agreement (Roosevelt),
  110–111, 114
Germany
  corporate governance, state
    administration roles, 116–117
  economic model, pressure, 179
Gibbons v. Ogden, 88–89, 90, 93
GI Bill, 130, 199
Gig economy
  jobs, creation, 17
  workers, employee treatment, 1
Gilded Age, 111
Girard, Stephen, 85, 97
"Giving Pledge" (Buffett), 201
Glass-Steagall Act (1933), 130
Glorious Revolution (1688), 10, 44,
  47–48, 57, 69
Golden Era, cessation, 47
Gold Rush (1849), 91

Google
  competition/innovation right,
      assertion, 191–192
  dominance, 172
  "Don't Be Evil," 16, 162
  European Commission actions, 180
  impact, 173
Gordon, Robert, 96–97
Gould, Jay, 91
Government
  constraints, reduction, 104
  control, invisible hand (power), 83
  disrupting, 158–159
  financing, Girard (impact), 85
  government-sponsored cartels,
      Roosevelt support, 129
  hands-off approach, 190
  intervention, 125–126
      limitation, 109
  limitation, 192–194
  openness, impact, 87
  policy, entrepreneurial energy
      (combination), 200–201
  reinventing, 151, 158–159
Great Atlantic and Pacific
      Tea Company
      (A&P)
  founding/success/backlash, 23–25
  pivot, 25
  pricing arrangements, 129
Great Depression, 120, 125
  bigness, test, 128–129
  overcoming, 140
Great dismantling, 134–137
Great merger movement, 112, 113
Great Resignation, 170
Green entrepreneurship, 18
Greenfield opportunities, 32
Greenwashing, 181
Growth share matrix, 132
Guerilla strategies, 34
Gulf, competition, 126
Gulf & Western, diversification,
      132

H

Hailo, FREE NOW merger, 2
Hamilton, Alexander, 49, 67,
      75, 81–82, 90
  states debt assumption,
      insistence, 84
  vision, competition, 83–85
Hancock, John, 53, 56–57, 64, 93
Hancock, Thomas, 53
Hartford, John/George, 23, 25
Hartford Sermon (Hooker), 51
Hartz, Louis, 11
Hatch-Waxman Act of 1984, 135
Headright grants, 46
Hedge funds, management, 156
Heinz, H.J., 106
Henry, Patrick, 56–57, 67
Hewlett-Packard
  competitiveness, 177
  division, 157
High-Tech Colbertism, 48
Home Depot, impact, 174
Homestead Act (1862), 104
Honda, brand acceptance/operations
      expansion, 135
Hong Kong, liberties (China
      crackdown), 184
Hooker, Thomas, 51
Hudson Henry, 51
Hyundai, brand acceptance/
      operations expansion, 135

I

IBM
  hardware units, sale, 156–157
  incumbency, attack, 161
  momentum, 160
  outmaneuvering, 147
  prosperity, 133
  shortsightedness, 137–138
Impact investing, impact, 159
Imperial incumbency,
      resistance, 55–57

Incentive systems, impact, 7
Inclusion, absence, 171
Inclusive entrepreneurship, 195–196
Incumbency, dangers, 138
Incumbents
  age/aging, 125
  barriers, creation, 107
  combination, 111–112
  decision-making/discipline, 28
  disruption, 150
  entrenched incumbents,
    development
    (occurrence), 52–54
  entrepreneurial economy,
    relationship, 34–36
  growth orientation, 27
  local incumbents, losses, 106–108
  problems, 29
  property rights, changes, 152
  prosperity, 133
  shortcomings/limitations, 27–28
  strengths, leverage, 193
  study, 26
  understanding, 26–30
  upstarts
    battle, 15
    challenges, 6
    collaboration, 169
    dynamism, 38
    weapons, 30–31
India, start-ups (increase), 7
Individual initiative, deference, 70
Individualism, 87–88
  lauding, 150
Individual Retirement Account
    (IRA), development, 157–158
Individuals, power (increase), 2032
Industrial democracy (argument),
    113
Industrial mutation, 36
Industrial Revolution, 73
  innovation, democratization, 44
Industries, transformation, 32
Inflection point, 169

Information, usage/core
    competency, 154
Infrastructure
  development, 193
  public investment, 5
Initial public offering (IPO),
    impact, 197
Innovation
  commercialization/
    development, 36
  continuation (US), 86
  dampening, 30–31
  democratization, 44
  deterrence, 112–113
  development, protectionists/rentiers
    (attack), 68
  economy, acceleration, 153
  entrepreneurial economy,
    relationship, 34–36
  impact, 193
  lauding, 150
  market access, support, 15
  pursuit, 116
  support, 16
Innovators, dilemma, 153–154
Innovator's Dilemma, The
    (Christensen), 28
*Inquiry into the Nature and Causes of
    the Wealth of Nations*
    (Smith), 83
Instagram, acquisition, 162, 174
Intel, formation, 137
International Telephone and
    Telegraph, diversification,
    132
Interstate Commerce Commission,
    formation, 108–109
Investors, company-level
    categorization, 119f
Invisible hand, power, 83
iOS (Apple), impact, 149
Irving, Washington, 87
Israel, innovation (growth), 8
Italy, "socialist lite" models, 131

J

Jackson, Andrew
  anti-monopoly tradition, 112–113
  finance decentralization, 91–92
James I, grants (issuing), 44
Japan
  Ministry of International Trade and
    Industry (MITI), impact, 131
  success, 135
Jefferson, Thomas, 48–49, 67, 75, 150
  anti-monopoly tradition, 112–113
  government perspective, 192–193
  vision, competition, 83–85
Jensen, Michael, 118, 136, 198
JetBlue, scale (gaining), 153–154
Jet.com, formation/success, 175–176
Jinping, Xi
  "common prosperity" focus, 183
  country control, 183
  "new development concept," 183
  private sector control, 3
Jobs, Steve, 34, 138, 161–162, 177
J.P. Morgan & Company, 196
  financial assistance, 110
  mergers, reduction, 116
  Pujo Committee investigation, 113
  rescue, 15
Junk bonds
  creation, 15
  investments, 136

K

Kalanick, Travis, 1–2
Keiretsu (Japan), growth, 7
Kent, James, 49
Kia, brand acceptance/operations
    expansion, 135
Killer apps, impact, 148
King James II, replacement, 47–48
Kingsbury Commitment (1913), 126
Kirzner, Israel, 33
Kmart, competition, 155

Kodak, decline, 177
Kohlberg, Kravis & Roberts,
    acquisitions, 137
Kopp, Wendy, 158
Kuaidi Dache, Didi Dache merger, 2

L

Laissez-faire innovations,
    democratization/
    dissemination, 128
Laissez-faire operation, 93
Laissez-faire populism, promotion, 91
Large corporate firms,
    importance, 26–27
Large-scale enterprise, control
    (organizational framework),
    112
Large-scale industrial capacity,
    government usage, 193
Law, due process, 108
Laws of Disruption, The (Downes), 178
Lean start-up, facilitation, 160
Lee, Richard Henry, 67
Legacy systems/processes, impact, 32
Legal origins, importance, 71
Legal realism, 111
L'Enfant, Pierre, 81
Leveling principle, 66
Leveraged buyout (LBO), usage, 137
Lexington (flagship), 90
Liberty (burning), 56
Lincoln, Abraham, 44, 104
Linux (open system), 149
Livingston, Robert, 89
Lobbying, increase, 192
Local banks
    number, decline, 196–197
Local banks, emergence, 85
Local incumbents, losses, 106–108
Locke, John, 10, 46, 48–49, 52, 57, 67
Lord Fairfax, 54
Lore, Marc, 175–177
Louisiana Purchase (1803), 84–85

Lowell, Francis, 87
Luddites, impact, 200
Lyft
  competition, 1
  intrusion, 194
  scale, gaining, 179

M

Macron, Emmanuel, 179
Madison, James, 11, 66, 67, 83, 192
Magna Carta (property rights
    recognition), 8
Ma, Jack (detention), 4
Managerial expertise, governmental
    usage, 193
Manhattan Project, 130, 138
Marconi Wireless
    Telegraph Company,
    133
Marginalism, doctrine, 111
Marketplaces, creation, 196
Markets
  access, 69
    bias, 194–195
  capitalization, decrease, 138
  crowding, 86–87
  development, 106
  entry strategies, 32
  market-based capitalism, 46
  public credit markets, role, 197
  start-up entry, 31–34
Marshall, John, 49, 88, 93
Marshall Plan, 131
Mason, George, 63–64
McCormick, Cyrus, 96
MCI, antitrust lawsuit, 126–127
McKinley, William, 113
Means, Gardner, 118
Mercantilism, theory, 45
Merger movement, 119
Merrill Lynch, investment ease, 200
Meta (Facebook), dominance, 172
Me-Too movement, 169

Microsoft
  commitments, 195
  competition/innovation right,
    assertion, 191–192
  DOJ civil antitrust case, 148, 153
  dominance, 172–173
  European Commission fines, 180
  intellectual property control, 138
  Netscape challenge, 148
  operating system, challenges, 149
  risk, competitor pre-emption, 148
  success, 147–148
Microsoft millionaires, creation,
    147
Mid-career re-skilling, 200
Middle-income trap, 183
Military spending, increase
    (Reagan), 151
Milken, Michael, 136, 156
Ministry of International Trade and
    Industry (MITI) (Japan),
    impact, 131
Mittelstand firms (Germany), growth,
    7
Monarchy, break (France), 72–73
Monopolies, progressive response,
    112–115
Montesquieu, Baron de, 49, 67
Morgan, J.P., 107
Morrill Land-Grants Acts
    (1862), 104, 199
Morris, Robert, 64, 75, 85, 93
Moses, Brown, 82
Motorola, displacement, 161
Mun, Thomas, 48
Musk, Elon, 202
Myspace, Facebook (impact), 176

N

Nader, Ralph, 135, 194
Napoleonic code, 89
Napster, copyright issues, 152, 192
Nasdaq, challenges, 155

National Banking Acts
(1863–1866), 107
National banks, development
(New York),
107
National Broadcasting Company
(NBC), RCA launch/
expansion, 133–134
National champions
creation, 119
favoritism, 140
promotion, 7, 34
National Industrial Recovery Act
(1933), 129
National Recovery Administration
(NRA), establishment, 129
Natural monopolies, 173
AT&T control, 125–126
doctrine, 108
Natural rights, concept, 48–49
Natural stagnation, 183–184
Navigation Acts (1650/1660),
51, 55
Net neutrality, issue, 152
Netscape, 160
initial public offering, 147–149
Networks
corporate strategy,
relationship, 36–38
effects, 37–39, 148
open networks, development, 37
power, Rockefeller
exploitation, 106
New Amsterdam, founding, 51–52
"New development concept," 183
"New Economy" (1999), 177
New Establishment, landing, 150
"New Freedom" (Wilson), 115
New knowledge, impact, 35–36
"New Nationalism" (Roosevelt), 115
New York Stock Exchange
capital, channeling, 107
challenges, 155

impact, 197
market, struggle, 95
Niche offerings/providers,
impact, 154
Nissan, brand acceptance/operations
expansion, 135
Noblesse oblige, 74
Nokia, displacement, 161
North (US)
economic model, validation, 104
innovation, 96
North–South division (US), 95–97
Northwest Ordinance (1787), 84–85
Nouveau riche class,
encouragement, 88
Nucor, market share impact, 154

O

Obama, Barack, 153
Occupy Wall Street movement, 169
Oglethorpe Plan (Georgia), 52
Oil Crisis (1970s), 127
Oil leases, Rockefeller purchase, 110
Oil supply shocks, 134, 135
Old World, opportunities, 45
Oligarchies, domination, 131
Oligopoly
"Age of Oligopoly," 131
success, 150, 183
Olson, Mancur, 12
Open corporation laws, shift, 95
Open networks, development, 37–38
Open systems, challenges, 149
Opportunity
sources, 35–36
zones, success, 194
Opt-in/opt-out marketing,
impact, 195
Organizational challenges, 29
Other People's Money and How the
Bankers Use It (Brandeis), 113
Outsourcing, development, 37

P

Paine, Thomas, 63
Palo Alto Research Center
    (PARC), 138
Panic of 1837, 92
Panic of 1907, 115
Paper money, substitution, 66
Partners in Health,
    founding, 158–159
Patent Office, impact, 83–84
Patents
    corporate entity holdings, 112
    laws, updates, 153
    radio patents, ownership
        (worry), 133
    trolls, control, 153
    US Constitution protection, 86
Paterson, founding, 81–82, 90
Patroonships, allowance, 51–52
Peace of Paris (1783), 65
Peale, Charles Wilson, 56–57
Penn Central railroad, bankruptcy
    (1970), 134
Penn, John, 52, 54, 64, 75
Pennsylvania, constitution, 64
Pension funds, investment ability, 137
"People's Line," 90
Personal computing
    growth, 137–138
    operating system, dominance, 147
"Personhood" (Supreme Court
    extension), 108
Philanthropy, impact, 201–202
Physiocrats, focus, 49
Platforms
    corporate strategy,
        relationship, 36–38
    technologies, impact, 148
Political CEO, characterization, 199
Political foundations, impact, 14
Political risks, 31
Political stability, 67
Political systems, economic systems
    (relationship), 12–13

Popham Colony, 44
Popham, John, 44
Porter, Michael, 30
Portfolio
    diversification, financial
        advantages, 132
    management, benefits, 132
Postwar affluence, impact, 135
Powers, separation, 68–69, 109
Private equity funds, management,
    156
Private initiative, opportunities, 48
Private ordering, 11
    orientation, 71–72
"Privileges and immunities"
    provision, 104
Proclamation of 1763 (Parliament),
    55
Production, improvements, 106
Professional manager, creation, 112
Property
    competition, balance, 88–90
    control, 66
Property rights, 67
    balance, 31
    competition rights
        balance, 201
    contrast, 92–93
    expansion, 151
    importance, 89
    incumbent property rights,
        changes, 152
    protection, 83–84
    rebalancing, 153
    recognition, 8, 10
"Prudent man" rule,
    establishment, 15
"Prudent man" standard
    adoption, 197
    relaxation, 107
Public credit markets, role, 197
Public equity market, strength,
    197
Pujo Committee investigation, 113

Puritan ideology, emphases, 50–51
Puritan theocracy, 54
Purposeful Darwinism, 177

Q

Queen Elizabeth I
  backlash, 10
  British East India Company
    charter, 47
  impact, 43–44
Quicken, acquisition, 153
Quidsi, acquisition, 175
Quill Corp. v. North Dakota, 152

R

Racism, undercurrents, 103
Radio Corporation of
    America (RCA)
  GE spinoff, government
    enforcement, 134
  National Broadcasting Company
    (NBC) launch/
    expansion, 133–134
Radio, development
    (acceleration), 133
Railroads
  capital, requirement, 105
  competition, government
    intervention (call), 105
  consolidators, impact, 107
  dethroning, 133
  Interstate Commerce Commission,
    federal regulation, 108
  progress, 104–106
  public market dependence, 197
Raytheon
  founding, 131
  prosperity, 133
RCA. *See* Radio Corporation
    of America
Reagan administration, deregulation
    efforts, 136

Reagan, Ronald (military spending/
    deregulation increases), 151
Reflections on the Revolution in France
    (Burke), 64
Regional ownership
    distribution, 118f
Regulatory capture, 31
  blame, 135
Research and development (R&D)
  business, government entry, 130
  failings, 27
Research, impact, 193
Research institutions, public
    investment, 5
Re-skilling, 200
Revlon Rule, 136–137
Rhode Island, charter (1663), 46
Rights of Man, The (Paine), 64
Risk-enabling finance, impact, 14–15
Risk-taking
  avoidance, 117
  encouragement (US), 7
Rivals
  buyouts, 106
  competition, 136
Robinhood, disruption/
    impact, 155, 200
Robinson-Patman Act
    (1936), 24, 129
Robotics, impact, 200
Rockefeller, John D., 106
  court beneficiary, 126
  oil leases, purchase, 110
Roosevelt, Franklin D.
  government-sponsored cartels, 129
Roosevelt, Theodore, 113
  activist approach, 114
  "gentlemen's agreement,"
    110–111, 114
  New Nationalism, 115
  statist approach, 114
Royalists, civil war, 47
Ruinous competition, chaos, 108
Rule of law, supremacy, 69

"Rule of Reason" (Supreme Court establishment), 114
Rush, Benjamin, 56–57, 75

S

Santa Clara v. Southern Pacific, 108, 158
Sarnoff, David (impact), 133–134
Scale. *See* Economies of scale
  advantages, usage, 111
  Carnegie, Andrew, 109–111
  gaining, 153–154
Schechter Poultry decision. *See A.L.A. Schechter Poultry Corp v. United States*
Schumpeter, Joseph, 6, 33, 35, 36, 94
Schwab, Charles, 127
Scientific Revolution, impact, 8, 10
Sears, competition, 155
Sears, Richard, 105
Secondat, Charles-Louis de, 49
Second Bank of the United States, 91
Securities and Exchange Commission (SEC), shareholder protection, 130
Self-made man (Franklin), 54–55
Shareholder
  activism, 182
  SEC protection, 130
Shareholder capitalism
  development, 130
  evolution, 198–199
Shareholdings, dispersal, 117
Shay's Rebellion (1786), 66
Shell, competition, 126
Sherman Antitrust Act, 114
  FTC usage, 24
  impact, 107–109
Shockley Semiconductor, "Traitorous Eight" exit, 137
Shopify, impact, 177, 196
Short-term borrowing, options (increase), 132

Silicon Valley
  creation, 131, 137, 150
  global model, 189
  inspirations, 160–161
Singer, Isaac Merritt, 106
Sixteenth Amendment, 114–115
Slater, Samuel, 82
Slaughterhouse Cases (1873), 104
Small businesses
  challenges, 196
  evolution, 103
  growth, 33
  unfair competition protection, 129
Smith, Adam, 10, 34, 48
Social business, engagement, 159
Social concerns, 170–172
Social entrepreneurship, 18, 158
  hybrid forms, emergence, 159
  impact, 201–202
Social issues, focus, 178
"Socialist lite" models, 131
Social rebellion, 149–150
Society for Establishing Useful Manufactures (SEUM), founding, 81–82
Software as a service (SaaS), concept, 160
Sons of Liberty, disguise, 56–57
South (US)
  agricultural commodities emphasis, 96
  anti-monopoly tradition, 112–113
  development, lag, 97
Spin-ins, strategy, 157
Spinoza, Baruch, 46
Spirit of the Laws (Montesquieu), 49
Spotify, attack, 163
Stamp Act of 1765, support, 55–56
Standard Oil Corporation
  breakup, 114
  competition destruction, 106
  holding company charter, 107
  price discrimination, 152
  Roosevelt actions, 114

Standard Oil Corporation
(*Continued*)
size/control, 125
trust regulation
circumvention, 107, 112
user prices, reduction, 126
Standard & Poor's 500 Index
company lifespan, 139f
study, 6
Starbucks, impact, 154–155
Start-ups, 31–34
activity, global investments, 4
enterprises, encouragement, 189
increase (China/India), 7
increase (US), 135
lean start-up, facilitation, 160
States
competition, impact, 69–70
debt assumption, Hamilton
insistence, 84
federal government,
relationship, 68–69
Statute on Monopolies, passage,
44
Steam power, impact, 86
Steam technology, investment, 89
Steel manufacturing, Carnegie
focus, 109–110
Stigler, George, 136
Stock ownership
encouragement, 157–158
usage, 200
Story, Joseph, 93
Substantive due process, 70, 108
Success, culture, 202
Sugar Act of 1764, 55
Supermarket, creation, 24–25
Supply-meets-demand
equilibrium, 33
Sustainable Finance Disclosure
Regulation (SFDR), EU
passage, 181
Sustaining innovation,
incorporation, 26

Swift, Gustavus, 105–106
Systematic management,
techniques, 112

T

Taft, William Howard, 113, 114
hands-off approach, 115
Taney, Roger, 93
Target, impact, 174
Taxes, postponement, 66
Technical debt, 29
avoidance, 160
Technological unemployment
cost, 17
fear, 200
Technologies
changes, 193, 195
leverage, 105–106
opportunities, 45
platforms/marketplaces, data
collection ability, 191–192
possibilities, 160
Telecommunications Act (1995)
criticism, 152
Section 230, effectiveness, 194
telephone number portability, 195
Telephone portability,
importance, 151
Tencent Holdings, investment, 2
Tennessee Coal and Iron Company,
acquisition, 110, 114
Terman, Frederick, 131
Tesla, founding/launch, 156, 194
Texaco, competition, 126
Third-party providers, marketplaces
(creation), 196
Thoreau, Henry David, 88
Throughput, volume (increase), 106
Tiananmen Square, crackdown, 182
TikTok
challenge, 163
growth, 176
Tocqueville, Alexis de, 73, 87

Townsend Duties (1767), passage, 56
Toyota, brand acceptance/operations
    expansion, 135
Trade, protection (absence), 104
"Traitorous Eight," 137
Transcontinental railroad,
    subsidization, 104
Travis's Law, 2
Trump, Donald (divisiveness), 169
Trustees of Dartmouth College v.
    Woodward, 88, 93
Trusts, regulation
    (circumvention), 112
Twain, Mark, 111
Twitter, power, 152
Two-party system, persistence, 72
Two Treatises of Government
    (Locke), 48

U

Uber
    expansion/success, 1–2
    founding, 156
    intermediary perspective, 192
    intrusion, 194
    local regulation exemptions
        claim, 152
    scale, gaining, 179
UberChina, sale, 2
Uber Eats, disruption, 175
Unicorns
    creation, 3–6
    US leadership, 4
Unionization, preemption, 116
United Kingdom
    Anglo-Saxon business model, 117
    economy, challenges, 7
United States
    Anglo-Saxon business model, 117
    balance, continuation, 191–192
    capitalism, corporate
        reconstruction, 115
    churn rate, 6, 139–140

colonial foundations, 43
colonial openness, 50–52
Congress, bankruptcy code
    establishment, 84
corporate-administered
    marketplace, approach, 116
corporate dynamism, 138–140
cultural shift, 137–138
development, Federalists (impact), 83
economic anarchy, 75
economic destiny, control, 184–185
economic elites, impact, 93–95
economic privileges, control, 67
economy
    consolidation, 111
    growth, 74
    transformation, 119
entrepreneurial economic system, 68
entrepreneurial economy,
    features, 13–15
entrepreneurial political economy,
    stability/security, 13
Fifth Amendment, 70
Fourteenth Amendment, 70,
    103–104, 108
individualism, 87–88
innovation, continuation, 86
liberal economic policy,
    impact, 164
local banks, emergence, 85
marketplace, incremental changes
    (impact), 86
mixed economy, strength, 69
North-South division, 95–97
political economic system, 69–70
political economy, origin, 67–68
pro-entrepreneur political
    economy, 68
property rights, 10
shareholdings, dispersal, 117
Sixteenth Amendment, 114–115
striving, government openness
    (impact), 87
success, continuation, 192–202

United States Constitution
  compromises, 65–67
  entrepreneurialism, 68–72
  passage, impact, 72–73
  supremacy, importance, 88
United States Steel Company
  antitrust attention, avoidance, 115
  creation, 110–111
  market share, loss, 153–154
  protection, loss, 127
  size/control, 125
Unocal, competition, 126
Unternehmergeist (entrepreneurial
  spirit), 35
Upstarts
  bias, 65–66
  change, 16
  entrepreneurial dynamism,
    continuation, 94–95
  entrepreneurial economy,
    relationship, 34–36
  entrepreneurship, 147
  focus, 128
  impact, 65
  incumbents
    battle, 15
    collaboration, 169
    dynamism, 38
  strengths, leverage, 193
  upstart-incumbent dynamic,
    American Revolution
    emergence, 75–76
Utilitarianism (concept), 111

V

Vanderbilt, Cornelius, 13, 89, 97, 202
  entrepreneurship, 90–91
  wealth, 94
Vanguard, investment ease, 200
Venture-backed companies, exit
  value (increase), 157
Venture capital, 198
  creation, 15
  expansion, 163–164

financial liberalization, impact, 137
GDP percentage ranking, 9f
pension funds, investment
  ability, 137
success, 189–190
Venture capitalists, race/ethnic/
  gender diversity (share), 171f
Venture funding, diversity/inclusion
  (absence), 171
Venture funds, investments, 157
Venture philanthropy, impact, 159
Vertical integration, 37, 112
Vietnam War, impact, 135, 150
Virginia Declaration of Rights,
  drafting, 63–64
VOC, impact/success, 47

W

Walmart
  Amazon competition, 175
  growth, 154–155
Walton, Sam, 154
War bonds, sales, 107
War Industries Board, business
  powers, 128
War of 1812, 84–85
Washington, George, 53, 55,
  64, 75, 83
Watergate, impact, 135, 149
Way to Wealth, The (Franklin), 54
Wealth
  concentration, economic/political
    power (relationship), 95
  generation, 202
Wealth of Nations, The (Smith), 48
Weber, Max, 50–51
Webster, Daniel, 93
Webvan, business closure, 155–156
Welch, Jack, 157
Western Electric, spinoff, 126–127
Western Union, 111
  divestiture, 126
Westinghouse, patents
  (ownership), 133

WhatsApp, acquisition, 162, 174
Whitney, Eli (cotton gin
    commercialization failure), 86
William of Orange, impact, 47–48
Williams, Roger, 51
"Will theory" (contracts), 89
Wilson, Woodrow, 113–115
  "New Freedom," 115
Winthrop, John, 51
Woke corporations
  concerns, 199
  limitations, 12
Wonder Group, 175
Workers
  entrepreneurial economy,
    impact, 16–17
  unions, challenges, 125
Workforce development/flexibility,
    199–201

World War I, 127
  bigness, era, 127–130
  economy, transformation, 119
World War II, 120
  postwar economic boom, 134
  war production, 130

X

Xerox, personal computing
    technology development, 138
Xiaoping, Deng, 182

Y

Yorktown, victory, 64

Z

Zaibutsu business groups, 117